Croydon Libraries

You are welcome to borrow this book for up to 28 days. (A)
If you do not return or renew it by the latest date stamped
below you will be asked to pay overdue charges. You may
renew books in person, by phoning 0208 726 6900 or via the
Council's website www.croydon.gov.uk

4 NOV 2008	- 3 SEP 2012	
	4 APR 2013	
5 JUN 2009		
29 OCT 2009	19 DEC 2012	
16 Jan 2010	LOAN ISCA	
1 MAY 2010		
26 AUG 2010		
23 SEP 2010		
1 MAR 2011		
03 MAY 2011		
6 OCT 2011		

**CROYDON
COUNCIL**
www.croydon.gov.uk

baby sleep
andrea grace

For over 60 years, more than 50 million people have learnt over 750 subjects the **teach yourself** way, with impressive results.

be where you want to be
with **teach yourself**

For UK order enquiries: please contact Bookpoint Ltd, 130 Milton Park, Abingdon, Oxon, OX14 4SB. Telephone: +44 (0) 1235 827720. Fax: +44 (0) 1235 400454. Lines are open 09.00–17.00, Monday to Saturday, with a 24-hour message answering service. Details about our titles and how to order are available at www.teachyourself.co.uk

For USA order enquiries: please contact McGraw-Hill Customer Services, PO Box 545, Blacklick, OH 43004-0545, USA. Telephone: 1-800-722-4726. Fax: 1-614-755-5645.

For Canada order enquiries: please contact McGraw-Hill Ryerson Ltd, 300 Water St, Whitby, Ontario, L1N 9B6, Canada. Telephone: 905 430 5000. Fax: 905 430 5020.

Long renowned as the authoritative source for self-guided learning – with more than 50 million copies sold worldwide – the **teach yourself** series includes over 500 titles in the fields of languages, crafts, hobbies, business, computing and education.

British Library Cataloguing in Publication Data: a catalogue record for this title is available from the British Library.

Library of Congress Catalog Card Number: on file.

First published in UK 2007 by Hodder Education, 338 Euston Road, London, NW1 3BH.

First published in US 2007 by The McGraw-Hill Companies, Inc.

This edition published 2007.

The **teach yourself** name is a registered trade mark of Hodder Headline.

Typeset by Transet Limited, Coventry, England.
Printed in Great Britain for Hodder Education, a division of Hodder Headline, an Hachette Livre UK Company, 338 Euston Road, London, NW1 3BH, by Cox & Wyman Ltd, Reading, Berkshire.

The publisher has used its best endeavours to ensure that the URLs for external websites referred to in this book are correct and active at the time of going to press. However, the publisher and the author have no responsibility for the websites and can make no guarantee that a site will remain live or that the content will remain relevant, decent or appropriate.

Hodder Headline's policy is to use papers that are natural, renewable and recyclable products and made from wood grown in sustainable forests. The logging and manufacturing processes are expected to conform to the environmental regulations of the country of origin.

Impression number   10 9 8 7 6 5 4 3 2 1
Year   2010 2009 2008 2007

contents

introduction

This book will teach you how to:

- understand the science of your baby's sleep
- recognize the nature of your child's sleep problem
- realize that you are not alone in having a sleepless baby
- get motivated for change
- choose the right solution for your baby and yourself
- design and implement your own tailor-made sleep plan – after all, you know your child better than anyone else.

The experience of parenting can be absolutely wonderful. The truth is that for many of us, it can also be exhausting and unnerving. This is especially the case if your child is awake and crying for much of the night.

If you have picked up this book, there is a good chance that you are one of literally thousands of parents with a baby who has a sleep problem. You may well be feeling tired, confused and be losing your confidence. Of course, you love your baby very much and you expected being a parent to be tiring, but this unrelenting exhaustion is more than you ever anticipated.

Well here is some very good news for you. No matter how severe your baby's sleep problem is, how fragile she may be in terms of her needs or how low your tolerance for seeing her upset is, there is always something that you can do to improve her sleep.

If your baby is not sleeping there is a reason why not, and in this book you will find the information that you need to identify what is preventing your child from enjoying peaceful nights. More importantly, you will learn how to introduce gentle changes that will make all the difference to her sleep.

This book recognises that each baby is an individual and that no single sleep solution is suitable for all. Once you have realized why your baby is sleeping badly, you will be able to choose from a range of solutions designed to suit both her needs and those of your family.

Not all babies and families fit into the same mould, thank goodness, and in recognising this, you will find sections on babies with special needs, specific medical problems and particular family circumstances.

Did you know?

Even if your baby is fragile, because of a medical condition or other disability, there is a great deal that you can do to improve her potential for sleep.

In the following chapters you will discover something about the nature and value of babies' sleep. You will find practical advice on how much sleep your baby needs, how to establish a perfect bedtime routine, when and how to drop night feeds and what to do when things go wrong. You will find out what your baby needs in order to sleep well, safely and happily.

Once you have read the chapter on the nature of sleep, you should use the book as a manual, referring to the clearly laid out chapters that address the needs of babies who are similar to your own. There are lots of real-life case studies which it is hoped will strike a familiar chord with you. Although no two sleep problems are the same, just as no two babies are the same, many problematic sleepers share strikingly similar stories. It is hoped that you will find these helpful, not only in recognising that you are not alone, but also in offering you some ideas about how to approach your own baby's sleeping problems. The case studies will inspire and motivate you to confidently make changes in the way that you handle your baby's sleep difficulties.

From Chapter 8 onwards you will find guidelines on how to identify your baby's sleep problem and you will then be guided through the planning, design, implementation and evaluation of a tailor-made sleep plan.

You will be amazed at what you can achieve and how quickly your sleep problem can be resolved. You will also see that teaching your child to sleep well can be a rewarding and positive experience. Given that you are already up in the night attending to your baby, it makes sense to use that time wisely, in helping your baby learn happily all by herself.

As your child grows and learns life skills, such as communicating, getting mobile and enjoying her food, she will need your help, guidance and support. Exactly the same is true for learning sleep skills. Sleep is not only essential for good health and development; it is also one of life's simple pleasures. Taking the time to teach her how to enjoy sleep is a great investment and a wonderful gift from you to her.

When your baby is well rested, she will be more content, secure and better able to play and learn. Not only this, but when you get the rest that you so badly need, you will have the energy to maintain your other important relationships and interests. Most important of all, however, is that by successfully tackling your baby's sleep problem your confidence as a parent will be restored and you will be able to truly enjoy your child's precious infancy.

Please note that the male and female pronouns have been alternated in each chapter of this book. This is for convenience only and not because sleep problems at different ages are necessarily gender specific.

01 sleep: the facts and background

In this chapter you will learn:

- how to understand the function of your baby's sleep
- how to help your baby to sleep safely
- how to recognize what your baby needs in order to sleep well
- about the nature of your baby's sleep
- about how much sleep your baby needs
- about daytime naps
- about bedtime routines
- about safe sleeping for babies – how to reduce the risk of cot death
- what your baby needs in order to sleep well
- how to recognize if your child has a sleep problem.

Given that this book is designed for parents of sleepless babies, it hardly needs to be stated that sleep is much more than just a functional state. Sleep is a wonderful, enjoyable process which, as well as helping us to function physically and mentally, is also a simple pleasure. Nothing can beat the feeling of slipping between the sheets of a cosy bed at the end of a hard day, or of staying in your warm bed for an extra hour on a weekend morning.

Babies can be helped to love their sleep, just as much as you do. During sleep, babies are able to grow, both mentally and physically. Their energy levels are restored and, as with adults, they are more likely to be cheerful and reasonable during the day as a result.

There are no clinical trials done on babies to asses the effects of sleep deprivation, because of obvious ethical reasons. It makes sense, however, to assume that babies are likely to suffer the effects of sleep deprivation, to some extent at least, in the same way that adults do.

Research into adult sleeplessness shows us that sleep is vital for maintaining a healthy mind and body. Adults who are sleep-deprived run the risk of developing depression, poor concentration and a greater tendency to sustain injury through accidents. We are also beginning to understand that when we are sleep-deprived, we are more susceptible to infections.

Despite this, we need to remember that babies on the whole are amazingly robust. Even those with pretty poor night-time sleep seem to cope very well during the daylight hours.

Joshua has always been a gorgeous and cheery baby during the day. This was the case even when his night-time sleep was bad. Our friends, family and even our health visitor just couldn't believe it when we told them how difficult he was during the night. It wasn't easy to get the support that we needed to manage his sleep, because he was feeding well and looked so happy and healthy. I think people thought we were exaggerating. Now that he is sleeping well at night, we are able to get the sleep that we need too. This means that we can fully enjoy our days with him.

Research from Cambridge University has shown that one very interesting difference between adults and children who are very tired is seen in daytime behaviour. When adults are exhausted, we are likely to move and think more slowly, as well as yawning a lot and feeling very sleepy. In contrast, however, babies and young children become *more active* during the day when they are tired.

This over-activity is often accompanied by irritability and crying. Doesn't that sound familiar? This is typical 'over-tired' behaviour and it can have a negative impact on your baby's ability to settle to sleep, both for his daytime naps and during the night.

Did you know?

Babies who are sleep-deprived during the night become more active during the day.

The nature of your baby's sleep

One of the most important things for us to understand when we come to assess our baby's sleep problem is that *it is perfectly normal for babies to wake up in the night.* Even those model babies who are 'good sleepers' will wake up several times during the night. What distinguishes good sleepers from those who have a sleep problem is the ability to re-settle without help from their parents when they stir or wake up during the night.

Top tip

If you want to increase the likelihood of your baby sleeping through the night, you need to encourage him to be aware that he is in his cot when he falls asleep at the beginning of the night.

Babies who are placed into their cots only when they have gone to sleep are understandably confused or even alarmed when they stir in the night and find themselves in a different place.

When a baby goes to sleep at the beginning of the night, he does not go into several hours of continuous deep unconsciousness. Sleep in many ways is still a rather mysterious process, but what we do know is that it comprises many different stages and cycles. These stages are made up of different types of sleep, which occur in cyclical patterns during the night, interspersed with brief arousals. In other words, he wakes up. The two main types of sleep are *rapid eye movement sleep*, or REM sleep, and *non rapid eye movement sleep*, or NREM sleep.

REM and NREM sleep

These are two terms which define the main stages of sleep. You may have heard of them, but what exactly do they mean?

REM sleep is often referred to as 'active sleep' in babies. In adults it forms the minority at just 20 to 25 per cent of the total night's sleep. During this kind of sleep, muscle tone is almost absent and the body's ability to regulate its own temperature is temporarily suspended; paradoxically, the brain's activity is at its highest level. During REM sleep, dreaming is most likely to occur – in fact REM sleep is sometimes called dream sleep.

NREM or 'quiet sleep' occurs in four varying stages and in adults takes up the majority of the total night's sleep, averaging 75 to 80 per cent. This kind of sleep is very deep and restorative. During NREM sleep, your body will be calm and still.

REM sleep in babies

In newborn, full-term babies, REM sleep accounts for at least half of the total sleep period and in premature babies, this 'active sleep' can account for around 80 per cent of all sleep. It is thought that the reason for this large amount of REM sleep in the early weeks is that is it is important for the development of a baby's brain. You can tell when your baby is in REM sleep as his eyes will move rapidly under his eyelids. You may also notice some twitching of his body and even smiling. During this kind of sleep, your baby is not able to maintain his body temperature by sweating or shivering. Because of this, you need to pay careful attention to helping him keep his body temperature just right. We will look at this more closely in the section on safe sleeping, later in the chapter.

NREM sleep in babies

During NREM sleep, your baby is less likely to be woken up by noise or movement. You may notice that his eye movements are slow and sweeping below his eyelids. Throughout his early weeks, he will begin to gradually increase the period of his NREM sleep, although it will take around six months of brain development before he moves into a mature pattern of NREM/REM sleep cycles and you are able to predict when his deep sleep is likely to occur. NREM sleep is important for your baby's growth and weight gain.

REM sleep

Looking at my baby: what do I see?
- His eyes are moving rapidly under his delicate eyelids.
- Although he is asleep, he is smiling occasionally.
- His breathing is fast and irregular.
- His little body twitches and jerks from time to time.

Why is he doing this?
- Even though he is sleeping, his brain is very active right now.
- He may be dreaming.
- This kind of 'active sleep' is normal, especially in tiny babies.

What should I do?
- Make sure that he is cosy, but not over-heated, as he can't maintain his body temperature very well during REM sleep.
- Don't pick him up or wake him. He may look a little unsettled, but this special kind of sleep is important for his brain development.

NREM sleep

Looking at my baby: what do I see?
- His eyes may be moving in slow, sweeping motions beneath his eyelids.
- His body is calm and still.
- The expression on his face is peaceful.
- His breathing is slow and regular.
- He is undisturbed by moderate background noises.

Why is he doing this?
- He is in 'quiet sleep', which is the deepest kind of sleep.
- His body is both resting and growing.

What should I do?
- Leave him to sleep peacefully, but be aware that after this deep sleep phase there will follow a period of more active sleep.

The sleep cycles

The term 'sleep cycle' describes the transition from NREM sleep to REM sleep followed by a brief 'wake up'. After the waking, a new sleep cycle begins again. These sleep cycles are repeated throughout the night.

Unlike older babies, new babies experience a phase of REM sleep at the beginning of the night, instead of the more usual NREM sleep. You will see, however, that when your baby has matured a little, this initial REM sleep phase is replaced by NREM sleep. This usually occurs at around the age of three months. You may indeed have noticed that your baby settles well into peaceful sleep at the start of the night, only to wake up confused and upset half an hour or so later. The reason for this is very likely to be that he is in transition from NREM sleep to a period of REM sleep and does not yet have the skills to re-settle by himself.

> When Emily got to four months old, she started to settle really well at bedtime with no crying or fuss. We noticed, though, that about half an hour later she would wake up and cry. Every night we had to go and re-settle her, and although this only took a few moments, it was disruptive and it meant that we could never leave her with a babysitter. In the end, we started to cut down on the amount of patting we used to get her back off to sleep and gradually, she learned how to re-settle herself. Although we still hear her call out occasionally at this time, we rarely now have to go to her.

In new babies, the usual length of a sleep cycle is around 50 minutes, but gradually extends to 90 minutes from the age of six months into adulthood. As a parent you may be only too aware that as the night progresses, your baby is more likely to become more restless and wakeful as dawn approaches. Typically, between three and six months, babies start to sleep in a relatively peaceful block at the beginning of the night, despite periods of REM sleep, but from the early hours onwards, sleep becomes much lighter and more fragile overall.

Top tips

- Early waking is normal in babies. You will find it easier to cope with if you are able to accept it and adjust your lifestyle to fit in with it.
- If at all possible, arrange with your partner to have one precious 'lie in' each, perhaps on a weekend morning. You will both feel better for it.
- Go to bed early. Even if you are usually a 'night owl', your body will adjust to its new timetable.
- Avoid drinking alcohol. As well as being unsafe, being under the influence will make getting up in the early hours ten times worse.

Biological clock

In very simple terms, your biological clock works to tell you the difference between night and day. Newborn babies do not automatically recognise bedtime. Their sleeping time is divided more or less equally between night and day. As your baby matures, however, he will begin to take the majority of his sleep during the night and nap for shorter periods during the day. This process is usually achieved by the third month, if not before.

There are a number of factors which influence your baby's biological clock. He has his own internal *circadian clock*, which is situated in an area of the brain known as the hypothalamus. This helps him to distinguish between night and day. The circadian clock does not work alone, however; it needs external clues such as light and darkness, noise levels and mealtimes. It also responds to conditions within your baby's own body, such as temperature, hunger and hormone levels. Hormones associated with sleep are:

- growth hormone
- melatonin
- cortisol.

How much sleep do babies need?

Nought to six weeks

In these early, precious but exhausting weeks, sleep is very closely involved with feeding. Your new baby will tend to live life in a milky, dozy state. It is quite usual to feed him every two to three hours. As we have already seen, few babies really settle into a period of quiet, deep sleep yet.

Babies of this age tend to sleep for 15–18 hours in a 24-hour period.

Six to sixteen weeks

By this stage many babies are beginning to sleep for longer periods and to feed less often. It is usual for a baby of about eight weeks old to sleep for six hours at night without waking for a feed, although many babies have managed to do this earlier and some will be a little later.

His total sleep requirement may have dropped slightly, to between 14 and 16 hours per day, but sleep will be becoming deeper and lasting for longer periods.

Four to six months

At this lovely age, your baby is becoming much more active. By six months he will have started to enjoy solid food and require less milk. Before six months, however, he may still need a feed during the night.

By now it is likely that he will be sleeping for between six and ten hours at night, with two to four daytime naps. This should total about 14–15 hours.

Six to twelve months

By now your baby is likely to be very active indeed. The 'average' baby sits up independently at six months, crawls at nine months and begins to toddle at one year old. These stages of your child's development are tremendously rewarding, but can be exhausting too. Both you and your baby need your sleep more than ever before. Babies of this age do not normally require a feed during the night. In fact, feeding at night may impair your baby's appetite for the food that he needs during the day.

Your baby requires 13–14 hours sleep in a 24-hour period. This is usually made up of a night-time sleep of 10 to 12 hours, plus a morning and afternoon nap.

Twelve months to two years

In the second year of life, when your baby is growing at a tremendous rate and is likely to be racing around, his sleep requirement remains at around 12–14 hours in a 24-hour period. He may, however, drop one of his daytime naps and instead take just one long nap in the middle of the day.

Babies' average hours of sleep

- 0–6 weeks (healthy full term baby) – 15–18 hours
- 6–16 weeks – 14–16 hours
- 4–6 months – 14–15 hours
- 6–12 months – 13–14 hours
- 12–24 months – 12–13 hours

02

what every baby needs for a good night's sleep

Watch the techniques in action on videojug.com

videojug
LIFE EXPLAINED. ON FILM.

In this chapter you will learn:
* how to establish a great bedtime routine
* how to keep your baby safe during sleep
* how to manage your baby's daytime naps.

Bedtime routines

Introducing a good bedtime routine is the single most important thing that you can do to help your baby sleep well through the night. Unfortunately, for many of us, at the end of a busy and tiring day, we have few resources and even less energy to make the effort to create a lovely routine for our babies. However, once you realize just what a difference it will make, not just for your baby, but for you too, you will find the motivation to put this into place.

The best bedtime routine provides *a familiar series of steps* leading up to bedtime and sleep. Each of these steps will in time become a mini sleep trigger for your baby. Your child's bedtime routine can be as short and sweet or as long as you like, providing that it can be worked into your daily life and is implemented in a loving and consistent manner. When you come to plan your bedtime routine you need to take into account your family's ethos, values and practical circumstances.

Getting the timing right

If a bedtime routine is to be really effective, it needs to conclude with your baby going off to sleep. For this reason, you need to pay attention to *timing*. There is no point going through the whole bedtime preparation process only to bring your baby back into the living-room to play or watch a video. You need to begin your routine around half an hour or so before you know your child is ready to go to sleep.

Top tip

You should only begin your bedtime routine when you know that your child is ready to sleep. The *process* of the routine is more important than the time at which it is carried out.

If you have been unable to prevent your baby from sleeping late in the afternoon, it makes sense to begin her bedtime routine later in the evening, rather than rigidly sticking to a set bedtime. This way, she will be nice and sleepy by the end of the routine and ready to go into her cot. Putting her to bed with lots of energy to spare is likely to result in her crying and calling for you, and can result in her developing negative associations with bedtime.

Sleep triggers

Any repeated action which is associated with falling asleep will very soon become a sleep trigger. This is why a consistent bedtime routine is so very important and so *useful* to you as a parent. Choose your sleep triggers carefully, and try to make them simple and fun – after all, you will be using them every day.

Sleep triggers

- A warm bath
- A familiar song or splashing game in the bath
- A massage
- A familiar spoken ritual or story book before going into the cot
- Familiar parting ritual before leaving your baby to settle for the night

---

Bath-time

Introducing a nightly bath early on in your baby's life will really help to promote good sleep for her. The action of taking a bath, if it is taken before bed provides a clear signal that daytime is now coming to an end and sleep time is on its way. This is particularly effective if you make sure that you have all you need to settle your baby for the night when you begin bath-time, so you can avoid having to return to the living-room.

Try to make bath-time a lovely part of the day for both or all of you. Turn off the TV and radio and let the answer machine deal with telephone calls. This is a special time for you and your child and an ideal opportunity to handle her in a loving way. Having this close contact and attention from you will make her feel happy and content – just the way she should feel before settling for the night.

Don't worry if bath-time is full of splashing and noisy fun. Your baby is simply expending her reserves of energy, and this is a good thing. The time for soft lighting and quiet voices is when you take her to her room.

In many families, it is Daddy's job to bath the baby when he comes home from work. This is a really lovely thing to do, as it helps to develop a loving bond between father and baby. Once again, if your baby gets really wakeful and excited at Daddy's arrival, this need not be a problem. Provided that this is built into the consistent ritual of the bedtime routine, it will *still* act as a sleep trigger.

Parents of babies with eczema and other dry skin conditions are sometimes advised not to bath their babies daily. Of course, you need to accept expert advice, but most paediatricians and dermatologists nowadays would advise a daily warm (not too hot) bath in water to which a special moisturizer has been added. Do check with your doctor or health visitor if you are unsure, as it is a shame for children with dry skin to miss out on this lovely and soothing bath-time ritual.

You may prefer to bath your baby in the morning or might not have access to bathing facilities, in which case you can introduce elements of the bath-time routine, such as a naked kick around on the changing mat and a gentle splashing song into your nightly wash and change routine.

If you do nothing else in preparation for bedtime you must at the very least wash your baby's face, hands and bottom; clean her teeth (if she has any) and put a clean sleep suit and nappy on.

Other sleep cues

Try to avoid the complicated use of mobiles, light shows, DVDs, music and so on during your bedtime routine. These things can be cumbersome and liable to break down. They also, potentially make life very difficult for you when you go away on holiday. The best sleep triggers are *portable*, and the most portable of all are those actions and words performed by you.

The wonderful thing about a good bedtime routine is that not only does it help a baby to feel sleepy; it also helps her to feel *safe* and content. Babies and children absolutely love ritual, routine and predictability. Try putting yourself in your baby's position: when you are little and dependent on others, routine helps you to feel safely contained and cared for.

A great routine

- Begin your routine shortly before you know your baby is ready for sleep.
- Take everything that you need for the night with you, to avoid having to come back into the living area.
- Follow a similar bedtime 'script' by using familiar phrases and actions at key points during the routine.
- Bath every night unless there are genuine reasons why you can't; sing the same 'action' song in the bath each night.
- Go directly to your baby's sleep room after the bath.
- Change her into a clean nappy.
- Give her a milk feed.
- Read a story or say a goodnight song.
- Place her into the cot, awake but sleepy, to settle for the night.

When Thea was newly born, I breastfed her on demand and didn't worry too much about establishing a bedtime routine. Her dad and I are both quite laid back and we didn't like the idea of our first baby having to fit in with some kind of strict regime. We were very happy to have her up with us evenings, especially as she was growing well and was such a delight to be with. However, when she was six months old I felt that Thea was becoming more and more unsettled and needed to have a little more structure. I think too that we needed to have more time together in the evenings as a couple.

We decided to try introducing a bedtime routine and to make it a loving family time. Her dad was responsible for bathing and changing her and I then fed her, read to her and put her in her cot. We found that far from being restrictive, the whole routine thing opened up a new way of enjoying her. Thea loved having daddy bath her and the special quiet time with me too. We have found that since introducing the routine, she sleeps much better and is generally much more settled.

I realise in retrospect that we could have started earlier on this, and that there were times in the evenings when she was unsettled and we were carrying her round with us – passing her between one another to try and comfort her, when she was in reality, just over-tired, needing some structure and her own space.

Later in this book you will learn how to teach your baby the skill of going to sleep without having you beside her. In preparation for this you need to establish a good routine and to be aware if your child is falling asleep in a way that is likely to cause her to wake and cry for you during the night, when she goes through the light phase of a sleep cycle.

Unhelpful settling habits include:

- falling asleep over her milk feed
- being cuddled or rocked in your arms until she is asleep
- twiddling your hair or pinching your skin (more common than you might think)
- using her dummy (pacifier) to induce sleep – unless in the early weeks if she has colic or reflux. (You might want to look at the later section covering this, as well as the one on dummy use.)

Safe sleeping for babies: how to reduce the risk of cot death

When undertaking sleep training of any kind, it goes without saying that the safety of your child is of paramount importance. Whether you are considering sleep training or not, you need to be sure that your child is safe at bedtime and during sleep.

Cot death or Sudden Infant Death Syndrome (SIDS), although relatively uncommon, is every parent's worst fear. Fortunately, there are some simple steps that you are able to take in order to reduce the risk of this tragedy occurring. The following guide is based on information from the Foundation for the Study of Infant Deaths.

Positioning

The safest position for your baby to sleep in is on her back. She should also be placed with her feet to the foot of the cot, with the bedding tucked in and made up to come no higher than her shoulders. This is so that she can't wriggle down under her blankets. Do not position your baby's bed near to a radiator or heater of any kind. The cot should be kept away from direct sunlight, too.

It is recommended that babies sleep in a crib or cot in the same room as a parent until six months old. In the very early weeks, many parents have the cot close to the side of their bed for ease of feeding. Once your baby is not taking night feeds, it is best to place the cot at the foot of your bed, where she can't see you so easily and gets used to the feeling of being alone during the night. This will help to prepare her for the move to her own room.

Bedding

Duvets and pillows are not recommended for babies under one year. It is far safer to use a cotton sheet and light layers of cotton blankets. Electric blankets and hot water bottles should *never* be used.

Sheepskins are safe to use provided that your baby is sleeping on her back. They are only really suitable for the early weeks before she is able to roll over (at around six months).

It is fine to use a baby sleeping bag. They are great for keeping babies cosy but they need to be cotton, light weight and not have a hood. They should never be used with a duvet or quilt. If additional warmth is needed, a light blanket or cotton sheet, or extra clothing is usually all that is necessary. It is most important that the sleeping bag is not too big around the neck, to prevent your baby from slipping down into the bag.

The cot

Ideally, your baby's mattress should be new. If yours was inherited from a family member or a friend, you need to make sure that it is clean, dry and free from cracks and tears. It should be firm, with no sagging and fit the cot snugly, with no gaps at the edges. Ventilated mattresses with holes are not recommended, as they are impossible to keep clean. Your baby should not sleep on a pillow, bean bag, sofa or water bed.

The use of cot bumpers has been discouraged in the past, but current opinion is that they do not cause overheating. It is advisable, however to remove a cot bumper once your baby is able to get onto her hands and knees, as she may potentially use it as a means to climb out of her cot.

Temperature

The recommended room temperature for a baby is 16–20°C. For many of us, this feels rather cool, but research has shown that it is a safe and comfortable temperature for a baby to sleep in. In ordinary circumstances it is not recommended that central heating be left on over night, unless it is controlled by a thermostat.

To see if your baby is too hot or too cold, you should feel her tummy or neck, but not her hands or feet, as they often feel quite cool.

Do check that your baby is not hot and sweaty during sleep.

Sleeping with you

The safest place for your baby to sleep is in her cot, on her back. For the first six months, it is best for her cot to be in a room with you. If there is not enough space, you should have her in the next nearest room, with the doors left open.

You should especially avoid having your baby sleep in bed with you if:

- either parent is a smoker (even if you don't smoke at home)
- either of you have been drinking alcohol or have taken drugs or medication which might cause drowsiness
- either of you is very tired
- your baby was premature or of low birth weight (less than 2.5 kg or 5.5 lbs)
- your baby is under three months old.

If you do choose to have your baby sleep in bed with you, you need to be aware of the dangers of rolling over and suffocating her; of her falling out of the bed or getting trapped between the bed and the wall. Watch out for accidents and make sure that her head is uncovered and not near the pillow and that her covers are light. Never sleep with her on a sofa or in an armchair.

> Before commencing any kind of sleep training that may involve leaving your child alone to cry, you should be quite confident that she is healthy, has no temperature and that her environment is safe.

Guidelines for reducing the risk of cot death:

- Cut smoking in pregnancy – this includes fathers too.
- Do not let anyone smoke in the same room as your baby.
- Place your baby on her back to sleep.
- Do not let your baby get too hot.
- Keep your baby's head uncovered – place your baby with her feet to the foot of the cot, to prevent wriggling down under the covers.
- If your baby is unwell, seek medical advice promptly.
- The safest place for your baby to sleep is in a cot in your room for the first six months.
- Do not share a bed with your baby, especially:
  - if you or your partner smoke – even if away from the home.
  - if either you or your partner have been drinking alcohol
  - if you or your partner take medication or drugs that make you drowsy
  - if you or your partner feel very tired
  - if your baby was born premature or was small at birth.
- Never sleep with a baby on a sofa or armchair.

Daytime naps

In recent years, there has been a swing back to the practice of offering babies structured feeds and a controlled regime of daytime naps, ideally taken in baby's cot. Parents often express concern that they are unable to achieve consistency with naps and that the needs of caring for older children mean that they are often out of the home at nap times and therefore unable to settle baby in her cot. However, so long as she is given the opportunity to sleep during the day, whether it is in the cot, pram, sling or even in the car seat, she will still benefit from her naps.

Important

Your baby does *not* have to be at home in her cot to enjoy the benefits of a daytime nap.

I already had two year old Pietro when Sofia arrived. I was worried that I wouldn't be able to give her the same structured nap regime that he had when he was small, as we were constantly on the move between various activities. Even when we were at home, the house never seemed to be quiet.

Sofia has managed to fit her naps in when she is out in the pram, and it hasn't taken her long to settle into a pattern where her main nap of the day is now taken in her cot at the same time as Pietro has his.

In the end, I really don't think she has suffered from the lack of structure during the day. In fact, if anything, I think that she has benefited by learning to be more flexible about where she sleeps. She is far more easy-going now than her brother was at her age.

In order to establish a pattern of napping, it makes sense to watch for the signs that your baby is becoming tired and to follow her lead. This approach is more likely to be successful than imposing a prescribed sleeping schedule on to her. You need, however, to avoid allowing her to become over-tired, as this will make it difficult for her to settle.

Signs that your child is becoming tired include:

- rubbing her eyes
- yawning
- crying
- becoming fractious.

The best ways to settle your baby for a nap are:

- Try not to over-handle her, as this may make her irritable.
- Put her down in her cot or pram with minimum fuss and then leave her to settle alone.
- If you do not like to leave her alone to cry, it is alright to stay beside her, with a hand resting on her.
- Avoid picking her up and putting her down again.
- Rock the pram or cot if you can, but avoid rocking your baby in your arms.
- Remember that patting her may irritate her if she is very tired.
- Try to schedule her naps at reasonably consistent times during the day, but allow her some flexibility.

- Above all, try not to get discouraged if her daytime pattern is erratic at times.
- Be aware that early on, babies' nap requirements change from week to week: you need to be open to change.
- Remember that sometimes over-napping in the day or napping too late in the day can cause problems with settling to sleep at night.
- Equally, not having enough daytime sleep can cause your baby to become over-tired and irritable at bedtime, leading to settling and sleeping problems.
- An over-tired baby will often either refuse her feed or fall asleep over it, resulting in her being hungry later on.

Top tip

If your baby is taking erratic, inconsistent naps during the day, concentrate your efforts on establishing good sleep habits at *night*.

Once your baby has learned good night-time sleep skills, she will be able to transfer them to her daytime naps too.

Averages for daytime naps

0–6 weeks	Four to eight naps a day totalling seven and a half to nine hours. Your baby will need to nap at least every two hours.
6–8 weeks	Four naps a day totalling approximately six hours. These normally consist of two to three short naps of between 30–60 minutes plus one longer nap of up to two hours.
4–6 months	Three naps a day totalling approximately three to four hours. These naps are usually arranged as a short morning nap, a long nap during the middle of the day and another short nap late in the afternoon.
6–12 months	Two naps a day totalling two to three and a half hours.
12–24 months	One nap, usually taken in the middle of the day and lasting for approximately one and a half hours, although there may be a second shorter nap taken either in the morning or later in the afternoon.

Does your child have a sleep problem?

Parents vary in their attitude towards their children's sleep and in their tolerance levels, too. For some, frequently feeding or rocking an older baby back to sleep during the night or having their child come into their bed during the night is simply not a problem. Others have very high expectations of how their child should be sleeping and worry that they will come to harm if they do not fit the norm described in the parenting manuals. Some parents need their child to sleep perfectly both day and night in order to cope with the pressures of their working lives.

Babies learn how to sleep through the night at different ages. For some this will be in the very early weeks and for others it might take six months or more. There is no doubt, too, that some babies need more sleep than others. In order to establish whether or not your child has a sleep problem, ask yourself the following questions:

1 Is she happy and content when she is awake?
2 Is she feeding well?
3 Is she growing well and putting on the right amount of weight?
4 Does she wake up gradually and happily?
5 Are you enjoying her infancy and being close to her?
6 Even though you are tired, do you have enough energy and time to spare for at least one activity that doesn't involve her?

If you have answered 'yes' to most of these, then the chances are that even if she doesn't sleep right through the night, she is getting enough sleep. If you answered 'no', then you need to ask yourself the next few questions:

1 Is she cranky and irritable when she is awake?
2 Does she often fall asleep during her feeds or struggle to feed?
3 Are you concerned about her weight gain?
4 Does she sleep for very short bursts and wake up suddenly distressed?
5 Are you finding being with her stressful and difficult?
6 Are you exhausted and have no spare time to yourself?

If you answered mainly 'yes' to these questions, and you have ruled out that she might be unwell, then your baby probably does have a sleep problem. Don't worry though; there is always a solution, no matter how severe the problem is. Find the section in this book that best describes your baby's age and make your way there. Help is at hand.

03 sleep advice for the first six months

Watch the techniques in action on videojug.com

LIFE EXPLAINED. ON FILM.

In this chapter you will learn:

- how to help your baby into good habits which will maximize his potential for sleeping through the night
- how to develop some effective ways to settle your baby when he cries or wakes up
- how to feed your baby in the night when he needs it, without creating a feed–sleep association.

Nought to six weeks

During these amazing first few weeks, your first concern needs to be that your baby's feeding, whether it is with breast or formula milk, becomes established and is working well. It is important that you are confident that your baby is growing steadily.

It is also very important that you spend lots of time holding and cuddling your baby. Remember that until very recently he was held securely in the warmth of his mother's womb. If constant holding is difficult for you, you might like to try using a well fitting and supportive sling-type baby-carrier for some of the day. This way, you can keep your baby close to you whilst getting on with any important household chores. Remember, however, that as a new mother, it is important that you rest as much as you can during these early weeks, so don't try and overdo things.

At night-time, if your baby seems to need constant holding, you might like to consider swaddling him. Swaddling has been an effective way of calming babies for centuries. It is a method of wrapping a baby to create a secure feeling of being held.

Top tip
How to swaddle your baby

1 Spread out a pure cotton baby flat sheet with the right hand corner folded down slightly.
2 Lay your baby onto the sheet facing up with his neck against the fold.
3 Pull the top left hand corner across his body and tuck it behind his right arm, smoothly under his back.
4 Pull the bottom right corner up and across to under his chin.
5 Bring the bottom left corner diagonally over his right shoulder and tuck it in at the back.
6 Now check that the swaddling is firm but *not too tight* and that his face and head are uncovered.
7 If your baby is wearing a vest and sleepsuit, this is probably all the bedding he will need.

Swaddling is a lovely alternative to being held, although not all babies like it. For obvious reasons, it is especially unsuitable for babies who like to suck their thumb. It is really only suitable for babies in the early weeks, as later on, the restriction in movement can cause annoyance and potentially impair motor development.

In Chapter 1, we have seen that babies of nought to six weeks tend to sleep for around 15–18 hours in a 24-hour period. If you think that your baby isn't getting this much sleep why not keep a simple sleep diary? This will give you a clearer picture of his sleep habits and will enable you to see if any pattern is beginning to emerge. Remember, though, that at this age babies' sleep tends to be quite light, and he may be sleeping during his feeds.

Try not to feel discouraged if your baby does not sleep through the night at this age. It might not feel like it, but most babies do not sleep through yet. Provided that you give him plenty of love, care and food and help him to feel safe and secure, you will be maximizing his potential for good sleep.

Remember that if you are breastfeeding, it may take a little longer for night feeding to stop than if you are using formula milk. These night breast feeds are necessary, as it is during the night that mothers' levels of prolactin (the hormone responsible for milk production) are at their highest. In these early weeks, night feeding will ensure that you have enough milk to meet your baby's needs during the coming day.

Nought to six weeks: your baby's top sleep needs

1 Enough milk: If you are breastfeeding this means feeding on demand; for formula-fed babies, you need to offer him about 2 $^1/_2$ oz milk (75 ml) per pound (0.45 kg) of his body weight in a 24-hour period

2 A warm, safe and cosy place to sleep

3 Frequent daytime naps to prevent over-tiredness

4 A different and darker sleep environment at night, to encourage the production of the light-dependent sleep hormone (Melatonin)

5 During the night, keep the lights down low and speak softly. Do not change his nappy unless it is very wet or is soiled. A Thermos with warm water for cleaning your baby will save you crashing around in the bathroom in the middle of the night.

6 Introduce a familiar gentle song that your baby will come to associate with bedtime.

Six weeks to four months

At around six weeks you will receive your baby's first smile. This wonderful moment often heralds the start of a period of more settled sleep too. It often takes about six or eight weeks for breastfeeding to become fully established and for a baby to grow to be truly settled and contented. We have seen, too, in Chapter 1 how babies' sleep abilities are beginning to develop at around this age. For many parents, it is at this time that you will notice that your baby is sleeping for longer periods during the night. This is partly because he is bigger and more robust, even though he is still just milk-fed and will not move on to taking solid food until he is six months old.

His total sleep requirement may have dropped slightly; to between 14 and 16 hours per day, but his sleep will be deeper and last for longer periods.

To encourage good sleeping habits at this age, keep up with the first six steps and in addition try to encourage your baby to sleep *without feeding*.

Six weeks to four months: your baby's top sleep needs

1 Regular feeds: try now to give larger, less frequent feeds.
2 A very simple bedtime routine: if possible set to coincide with the time just before your baby usually sleeps for his longest period.
3 The same comfortable, safe sleeping environment: you may need to move from Moses basket to cot.
4 Encourage your baby to sleep without sucking: feed him until he is full and sleepy and then wind him well. Place him into his cot and settle him by patting or stroking if necessary.

Of course, for many babies this age can represent a difficult rather than a settled time. Common ailments such as colic, reflux, milk allergy and infantile eczema will have an adverse effect on the development of good sleep skills. Please see Chapter 7 for advice on how to manage the sleep of these special conditions.

Four to six months

By now, your baby is becoming more settled and his sleep patterns are more predictable. Daytimes are easier too, as your baby learns how to watch you and be entertained by what is going on around him. You need to provide him with a rich and varied environment to keep him stimulated. Rather than keep him in the same room all day, take him with you in his baby chair as you go from room to room. Chat to him as much as you can and give him lots of smiles. This will encourage him to develop his own lovely language. When he begins to make cooing and then babbling sounds, respond to him warmly and encourage him to carry on. If your baby uses a dummy, just keep it for sleep times. Putting a dummy into his mouth every time he makes a sound may impair the development of his speech.

When he is awake and at home, take advantage of the fact that he can now hold a toy and reach out to his baby gym by providing him with lots to look at, hold and touch. Also, change his position regularly, both to encourage his physical strength and motor development and to prevent him from becoming bored. Try alternating laying him on his back and tummy as well as having him reclined in his baby chair. Many babies are able to sit up straight and unsupported at around six months, and this independence increases the scope for activities.

Try to make sure that you go outside at least once a day, so that he can experience some sunlight. Although you need to protect his delicate skin with shade and sun block if the weather is warm or the sun is strong. Unfortunately, all too often, parents are reluctant to go out during the day as they feel they have to stick to a schedule whereby their baby naps only in his cot. Don't worry if he falls asleep in his pram. A nap taken in the pram (or car or sling for that matter) is every bit as valuable as one taken in the cot.

Provided that he is able to fall asleep in his cot at the start of the night and for daytime naps reasonably often; allowing him to nap in his pram each day will not hamper his self-settling skills.

Most babies now sleep for between six to ten hours at night, with two to three daytime naps, totalling about 13–14 hours.

It is at this age that your baby will begin to respond to a bedtime routine. Look back to Chapter 2 for advice.

> **Four to six months: your baby's top sleep needs**
>
> 1 Plenty of stimulation during the day
> 2 Two to three daytime naps
> 3 Establish a consistent bedtime routine
> 4 Encourage your baby to fall asleep without feeding or being rocked in your arms

Why do babies cry?

Before the development of speech, the primary way your baby has of communicating his needs to you is through crying. For lots of parents, hearing their baby cry can be stressful and worrying. Sometimes it is possible to interpret the nature of your baby's cry and to be able to tell the difference between a hungry cry, a tired cry or a cry of discomfort, for example. This is not always the case, however, and it can be utterly demoralizing having a crying baby on your hands and not knowing how to comfort him. It is important to realise that in these early weeks and months, picking your baby up, cuddling him and soothing him *will not spoil him*. He needs to know that if something is wrong, you are there to comfort and help him. By consistently responding to his needs when he is very little, you will build the foundations of trust and security that he needs in order to mature into independence. To establish why he is crying, try the following checklist:

> **My baby is crying. What might be wrong?**
>
> 1 *Is he hungry?* Try offering a feed. Even if he is not yet due for one, he may be having a growth spurt and need a little extra.
> 2 *Is he tired?* Try putting him down to sleep.
> 3 *Does he have wind?* Try holding him upright, supporting him firmly against your shoulder and applying firm circular strokes to his lower back until he manages to pass his wind.
> 4 *Is he too hot or too cold?* Look for signs that he is sweating or cold. Feel his abdomen to get a rough idea of his body temperature. Check the room temperature; it should be around 18°C (63°F). Also, during the day, check that he or the pram or cot are not placed in direct sunlight.
> 5 *Does his nappy need changing?*

6 *Is he in pain?* Check that his clothing is comfortable and not over-tight and then check him for wind and nappy rash. Look at his gums to see if he is cutting a tooth. If he is hot and/or crying inconsolably, if the nature of his cry is different to normal, or he is listless, you will need to seek immediate medical help.

7 *Is he being over-handled?* Sometimes, if a baby is crying miserably, is restless and is difficult to comfort, it can be a sign that he is just tired and irritable. The best thing to do is put him in his cot or pram and allow him to settle by himself.

Common medical reasons for excessive crying at this age include:

- colic
- teething
- nappy rash
- ear ache/infections.

These conditions, although challenging at the time, tend to be temporary and respond well to medicine prescribed by your GP. Of course there are more serious illnesses which might account for your baby's excessive crying and it needs to be stressed once more that if your baby is unsettled and seems in any way different to his normal self you should always seek immediate medical help.

Coping with a crying baby

It may be the case that your baby cries more than others do. You might have noticed that yours is the baby who cries the most during visits to the clinic, at baby groups and (especially stressful) as you try to do some shopping. On the other hand, it may be that your baby doesn't cry more than others but that you, as a parent, for whatever reason, find your baby's crying to be very stressful. If this describes you, you are by no means alone.

If you have gone through the above checklist and ruled out any physical cause for your baby's cries, try the following tips to learn how to deal with it.

Top tips
Coping with crying

- Don't be afraid to hold and comfort your baby if that calms him.
- Try not to worry about getting behind with the housework. Nothing is as important as your baby's needs. If ignoring household tasks makes you even more stressed, however, consider carrying your baby around with you in a very supportive sling, so that you can get on with what you need to do.
- Allow others to comfort him if they offer; and try not to feel undermined if they succeed. Sometimes it is just the change of scene that helps.
- Try placing him in his cot, on his side with one of your hands in the small of his back and the other against his tummy. Gently rock him to and fro until he falls asleep and then reposition him onto his back.
- Remember that *your baby is not crying on purpose*. If you find yourself getting angry, put him in a safe place and leave him on his own for a few minutes whilst you walk away, have a little weep, take some deep breaths or telephone someone for moral support. When you feel calm again, you can return to him.
- Make some time for yourself. Even if it is just half an hour for a relaxing bath.
- Talk to your family, partner, health visitor or GP if you feel that you are not coping.
- Ring the 'Serene' (formerly 'Cry-sis') helpline. This is an organization set up to support and advise the parents of crying babies.

How to settle a crying baby during the night

If your baby cries a lot at night at under six months old, rather than going for one of the 'controlled crying' solutions, it is best to try some more gentle alternatives. After all, he is still very little and often babies of this age will still require a night feed at some stage.

- The most important thing that you can do to prevent night-time waking and crying is to always place your baby into the cot after his bedtime feed whilst he is still awake and to settle him in his cot rather than in your arms.
- If you are offering a 10–11 p.m. 'dream feed' it is important that your baby is awake when placed back into his cot after this feed too, especially if he is over eight weeks old. The same goes for any later night or dawn feeds.
- If your baby's night-time cries are merely 'grumblings' and he is not yet due for a feed, you should briefly check that he is comfortable, warm enough but not too hot, and that his nappy is not sodden or soiled. If all these things are alright, you should encourage him to re-settle in his cot without a feed or a cuddle.

If he continues to cry, try the tips in the box below.

Top tips

What to do when your baby wakes in the night: settling tips for four- to six-month-olds

1 Keep the lighting low and remain quiet as you re-settle him. Do not attempt to entertain him or distract him with play. You need to offer a clear message that it is night-time.

2 Pick him up and hold him closely and firmly against your shoulder in an upright position to help him to bring up any trapped wind. Stroking the base of his back rather than patting his upper back is a more effective way of helping to bring relief.

3 Place him on his side with one of your hands in the small of his back and the other against his tummy. Gently rock him to and fro until he re-settles, then reposition him onto his back.

4 Offer him a drink of water.

5 Rock him in your arms, but as soon as he begins to calm down and become sleepy, place him back into his cot and comfort him there.

6 Offer him a milk feed, but *do not allow him to fall asleep whilst sucking*. As soon as he has had enough or is starting to become sleepy, stop the feed, wind him well and then place him back into the cot. Comfort him there if you need to until he has gone to sleep.

I was 42 when I had Abigail, and she was so very precious to us. Even before I was pregnant I used to visualize myself as a mother; holding my baby in my arms, playing games, feeding her, etc. I had a difficult birth, but I loved Abigail on sight and bonded with her immediately. What I wasn't prepared for was the impact that her crying had on me. She was a colicky baby in those early weeks and sometimes I felt really helpless when I couldn't comfort her. In the evenings, she would cry and cry, but would refuse to be comforted by the breast. Sometimes she would be rigid in my arms, crying continuously. I felt like I was a hopeless mother and that I must be doing something wrong. I even began to suspect that Abigail didn't like me! Her constant crying made me feel tense and panicky. I began to be afraid of being with her and the whole thing absolutely knocked my confidence. She grew out of the colic when she was three months old, thank goodness and I was able to feed her, hold her and comfort her as I had wanted to. She's a year old now and a delight to be with. I will never forget that difficult time, however, and I always feel sympathetic towards parents when I see them struggling to comfort a crying child.

Babies who will only sleep in your arms

Some babies are only happy and content when they are held in arms and will cry whenever they are put down in the cot. We have already looked at how to cope with this during the daytime, but during the night it is both impractical and unsafe to have your baby strapped to you in a sling. It is exhausting having to spend the night pacing up and down the room, rocking him in your arms.

Babies need to feel both sleepy and safe in order to settle and sleep well at night. One way of achieving this, as we have already seen, is to follow a consistent bedtime routine.

Another way of helping your baby to feel safe and contained is to reproduce the feeling of your touch by artificial means. One way of doing this is to use light swaddling. As discussed earlier, the gentle pressure of being wrapped mimics the feeling of being held. At this age, your baby might prefer to be swaddled just up to chest height, with his arms free. Alternatively a light sheet tucked into either side of the cot can produce a light and reassuring pressure. It is possible to buy a baby 'positioner' – a soft structure of two adjustable bolsters attached to a fabric base. This helps to keep your baby in a safe position and provides gentle pressure against his body. Alternatively, before your baby is able to roll over, you could use two small cotton towels placed either side of him, below chest height.

A baby's need to be held can prevent him from being able to settle and sleep for a sustained period. To maximize the sleep potential at this age of a baby who likes to be held close, use one of the above suggestions for reproducing your touch and then place him into the cot when you know he is tired. Stay beside him, with the additional soft pressure of your hand on his tummy until he ceases crying and goes to sleep. Over time, once he has got used to falling asleep in his cot, you can begin to withdraw your contact until he is able to go to sleep without help.

Top tips

Tips for settling four- to six-month-old babies who like being held in your arms

- Swaddling
- Tucking in
- Using a special positioner
- Positioning rolled up towels

Feeding at night – to feed or not to feed?

Your baby may still require a night feed up to the age of six months even if his weight is 14 lb (6.35 kg) or more. However, if your baby is gaining weight nicely, is over six weeks old, is not unwell and decides to drop feeds by himself, you should allow him to.

If you are still waking your baby for a 10/11 p.m. 'dream feed' at four months or more, you should think about stopping. The reason for this is that by establishing a milk–sleep connection during sleep, you may be unwittingly encouraging your baby to feed unnecessarily, not just at this time, but at other times during the night, when he stirs during the light phase of a sleep cycle.

Rather than wake him up, allow him to wake naturally for this feed and when he does, offer an increasingly smaller feed, making sure that he doesn't fall fast asleep whilst taking it and before you place him back into his cot.

Did you know?

If your baby is waking for feeds more frequently than every three hours after the age of eight weeks, he is almost certainly developing a sleep problem.

As we will see in coming chapters, lots of babies' sleep problems are caused by nutritionally unneeded feeds and by feeding to sleep. Provided that you are able to put your baby back into his cot following his night feeds whilst he is *awake*, there is every chance that you will avoid later problems.

It is very important to wind your baby well after any night feeds, especially if he is formula fed. This prevents him from being woken with a tummy ache later and will provide you with an opportunity to wake him slightly before he goes back into his cot.

Top tips
Night feeds

- After the age of eight weeks, discourage falling asleep over a night feed.
- Make sure that when the feed is finished, your baby is aware that he has been put back into his cot.
- Do not try to drop night breastfeeds in the early weeks. Night feeds ensure that you establish a good supply.
- Always wind him well after a feed.
- Feed him in a comfortable chair next to his cot rather than in your bed.
- Stop the 'dream feed' after four months if your baby is gaining weight nicely.

Case study
Ten-week-old baby girl: unsettled during the day and sleeping badly at night

Carla was the first baby of two investment bankers, living and working in London. Her mother was currently taking maternity leave, but father was back at work and putting in very long hours. Carla, a bottle-fed baby, was feeding well and gaining weight. At times, she was a happy, smiling baby... but not always.

The problem

Baby Carla was restless and irritable at times during the daytime. She took frequent short naps and often woke up crying, appearing to be still tired. During the night, she was feeding very small amounts every two hours or more. She would only ever go to sleep if she was held and rocked in a parent's arms.

The solution

1 Carla needed to regulate her daytime sleep routine and learn how to be less dependent on her parents helping her to settle.
2 She also needed to drop any unnecessary night feeds.

The sleep plan

Daytime

- Aim for three daytime naps, the first two lasting around one and a half hours and a shorter late nap.
- When at home, settle her in her cot, but if it suits, once a day allow her to sleep whilst out in her pram.
- Schedule naps approximately two hours after each feed *but* use this schedule as a rough guide only. It is better to work with Carla's natural tendency for sleep rather than impose a schedule that doesn't suit her needs.
- Having given her first feed at 7 a.m. at around 9 a.m. observe Carla for signs of tiredness, i.e. yawning, rubbing eyes, becoming grumpy. Before she becomes over-tired, take her to her cot, draw the bedroom curtains and instead of rocking her to sleep, put her down whilst she is awake.

- Once in her cot, stay beside her, patting her if necessary until she settles to sleep.
- If she wakes up after less than one hour, go back to her and pat her again for up to 20 minutes. If she goes back to sleep, leave her until she wakes up again naturally. If she is unable to go back to sleep, abandon resettling her, get her up, give her her next bottle a little early, but do not allow her to fall asleep during it and then settle her for her next nap up to an hour earlier than its due time.
- Give her her second feed of the day some time between 10.30 a.m. and 11 a.m. The fact that she has napped prior to this feed will enable her to have the energy to feed well and enjoy her milk.
- Around two hours later, take her out in the pram for her lunchtime nap. (Babies tend to enjoy napping on the move, and it gives you some space, a little exercise and even the chance for a peaceful cup of coffee.)
- If necessary, give Carla her 3 p.m. bottle whilst out and about.
- Offer a final, shorter nap at home in her cot at around 5 p.m. Settle her in the same way as for the morning nap.

Bedtime

- On waking at around 5.30 p.m., Carla should have a little play time and by 6 p.m. give half of her bedtime bottle whilst still downstairs. (The reason for this is that by bedtime she was often so tired that she fell asleep over her bottle and couldn't therefore manage a full feed.)
- Begin her bedtime routine around one and a half to two hours after she has woken from her final daytime nap.
- Bath her every night and sing the same song in the bath each night.
- Use familiar phrases at key stages during the routine, such as when she enters the bedroom. These phrases will in time become part of a series of little sleep triggers.
- After the bath, go directly to the bedroom to put her night clothes on. Once ready, offer the second half of her bottle, sitting close by the cot.
- Keep a soft light on in the room and *do not* allow her to fall asleep whilst taking this feed.
- After the feed, wind her well; during this process, hold her upright and sing a little bedtime song. It needs to be the same song each night in order to give Carla a feeling of safety and familiarity.

- Then turn the lights down or off and place her into her cot whilst awake. If necessary, comfort her there until she falls asleep. As she becomes accustomed to falling asleep in her cot, gradually withdraw the amount of patting until you are just sitting quietly beside her as she falls asleep.
- When Carla is able to go to sleep without being patted, you need to move gradually out of the room until she is able to settle to sleep without you.

During the night

- Go to bed as early as you can and divide the night into shifts, so that each of you can be sure of getting some rest.
- Do not wake Carla for her 11 p.m. bottle, as you have been doing, but wait for her to wake of her own accord and feed her then.
- This feed should be given sitting beside the cot rather than in your bed and after it, Carla should be burped, put back into her cot whilst still awake and then settled there as she had been at the start of the night.
- If she wakes up again before 5 a.m. she should be offered a drink of water only and settled in her cot as before.
- At any waking between 5 and 6 a.m. she can be offered a 3 oz bottle of milk, provided that she doesn't fall asleep on it and is put into her cot afterwards. This is to encourage her to sleep on until 7 a.m.
- If she has taken this small dawn feed, expect her to take less milk than normal at her first daytime feed.

The outcome

Carla's parents were able to help Carla sleep through the night in less than ten days and with minimal crying. For the first two nights that they dropped her dream feed, she did not wake up until 2 a.m. She fed well and then re-settled from awake with minimal help. She stirred briefly both mornings at 5.30 a.m. and was settled by patting only and then woke for the day at 6.45 a.m. On the third night she did not wake for her bottle until 5.00 a.m., and they just gave her 3 oz milk. She settled very easily and woke for the day at 7.15 a.m. This became a pattern for the next few nights until they decided to try just patting her at 5.30 a.m. It took two mornings of patting her for half an hour for her to re-settle, but soon after that she was back to waking up at around 7 a.m.

Her daytime sleep improved enormously too, due to her improved self-settling skills. She soon settled in to a pattern of a one and a half hour nap in the morning, followed by a two-hour nap in the early afternoon and then a half hour nap at tea time. Because she was well rested during the day, she was happier and she fed better too. This meant that she was able to enjoy her bedtime routine and her night-time bottle.

Conclusion

By removing the link between feeding and sleeping and by teaching Carla to go to sleep alone, her parents were able to dramatically improve her sleep skills. They were delighted that they had not had to leave her to cry alone to achieve this. *By addressing the cause of a baby's sleep difficulties, it is rarely necessary to use harsh sleep training methods.*

04 sleep advice for six- to twelve-month-old babies

Watch the techniques in action on videojug.com

In this chapter you will learn:

- how to safely and gently drop your baby's night feeds
- how to understand and address the reasons why she wakes up during the night
- how to cope effectively with both separation anxiety and increased mobility at night-time.

Is your baby still waking during the night?

Your baby may still seem very little to you, but by six months old, provided that she is gaining weight and is healthy, she almost certainly has the ability to sleep through the night. So what is stopping her?

We have seen already that by six months old, babies are likely to have settled into a mature pattern of 90-minute sleep cycles. Whilst for many babies, this heralds a time of more peaceful nights, for others, it can mean that there are more definite wake-up periods during the night. For those babies who have learned good settling skills early on, this rarely presents a problem. For other babies, however, whose sleep skills may still be a little fragile, hitting six months can signal a real deterioration in sleep.

In addition to the natural change in sleep structure, six months is the age at which certain physical and developmental changes can have an adverse effect on a baby's sleep. These factors include:

- teething
- becoming more mobile
- separation anxiety
- introduction of solid food.

Teething

The average age for a baby to cut the first tooth is around six months. For some babies this occurs, earlier and others will wait for a year or more before teeth appear. Lots of babies have only very minor discomfort during teething (if any at all), but just as many babies can really suffer during this time. One thing is for sure, however, most babies get grumpy and unsettled during this time and most will need some form of painkilling medicine at some point. For advice on managing your baby's teething problems, see Chapter 7.

Becoming more mobile

By the age of six months, many babies are able to roll over. Unfortunately, there is often a period of a couple of weeks or more before they learn how to roll back again. Many parents experience a worrying and tiring time at this stage, where they are up several times in the night, repositioning their baby who has got stuck in an awkward position. The good news is that although it might feel never-ending, this developmental phase rarely lasts for more than a week or two. Once your baby can confidently roll onto her front and back again, you need not be up in the night constantly checking her position.

> Rosalind had slept well from about the age of three months. However, just after she was six months old, she began to cry out in the night, almost in panic. When we went in to her, she was invariably stuck face down, in an awkward position and couldn't get herself right again. We were absolutely terrified, as we knew that it was safest for her to sleep on her back. We even thought she might suffocate.

> At first, one of us would pick her up and comfort her in our arms until she fell asleep and then we would put her down on her back again. This worked for a while, but we were often woken later to find Ros in the same awkward position. We spoke to our health visitor who reassured us that this was a phase, which would soon pass. She advised us to go to her as soon as we heard her cry out and to reposition her in her cot rather than getting her out and rocking her back to sleep.

> This worked very well for us. We decided to divide the night into two parts. One of us was to be on 'Ros duty' between 7 p.m. and 2 a.m. and the other one would take over until 7 a.m. This meant that even though we might both be disturbed, we each had some uninterrupted rest in bed.

> Thankfully, this phase did not last for very long, as Rosalind soon got the hang of settling herself into a comfortable position and sleeping through again.

The next stage in your baby's mobility comes when she is able to either sit up or climb onto all fours. Suddenly, it becomes more difficult to keep her in the lying down position if she wakes during the night. What begins as a cuddle and an attempt to lay her back down can turn into a rugby tackle and pin-down. Her ability to move around and especially to get up when she rouses in her sleep will wake her further. When you go in to attend to her and find her sitting or kneeling in her cot rather than lying down, you can be sure that it is going to take some time before she re-settles. Once again, provided that you do not get into the habit of rocking or feeding her back to sleep, it will very quickly pass.

As your baby approaches her first birthday she will learn how to stand up in her cot. Suddenly you may be aware of her not just crying, but often calling and rattling the cot bars, too!

What do I do if she won't lie down?

It is important, when your child sits, kneels or stands up in the cot that you show her how to lie down, get comfortable and go to sleep. First of all, you should physically place her into a good sleeping position again. If she immediately springs back up, you need to choose your approach.

Option one

Rather than keep tackling her back down, just place your hands reassuringly on her (or around her if she is standing up) and wait for her to lie down in her own time. Help her to get comfortable if she needs you to, but follow her lead. Do not get her out of the cot even if she indicates that she wants to unless you feel that she is unwell. This process may take a long time, so you will need to be very patient. As soon as she does lie down you should reward her by praising her warmly. Stay beside her until she has gone to sleep. By using this gentle approach she will learn how to re-settle and reposition herself with your support rather than your direct intervention.

Option two

Reposition her and reassure her briefly before leaving the room. Still leave the room even if she is standing or kneeling up before you get to the door. Return to her every five minutes for the briefest period, just to lay her back down. Reinforce your actions by saying, 'Lie down now' in a calm, non-aggressive voice. Each time you reposition her, try not to get into a physical tussle with her and do not hold her down. It is more important that she lies down, than she stays down. Staying down will come later, when she gets tired – and gets the message. By using this firmer approach, your baby will learn to settle back to sleep by receiving a very clear message that you expect her to lie down in the cot.

As soon as your baby is able to sit, stand or kneel in the cot you need to lower the base of the cot to the bottom setting and get rid of her bumper, if you have one. These measures are to prevent her from toppling out of the cot. The bumper, if firmly fitted can potentially provide her with a step-up to climb over the cot side.

Tiffany had never been a great sleeper, but my mum had told me that when she became more active, she would wear herself out and start to sleep better. I had really looked forward to the time when she started crawling, but unfortunately this was when things started to go from bad to worse. Being more active certainly tired her out; so much so that she rarely managed to finish her night-time bottle before she crashed out in my arms.

She would sleep deeply until about 2 a.m. when she would wake up, pull herself up and stand holding the top of the cot side. She cried like her heart would break. The first few times this happened, I would lift her out of the cot and hold her in my arms until she calmed down and went back to sleep. Then I could put her back into her cot. More often than not, she would wake again and I would have to go through the same process to get her to go back to sleep. After a time, she began to really struggle to go back to sleep and at that point I started to bring her into bed with us.

Finally, we all managed to get some sleep! Before long though, she started refusing to go into her cot at the beginning of the night and during the night she was very fidgety. It got to the point where we were all exhausted and I knew that I had to do something about it.

We were advised to make sure that Tiffany was awake when we put her into her cot at night. If she stood up, we were to leave her standing, cheerfully say goodnight, leave the room and come back into the room every five minutes. Each time we went back to her we were to lay her down gently and praise her when she was in the lying-down position before leaving her again. Because she was so active, she was exhausted at bedtime and we actually only needed to go back in to her three times before she went off to sleep.

On the first night she woke just after 2 a.m., standing up as usual. We responded by laying her down again, as we did at the beginning of the night and she must have known what to do, because she went straight back to sleep. I couldn't believe how easy it was and I'm kicking myself that we waited so long before tackling her sleep issue.

Sometimes it is not possible to leave your child to cry alone. It may be that you feel instinctively it is wrong or just that you are afraid of disturbing others in the family or even neighbours. The good news is that gradual withdrawal techniques work just as well, provided that you have a clear plan and follow the plan to its conclusion.

Our problems with Joshua's sleep began after a bout of teething, when he had got used to having medicine and cuddles in the night. Even when he was no longer teething or poorly, he would wake in the early hours, almost like it was a habit. He didn't just cry when he woke up; he screamed! The moment I picked him up, he would stop crying and settle to sleep in my arms. I knew that I had to get him used to staying in his cot again, but it was so difficult as when he woke up he was invariably sitting or kneeling up, crying and bashing the cot. I didn't want to leave him alone to cry, as it seemed too harsh. Just a few nights ago I had spent so much time soothing him in my arms and I felt he may be hurt and confused by the change in my attitude towards him.

I decided to try the gentle approach where my task was to keep him in his cot, help him to get comfortable, but not force him to lie down if he didn't want to, and to stay beside him, giving whatever comfort I felt was necessary. Over the coming nights, as Joshua became accustomed to staying in his cot, I was to gradually withdraw from him until he was sleeping independently again. He protested so much on that first night that I thought he might be sick. It was horrible, but I knew that he was frustrated rather than feeling abandoned. I did not force him to lie down if he didn't want to, but I stayed beside him, holding his hand. Each time he made a made a move to lie down I praised him warmly.

On the third night, he lay immediately back down the moment I walked into his room and I knew that I was getting somewhere. Soon after that I cut the amount of time that I stayed beside him and also stopped holding his hand. By the fifth night I knew that he no longer expected me to get him out of his cot and cuddle him back to sleep, so after checking him briefly when he woke up, I left him to settle alone. He cried for about half an hour, but his cry was more of a 'grumble'. It was completely different from the intense screaming he was doing at the start of the week. I felt OK about leaving him to cry at this point and, in fact, has not woken in the night since.

I have always felt uneasy about sleep training, and I know I'm a bit of a softy, but I believe the whole process has not harmed Josh in the slightest. He is still his normal sunny self during the day, and he sleeps like a dream at night.

Separation anxiety

Did you know?

Newborn babies think that they and their mother are one and the same person?

At around seven to eight months old, you may notice that your baby becomes upset when you leave the room. Prior to this, she may have been happy for you to be around, but not over-stressed when she couldn't see you.

Similarly, when she was very little she will have found that being passed to another adult, even if that person was a stranger, was no problem to her. Suddenly, at this age she will cry when she is held by another person that she doesn't know very well, even if you are close by.

This is an absolutely normal stage in her development and not at all a sign that she is emotionally fragile in any way. It is a fact that a new baby thinks that she is part of her mother. At first, she has no sense that she is an individual. It takes time for her to realise that she is a separate person and not one and the same as her mummy.

This realisation tends to occur at around eight months old and it usually brings with it a real sense of anxiety. Your baby will demonstrate this by becoming clingy and upset when you leave her. By now she understands the concept of *object permanence* (when she throws a toy from her cot, she knows that it still exists even though she can't see it) so she knows that you will come back to her. What makes her anxious is that she has no real sense of time yet. If you leave the room even for a moment, she has no idea when you are coming back.

Clearly this has huge implications for sleep training your baby. No parent wants their child to feel fearful and anxious, especially at night-time. Unfortunately, there are no magical solutions to dealing with this difficult time, but there are some measures that you can take in order to help your baby feel more secure about being apart from you.

Top tips
Helping your clingy baby

- Play 'peek-a-boo' games with her, where you hide first of all behind a newspaper, then behind a piece of furniture and finally behind a door. Keep your disappearances brief and your reappearances loving, with lots of cuddling.
- Before leaving her with another caregiver, make time for a relaxed and lengthy settling-in period. You should be present for as much of this time as you can.
- If you intend to leave your child with a nursery or childminder, try to schedule this before she is seven months old.
- When you are in another room, chat to yourself or sing, so that even though she can't see you, she can hear you.
- Consciously follow familiar daytime and evening rituals, so that she feels safe and contained.
- *Never* leave her in the care of others without saying goodbye to her. Sneaking away will only increase her anxiety in future.
- If you are back at work, make the most of your time with her before you leave in the morning and especially when you return at night. Make sure that your time together takes priority over housework and telephone calls.

Separation anxiety can last anything between a few weeks and several months and may have an impact on your baby's sleep. Even if you have managed to avoid problems at six months when her sleep developed into the mature sleep cycle pattern, there is still a chance that you may encounter problems at the seven months plus point.

No form of sleep training should be traumatic for a baby, no matter how tempting the benefits of unbroken nights are. Psychologically, it is better for your baby to either remain close to you during this period of separation anxiety or to experience only very sensitive, gentle and gradual training.

Top tips
Sensitive sleep training

- Follow a highly consistent bedtime routine, to help her feel safe.
- Be especially close, loving and physically warm with your baby in preparation for bedtime.
- At bedtime, make sure that she is in a safe place, then pop in and out of the bedroom briefly, to bring her nightclothes for instance. Be cheerful and calm each time you return.
- After a familiar story and good-night ritual, place her into her cot whilst she is awake, then stay beside her until she goes to sleep. Gradually move yourself away from the cot over the period of a week or two until she feels secure in her room alone.
- If you decide to leave her to settle alone from the start; return to her briefly and frequently to reassure her. *Act like your normal self* when you go in to her. It will unsettle her if you avoid eye contact and voice contact with her and will only make her feel more anxious.
- After a night of sleep training, be especially responsive to her on the following day.

When Aiden was six months old, I returned to work. I found it very hard to leave him as I had enjoyed every moment of his life, and was anxious about how his childminder would fill my shoes. At first, he was fine and I really felt that I had got the 'work–life balance' sorted. After a few weeks, however, he became very clingy towards me and cried whenever I moved more than a few feet away from him. He was OK with his childminder, but would avoid other new adults. Previously he had been happy to go to sleep in his cot alone at the beginning of the night, but all of that suddenly changed. I found that I had to hold him close to me to get him off to sleep and then he would wake up with real tears looking for me during the night. I was absolutely sure that I had caused this anxiety by returning to work and if we hadn't needed the money, I would have handed in my notice immediately.

On talking to other mothers in my post-natal group I found that most of them were experiencing similar issues with their own babies. Some of us were back at work and some were staying at home, but whatever the circumstances, all the babies were becoming clingy. I know it's awful, but I felt so much better! I did some reading and found that Aiden's behaviour was typical of a baby with normal separation anxiety and that I was not to blame. This made me feel much more confident, and I knew that in time he would be alright. His behaviour lasted for maybe three months and I'm glad to say that he is fine now, and back to his easy-going self.

Top tip

Don't automatically blame your baby's increased anxiety on the fact that you've returned to work. At seven months plus, this was likely to have happened anyway.

Why won't my baby sleep in her cot?

It is usually between six and twelve months that your baby makes her needs and wants very clear to you. For many families this is the time that baby firmly entrenches herself into the parental bed. A combination of teething, standing up and crying in the cot, worry or guilt over your baby's separation anxiety and, to be honest, your own tiredness and exasperation can make you take the line of least resistance and bring her into bed with you. Whilst there is no doubt that this might bring some initial relief in that you all get *some* sleep at least, the quality of that sleep is often poor and, over time, everyone can end up exhausted.

It is a fact that babies fidget and wriggle during the night. They also sleep horizontally across the pillows and have absolutely no regard for the well-being of their parents, who invariably end up sleeping so close to the edge that they are hanging half in and half out of the bed by morning. Parents who share their bed with the baby often suffer from stiff necks, bad backs and bad moods.

On a more serious note, sleeping in your bed is not recommended for safety reasons. Not only this, but over time, the initial benefits of having your baby sleep you with can end up working against you. Often babies who get into the habit of sleeping in bed with you during the night will refuse to settle in their own cots at the start of the night too.

How to help your baby sleep all night in her cot

In order to help your baby sleep all night in her own cot:

1 Help her to settle in her cot at the start of the night.
2 Help her to overcome the expectation that she will transfer to your bed during the night.
3 Teach her that her cot is a safe and permanent sleeping place.

Case study
Seven-month-old baby boy: feeding to sleep and sleeping in his parents' bed

The problem

Leo was the first baby of an art teacher and a civil servant. They lived in Hertfordshire, and had no family living nearby. He was a well-grown baby who was enjoying solids and developing well. At bedtime he was settled to sleep with a breastfeed and was then transferred to his cot. He would wake up any time from half an hour to two hours later in a very upset state. The only way that he could be comforted was by being breastfed back to sleep. At each waking, he would become increasingly difficult to settle, until his parents moved him into their bed in the early hours of the morning. Here he would settle but continue to breastfeed frequently during the night.

The reason

It is perfectly normal for babies to wake at night. Leo's difficulties were down to the fact that he was unable to re-settle without help. His parents thought that the reason for his frequent feeding was because he was a hungry baby. A vicious cycle had been established whereby Leo fed little during the day, because he was so used to feeding during the night. They needed to be reassured that he would be able to establish a better feeding pattern, and that his night feeds were being used mainly as sleep prompts.

They also learned that Leo was not yet able to accept his cot as a safe and permanent sleeping place. This was because he only ever went into it when he was asleep. Each time he woke, he felt alarmed to find himself in a strange place and he cried. The natural response of his parents was to remove him from his cot, and bring him to their bed, where he was comforted and fed back to sleep. He had learned that the right and proper place for his sleep was in bed with his mum and dad!

The solution

In order to help Leo sleep through the night, the family needed him to:

1 Fall asleep in his cot at the beginning of the night aware of where he was.
2 Drop his night breastfeeds and lose his suck–sleep dependence.
3 Overcome the expectation of the transfer to his mum and dad's bed and to learn that his cot was his safe and permanent sleeping place.

The plan

- Establish a lovely consistent bedtime routine. This will provide him with a clear series of steps leading up to bedtime. In a very short time, each of these steps will become sleep cues.
- Incorporate familiar phrases and songs into the routine, as these are very effective as well as highly portable cues. A good routine will not only help Leo to feel sleepy, but also help him to feel safe.
- The ideal time to begin the routine is around two to three hours after he has woken from his last daytime nap.

- After his nightly bath, take him directly to his room for his final feed. The room should be softly but well lit.
- You need to limit the duration of the feed to prevent him dozing, as it is very important that he is awake when he has finished.
- After the feed, whilst he is still awake, one of you should hold him in your arms and then look at a simple picture book for a few moments. If you keep to the same one each night, it will become a sleep prompt for him.
- Following the story, turn down the light and say goodnight to him. Regardless of whether or not he is still wide awake, you should place him into his cot.

Nights 1 and 2

- One of you should kneel or sit next to the cot and stroke his chest (or his back if he is kneeling up). As he eventually gives in to sleep, you should just have a hand resting on him.
- You should stay beside him, patting and stroking him if he needs you to until he eventually gives in to sleep. It is OK to speak softly, using repetitive phrases or to hum to him.
- Demonstrating a confident and calm demeanour will really help Leo to feel safe. It is best not to lift him out of his cot, but if you have to, place him back down once he is calm but still awake. There is no need to leave him alone, at this stage. Your first aim is to allow him to go to sleep in his cot, without the breast in his mouth. It is important not to be alarmed when he cries, as he is merely protesting at the change. He is also expressing his frustration at wanting to go to sleep, but not being able to yet. This is what you are teaching him now.
- Eventually, he will give in to sleep but this may take an hour or more. As he goes to sleep you should try not to be touching him, although it is OK that one of you is beside him. In time, when he has learned how to sleep without sucking, you should withdraw your presence so that he learns to sleep independently.
- When Leo wakes before 10 p.m., it should be relatively easy to re-settle him in his cot without feeding him or getting him out for a cuddle. You should offer him the same patting or stroking as you did at the beginning of the night.
- Each time he wakes up after 10 p.m., his mother needs to feed him in order to calm him and to address any possible learned

hunger. You must, however, cut the duration of the night feeds to *five minutes maximum*. This is to prevent him from going to sleep on the breast and to wean him off having significant amounts of milk in his tummy during the night.

- After each night feed, place him back into his cot whilst he is still awake. You should expect some more crying, and it is fine to stay beside him if he needs you to. Even though it is stressful, you should keep calm and resolute, he is learning all the time.
- Following this approach, most babies spontaneously stop waking up for night feeds and will sleep through the night.

Nights 3 and 4

- It is likely that by now, Leo will settle down willingly when placed into his cot. If he wants you to stroke him, you can do so, but cut down on the duration. You should also try to reduce eye contact with him as he enters sleep; nor should you be touching him at all.
- During the night, you should continue to withhold feeds before 10 p.m. but now restrict any later feeds to three minutes maximum.

Night 5 onwards

- After placing him into his cot at the beginning of the night, and sitting next to him for a moment or two, you should begin to gently potter around the room. After a short time you need to leave the room. If he calls out or cries, you should go back to him briefly to reassure and reposition him. You should not lift him out of the cot. After this you need to leave him again, regardless of whether he is calm and then return to him every five minutes. It is not necessary to go back to him if he merely 'grumbles' or cries in a rhythmic or 'fussing' way. By now, as he is used to his cot and going to sleep without the breast, this kind of cry is not a sign of any real distress. In time the crying will become almost tuneful and is a natural prelude to sleep in many babies.
- During the night, he should not be fed at all when he wakes up. You can offer a little water, but provided he has had enough to drink during the day, it is unlikely that he will be thirsty.
- You should treat any night waking with the same consistent response that you have used at the start of the night, i.e. returning briefly to reassure, but not feed or pick up.

- Very soon he will take more food during the day to compensate for the lost night feeds, and the balance will be redressed.
- Throughout the plan, demonstrate a calm, loving and resolute manner.

The outcome

Once Leo's parents understood the reason for his frequent waking and feeding, they felt confident about tackling his sleep problem.

They were relieved that they did not have to leave him alone to cry.

On the very first night of sleep training, Leo cried for half an hour at the beginning of the night. After this, however, he slept for a four and a half hour stretch, in his cot, which was far longer than he had ever done. He still, however, woke another twice in the night and was re-settled back into his cot after the recommended short feeds. There was little or no crying when he went into his cot. Although the two short feeds were hard going, Leo's mum was used to very little sleep, and realised that she was now using her time with him during the night in a much more positive way. On the fourth night of the plan, Leo's mother stopped feeding him altogether. Instead, she went to him, repositioned and reassured him and then left him to re-settle without her. Given that he now had the skills to sleep without the breast in his mouth and was no longer expecting to come in their bed, Leo settled very quickly.

On the fifth night, his parents were delighted that Leo slept through the night from 7 p.m. until 7.30 a.m. He has managed to maintain his good sleep habits, and the family now enjoy peaceful nights.

Conclusion

By understanding the reason for Leo's sleep difficulties and breaking the solution down into manageable tasks, his parents were able to solve the problem effectively and with minimal trauma.

Introducing solids

For the first six months of your baby's life, all of her nutritional needs can be met with either breast milk or formula milk. She even has her own in-built stock of iron which will last her until she begins on solids. In the past, the weaning of babies happened much earlier, but in recent years we have learned that early weaning is not only unnecessary, but can sometimes also be unsafe, as your baby's body may not be mature enough to cope with foods other than milk.

If your baby has had digestive difficulties such as colic, allergies, food intolerances or reflux, you need to give careful consideration to the timing and method of weaning. Always follow the advice of your doctor, health visitor or dietician. Sometimes, introducing solid food to vulnerable babies can actually worsen, rather than alleviate a sleep problem. This is due to tummy ache, diarrhoea or a worsening of allergic skin conditions such as eczema.

However, if your baby has already learned good self-settling skills and is taking just one small feed during the night before re-settling and sleeping until the morning, the chances are that introducing solids *will* help her to sleep through the night.

Did you know?

You may think that introducing solids early will improve your baby's sleep but this is not usually true. Babies who are exclusively milk fed will sleep through the night by six months when they have learned independent sleep skills.

Bethany had never been a brilliant sleeper, but I thought that when she began taking solid food her sleep would improve. I introduced baby rice early, at four and a half months old and she loved it. She seemed to want to take more than the two teaspoons which was recommended for her. This confirmed to me that she was hungry, and that this was the reason for her needing to feed during the night. I gave the rice during the afternoon, so that her tummy was nice and full for bedtime.

When I came to give her 7 p.m. bottle she was not so interested, and instead of her usual 8 oz, she only took

5 oz. This concerned me a bit but I realised that she might not be so hungry because of the baby rice she had taken earlier. That night, I won't say that she slept any worse than normal, but she certainly didn't sleep any better.

It was only after I saw a sleep specialist that I realised that the reason for Bethany's sleep problem was not that she was hungry. She was very well fed really, but her problem was that I used to feed her to sleep at the start of the night. When she woke in the night, the only way that she would settle was by taking another bottle. I'd always presumed that this was because she was hungry, but I came to realise that she fed not out of hunger but as a means of getting off to sleep. Once I taught her how to go to sleep without the bottle at the beginning of the night, she no longer needed it when she woke up during the night. I carried on giving the solids once I had started, but I can see in retrospect that I needn't have started her so early.

For advice on early weaning foods, consult your health visitor or look at some of the many excellent books available on the subject. From a sleep point of view, it is better to introduce solid food initially during the mid-morning period. This way, if there is any danger of the food causing an adverse reaction, there is time for it to get out of your baby's system before bedtime. There is nothing to be gained by filling your baby up with solid food just before bed. She will still benefit from the increased calorie and nutritional input, even if the food was given early in the day.

When do I know that my baby is ready for solid food?

- if she has been previously sleeping through the night, but is suddenly more wakeful and difficult to settle;
- if she begins to show an interest in the food that you are eating;
- if she drains her bottles and is unable to make it to the next feed without getting hungry;
- if she can hold her head and sit up straight with minimal support;
- if you notice that her weight gain has dipped below her normal percentile line.

From the time that Michael was very small we had established a very consistent bedtime routine. By three months old he was able to settle to sleep by himself and he would always sleep well until we woke him for a feed at 10 p.m. He would take his milk very well and then generally sleep through until 4 a.m. We then gave another feed and he would sleep until 7 a.m. At about four months old, he stopped waking for his 4 a.m. feed. He would wake at 6 instead and have a little water which helped him go through until morning. At four-and-a-half months we stopped offering the 10 p.m. feed, as he really didn't seem to be interested in it any more. From then on he would sleep from 7 p.m. to 7 a.m. each night and we were the envy of all our friends. Just before he was six months old, however, he began to wake at about 3 a.m. and was impossible to re-settle. In desperation, we offered him a bottle of milk which he demolished. We had read enough about sleep issues to know that he did not need the feed out of sheer habit; we knew that it was real hunger. If we needed a sign that it was time to introduce solid food, this was it. The following day, we gave him some baby rice and he really loved it. We carried on with our good sleep settling practices and continued giving Michael baby rice during the day. Within a week he was sleeping through the night again.

We have always felt that by being sensitive to the signals Michael gives us, we haven't gone far wrong, and following his lead on when to start solids has confirmed to us that this is the best way.

Daytime naps between six and twelve months

During this time of rapid growth and development, it is really inadvisable for your baby to go through the day without at least one nap. The average for daytime sleep at this age is two naps a day totalling two to three and a half hours. *However*, some babies may take three naps and others just one. Difficulties arise when your baby takes very frequent, short and reluctant naps. Often, babies who do this will sleep for hours if they are in the pram or in your arms. Clearly, this is not always practical or even desirable. At times even the most selfless of parents needs a little space during the day to attend to business or household matters.

From your baby's point of view, you need to remember that at this age, she is constantly being bombarded with new sights and experiences, not to mention discovering her own new skills and abilities. The world is a fascinating place, full of wonder and challenges, and she is using up masses of energy in her discovery of it. If she is to appreciate and enjoy all this newness, she needs at regular intervals to step back, have a rest and then start again afresh. If she doesn't do this, she will end up over-tired and over-stimulated. This will lead to tears and irritability and this can even affect the way that she sleeps at night.

For many babies, being well rested during the day means that they will sleep better at night.

> Simone had never been easy to settle for her daytime naps but we thought that when she became mobile, she would be so exhausted that she would be easier to settle. In fact, she got even worse! We could see that she was tired, as she was so cranky and kept crying and rubbing her eyes, but as soon as we put her into her cot she would be hysterical.

> The only way that we could get her to sleep was by putting her into the car and driving around with her. I couldn't always do this, as there were times that my husband needed the car for work.

> At about eight or nine months old, her night-time sleep got worse too. Soon we found that she hardly (if at all) slept during the day and then was up in the night several times, only to start the day at 5 a.m. We worked out that she was only getting about ten hours sleep in total out of 24 hours.

> The funny thing was that she didn't seem to be tired, actually. She was very active and into everything. Looking back, though, I realise that at this time she was very irritable indeed. I think that she was over-tired and struggling – just as I was!

Does this sound familiar? It is all too easy for babies to get into a vicious circle, where lack of sleep during the day leads to unsettled nights. Given that we know that babies who do not get enough sleep become *extra active* rather than lethargic and sleepy, this wound-up tiredness leads to an inability to relax and nap during the following day and so the pattern is repeated.

The best way to break this pattern is to begin with optimizing your baby's sleep skills at *night*. This might seem the wrong way around but in fact at night your baby is surrounded by other sleep prompts and has more chance for a 'wind down' time. You need to begin by making sure that your baby is consistently going to sleep all by herself at the beginning of the night. It is absolutely tempting after an exhausting day with an active baby to allow her to fall asleep over her milk feed or be rocked in your arms until she is at the point of sleep. If you do this, however, it will soon begin to work against you, and she will wake up later looking for you. Not only this, but if she crashes to sleep in your arms at bedtime due to sheer exhaustion, she has no opportunity to develop the settling skills that she needs for her daytime naps.

You might think that your baby goes into her cot whilst awake, but ask yourself if she *really knows* that you are no longer beside her. Working with her to encourage self-settling needs to be done at the beginning of the night, rather than if she wakes up during the night. This is because at this time, she is more likely to *succeed*. Once she has gone to sleep by herself she is more likely to sleep for a longer period. You need her to have had a good night's sleep and be well rested and not over-tired if you are to help her nap well during the day. Don't be discouraged, however, if when at first you begin to teach her how to fall asleep alone, she still wakes in the night. This will soon stop, but in the meantime, consider these wakings as an opportunity to reinforce the good settling skills that you are teaching her. Look at Chapter 9 for practical help on teaching your baby to sleep alone.

Once you are confident that your baby has the necessary self-settling skills, you can address her daytime sleep problems.

Case study

Nine-month-old baby boy: refusing daytime naps and needing to be rocked or fed to sleep at night

Morton was the second baby of a graphic designer and a landscape gardener. He had a five-year-old sister, Iris. He was a healthy baby, who was feeding well on formula milk and solids and was growing well. He was happy, responsive and had recently started to crawl.

The problem

Morton had recently begun to refuse to go into his cot for daytime sleeps. This meant that he was often irritable, crying and needing to be carried around in Christina's arms when awake. He would only ever go to sleep when he was being pushed in his pram or when in the car, and even then, he would try to resist sleep. When he did manage to go to sleep, he woke after just half an hour, crying and rubbing his eyes. Despite appearing to be tired, it was impossible to get him to go back to sleep.

In addition to this, Morton was becoming very difficult to settle at bedtime. He was clearly over-tired, but unable to relax and let go into sleep. This meant that his mother had begun to feed him to sleep in the dark in his room and if he didn't fall asleep on his bottle, she would rock him in her arms until he'd settled and then place him into his cot once he was in fairly deep sleep. As a result of this, he was waking often in the night, needing to be rocked again. He regularly woke up at 5 a.m. and at this time in the morning, it was impossible to get him to re-settle.

The solution

In order for Morton to establish a pattern of consistent daytime naps and peaceful night-time sleep he needed to:

1 Learn how to fall asleep independently and happily at the beginning of the night.
2 Apply his night-time sleep skills to his daytime naps.

The plan

- Follow a highly consistent bedtime routine, comprising a series of familiar steps leading up to bedtime. In time, these steps will ensure that Morton feels not only safe and contained, but sleepy too.
- Start the routine at around 6 p.m., unless Morton has inadvertently fallen asleep at teatime, in which case, he should be allowed to sleep for no more than 40 minutes and the bedtime routine should begin two and a half hours later, i.e. if Morton slept between 4.30 and 5.00 p.m., the routine should start at 7.30 p.m.
- After his bath, offer his milk as usual in his room, but keep a soft light on and discourage him from falling asleep during the feed.

- During the time that one of you is settling Morton, the other should put Iris to bed. Warn her that she might hear her baby brother crying, but to be reassured that Mummy or Daddy is with him, teaching him how to sleep, and that he is not alone.
- After Morton's milk, introduce a familiar good-night story book in his room before placing him in his cot. This will help to provide a new sleep trigger for him instead of the ritual of being rocked or fed to sleep. The book needs to be the same one each night until his settling skills are very strong.
- When the story is over, Morton needs to go into his cot whilst wide awake.

Nights 1 and 2

- Lean over the cot and cuddle/stroke/pat him until he begins to settle. As he eventually calms down, withdraw the amount of your contact until just your hand is gently resting on him or holding his hand.
- If Morton struggles to get up, kneel next to him with your arms around him, but do not lift him out of the cot. Speak softly, using repetitive phrases or hum to him. As he eventually becomes sleepy, lie him down and then, if necessary, lean right over into the cot and cuddle him. *Do not* pick him up and cuddle him to sleep. It is very important for Morton to know that he is in his cot as he falls asleep. Throughout his crying and protest at the change, maintain a calm and loving demeanour.

Night 3

- Maintain the new settling measures that you have introduced on the previous two nights but begin to move away from him slightly. Cut down on eye contact, and avoid touching him after your initial kiss goodnight and tuck-in.

Nights 5 and 6

- After placing him into his cot, quietly potter around his room. You can return to him to pat, reassure and lay him back down whenever he needs you to.

Night 7

- Say goodnight to Morton in your usual way, stay for a moment or two and then quietly leave. If he calls out or cries go back to him, stroke his back or tummy for a moment, then go through the withdrawal stages (taking about five minutes over this) and then leave again. If necessary, keep on returning to him and do not allow him to become distressed at any stage. Most important, however, is that however long it takes Morton to settle, you should not be in the room with him as he falls asleep.
- From night 1, both of you go to bed early, and be mentally prepared to be up in the night. He might wake up more often than ever at first, due to insecurity at the changes in his settling routine. When he wakes in the night, leave him to see if he can re-settle by himself. If his crying becomes more persistent, however, go to him and settle him as you did at the beginning of the evening, without getting him out of his cot.
- Treat any time before 7 a.m. as a night waking. After this, you should open his curtains and welcome him to the day, with as much cheerfulness as you can muster!

Daytime

- For the first week of the sleep plan, whilst Morton is learning how to settle to sleep at night, help him go to sleep at regular times in the day, so that his body gets into the rhythm of napping. At first you can help him to go to sleep by pushing him out in the pram or taking him in the car.
- Daytime sleep skills tend to be more fragile than night-time ones, so you can expect Morton to require extra help to wind down for his naps. What is very important is that he is well rested during the day, as over-tiredness will impact on the ground you are making in establishing his night-time settling skills.
- Offer two daytime naps, with one of these being shorter than the other. It doesn't matter which one that is. Watch out for signs that Morton is becoming tired during the day. These include yawning, eye rubbing, becoming short-tempered or crying. Before these signs go on for any length of time and he becomes over-tired, help put him to sleep in whatever way that you can.

- Timing of the naps should be scheduled for around 10 a.m. and 3 p.m. (or one hour either side of these times) but be flexible about this. It is more important to watch for Morton's sleepy signs.
- If he wakes up from his nap after less than 45 minutes and still appears to be sleepy, try and resettle him for up to 20 minutes. If at the end of this time he shows no signs of going back to sleep, you should allow him to get up.
- After one or two weeks of implementing the sleep plan at night, you need to encourage Morton to apply the skills that he has learned to his daytime naps. Instead of taking him out in his pram or the car for his naps, settle him at home. By now he should have established regular times and durations for his naps, so you will have a better idea of when to settle him.
- Follow a mini-bedtime routine when settling him down during the day. Go to his bed room, close the curtains and change his nappy if necessary. Remove his outer clothing and put him into his night-time sleeping bag. Read his usual bedtime story book and after this place him into his cot whilst he is awake. Leave him to settle alone. If he cries return to him every five minutes or so to reassure him, but do not stay with him. Eventually, he will settle to sleep without you, but this might take some time.
- If Morton sleeps for longer than usual, don't worry. There is no need to wake him up unless it gets to 4 p.m., after which time his late napping might interfere with his usual bedtime.
- Morton is not yet ready to have just one long nap in the day, but he soon will be. You need to follow his lead on this.

The outcome

It took around two weeks for Morton's sleep difficulties to completely resolve into a pattern of good night-time and daytime napping, but there were some great improvements from the very moment they started the plan.

Once his problems had resolved the change in him was remarkable. He was better tempered and less clingy to his mother. The whole family benefited from Morton's improved sleep skills: Iris found that her parents were less tired and they had more time for her on her own.

His mother hadn't realised just how exhausted she had become through constantly trying to comfort Morton, both during the night and in the daytime too. She was at last getting time to catch up on her own sleep.

The family liked the idea of tackling Morton's sleep troubles in two stages. They felt it was a gentle and sensible approach. Given that they had faith in the plan and were motivated to change, they had very good results.

Top tips

Daytime naps, six to twelve months

- Take note of the times that your baby appears to be sleepy during the day and follow her lead.
- Encourage your baby to establish good independent sleep skills at night, which can then be transferred to daytime.
- Just as at bedtime, allow your baby to self-settle.
- Follow a mini-bedtime routine before settling your baby in her cot during the day.
- If she wakes after a short time, allow her the opportunity to self-settle if she is just 'fussing.' Help her to re-settle by patting, etc., only if she really needs you to.
- Recognize that your baby is an individual and may not fit the textbook norm of daytime sleep patterns set out for babies of her age.
- Don't become a prisoner in your home. Sleep taken when out and about in the pushchair or car is just as restorative as sleep taken in the cot.
- Be flexible: your baby's daytime sleep needs will change as she grows.
- Do not rush to get your baby up if she wakes after a short nap. If you allow her to re-settle, she may sleep for longer and wake up better rested.

Older babies who will only sleep in your bed

There are two main reasons why babies of six to twelve months old want to sleep in bed with their parents:

1 They fall asleep in your bed at the beginning of the night.
2 They are used to the ritual for being brought into your bed at some point during the night or early morning.

It might at times appear that your baby hates or fears her cot. Babies are very good at letting us know when they are unhappy about something, and if your baby cries each time she is in her cot, you cannot be blamed for thinking that there is something the matter *with the cot*. It is very rarely the case that the cot is wrong, however. What babies do not like is *the unfamiliar*.

Look at this scenario:

> *You follow a perfect bedtime routine and then give your baby's bedtime feed cuddled up on your bed. She either falls asleep on her milk or you hold her in your arms before she snuggles down and goes to sleep. You gently place her into her cot and tiptoe out of the room. It may be shortly afterwards or several hours later that she wakes up with an outraged and upset cry. You hurry back to her and comfortingly scoop her up into your arms. You either feed her or cuddle her again until she is soothed back to bed. You may put her back into her cot if it is still early on, or if it is nearly morning, she will stay in the bed with you. Even if you have put her back into her cot, it is really only a matter of time before she wakes again and you bring her into the bed with you. She then sleeps peacefully until morning, perhaps with the odd tiny feed or cuddle when she stirs.*

Does that sound familiar? How about this other scenario:

> *Your baby always goes to sleep beautifully in her cot at the beginning of the night. She has a good bedtime routine followed by a story and a milk feed in her room. She goes into her cot either asleep or even awake sometimes, and then settles with minimal, if any crying. Despite this, she still wakes up in the night. By this time you are very tired, and you bring her into bed with you, where she settles immediately and sleeps well for the remainder of the night. Occasionally you have resolved to keep her in her cot for the night, but each time you try, her crying is upset to the point of hysteria.*

In the first scenario, it is clear that the baby is *never aware* of being put into her cot. Each time she wakes, she panics to find herself in an unfamiliar place. Her parents' response is to remove her immediately and to take her to their bed (a place that feels safe and familiar). Unwittingly, by doing this, the baby's feeling that the cot is the wrong place for her to be in is being reinforced.

In the second scenario, the baby is happy to settle into her cot, but has become accustomed to the *ritual* of transferring to her parents' bed. Babies and children get hooked on to rituals very early in life, and these familiar, predictable behaviour patterns are hugely important to them. When you try to change a ritual (in particular a night-time ritual) the protest from your baby will be massive. When you do decide to alter your baby's night-time ritual, it is important to realise that this protest is not an expression of fear or abandonment. Neither is it to do with fear of her cot.

It is easy to see why this extreme protest may seem like fear of the cot. Before you move her to a bed or travel cot or before you rush out and spend money on a set of new bedding, consider what the benefits will be of gently teaching her to accept her cot as a safe and permanent sleeping place.

> *At the age of 6 months, we moved William into his own room, but from the start he seemed to hate his cot. I was upset, as I'd put lots of thought into making his room and bed lovely and welcoming. We'd splashed out on a gorgeous cot, which would convert to a bed when he was bigger. It seemed like he was never going to be happy sleeping there though.*
>
> *At the beginning of the night, he would fall asleep during his last breastfeed which I gave in my bedroom. The reason for this was that I liked to relax and watch the soaps on TV during this feed. It was a good way for both of us to unwind and I felt that this feed was very unrushed and relaxed. I'm sure that some of the programmes theme tunes acted as 'lullabies' for William too!*
>
> *Once he fell asleep I would always place him into his cot. The problems began some time after midnight, when he would wake up and I couldn't re-settle him in his cot. I knew that he wasn't hungry, as he was feeding well in the day, and a breastfeed didn't settle him anyway. He used to actually point to his doorway, as if he was telling me that he wanted to come to my bed. As soon as I walked out of his room, he would clearly relax in my arms and he fell asleep virtually the moment he came into my bed.*
>
> *It became a routine that my husband would silently get up and almost sleep walk to the sofa, where he would spend the rest of the night.*

After taking advice, we decided to teach William that his cot was a safe and permanent sleeping place. We began by giving his bedtime feed in his room, rather than in ours. (My husband taped the soaps for me!) After this, I would put him into his cot whilst he was still awake. He protested for a couple of nights, but was tired and settled after half an hour or so. During the night, I would go to him, feed him very briefly and then place him back into his cot before he fell asleep. One of us would stay beside him, to comfort him as he got used to sleeping in what was actually a new place for him.

It was a difficult but ultimately rewarding experience, as within a week, William had stopped waking up during the night. We had our bed to ourselves and William was much happier. This was due, I'm sure, to the improvement in the quality of his sleep.

Neither of us had realised just how tired we had become, having our baby in bed with us each night. It is only now that we feel rested enough to really enjoy William's babyhood.

Did you know?

- Your baby *wants* to sleep all night in her cot. She demands to come into your bed because she is accustomed to the ritual.
- Her coming into your bed is habitual and *not* an emotional plea for your attention.

Dropping night breastfeeds

By the time your baby reaches the age of six months, provided that she is healthy, gaining weight nicely and has started solid food, she no longer requires a night feed for nutritional reasons. Lots of babies will drop night feeds without help once they reach a certain weight and when their sleep skills have matured. For many babies, however, night feeds will continue long after they are still needed. The reasons for this unnecessary feeding include:

- needing to feed as a sleep prompt
- learned hunger
- habit and ritual.

Case study

12-month-old baby girl, dependent on breastfeeding for sleeping

Felicity was the youngest of three girls. Her older sisters, Hannah and Isobel were five and three years old. They both shared a bedroom and slept through the night. Felicity had her own little room and cot. As babies, Hannah and Isobel each had had sleep difficulties similar to their baby sister. Both were breastfed during the night until well after their first birthdays. Their mother, Ruth, an ex-schoolteacher was now at home full-time, caring for the family. Their father, Mike, worked full-time as a telephone engineer, and often did overtime too. They lived in a bungalow on the outskirts of London.

Felicity had no health problems; she was developing well and had recently started walking.

The problem

Despite Felicity's recent increase in expended energy, she was not sleeping well at all. Typically she would fall asleep on the breast at the beginning of the night and then wake up to six times a night for short 'top-up' feeds. She was clingy and tired during the day and was taking virtually no solids. Clearly, the reason for her poor daytime appetite was due to excessive milk intake during the night.

The solution

Felicity needed to drop all of her night breastfeeds if she was to learn how to sleep through the night, and for her daytime appetite to improve. Whereas once, breastfeeding had been a lovely way of settling Felicity to sleep at night, it had now become the very reason for her wakefulness.

The plan

Stage 1

- Ruth needs to work to break the breast–sleep connection. It will prolong the process if Mike is to take over the night care, as Felicity will still expect a breastfeed each time her mummy tries to settle her. Mike can support Ruth by taking over the girls' care in the morning, to give Ruth a much-needed sleep in the morning. For this reason, you should start the sleep plan on a Friday night.

- Avoid allowing Felicity any daytime sleep or breastfeeds after 3 p.m.
- Offer a carbohydrate-rich supper and plenty of fluids (breast or water) during the day. As her daytime appetite is small, and she can easily become overwhelmed with food, it is best to give tiny portions and then offer second helpings, rather than overwhelm her with a large dish of food.
- Develop a highly repetitive and consistent bedtime routine. Always give Felicity a bath, and after this, go directly to her room to settle her to sleep. Aim to have her in her cot by 7.30 p.m.
- Daddy is to put Hannah and Isobel to bed as Mummy concentrates on Felicity.
- Breastfeed her on a chair in her own bedroom but *do not* allow her to fall asleep at the breast. If she does this, gently wake her by speaking softly to her. It is most important that you are sitting up when you feed her. If you lie down, you are giving Felicity the message that you will be staying with her for the night.
- After the feed, cuddle up and look at a familiar picture book – the same one each night. If she refuses this, remain calm and just show her the book cover before moving on to the next stage.
- Start a 'kiss goodnight' ritual prior to putting Felicity into her cot awake.
- When/if she cries, give her as much physical contact as she needs to help her to feel safe. You can stroke and pat her and even lean right into her cot and put yourself close beside her. You must not, however lift her out of the cot. If you do this, Felicity will expect another breastfeed, and it will be difficult for you to refuse. *If she goes to sleep, aware that she is in her own cot, even if she has cried and even if you have been beside her, that is marvellous progress and she is well on the way to sleeping through the night.* As she is crying, remind yourself that Felicity is neither hungry nor frightened. She is tired and frustrated, because she wants to sleep and doesn't have the skills yet. Stay positive as this is what you are teaching her now.
- As she enters sleep, withdraw the amount of physical contact, so that you are just quietly sitting by her cot.
- When she goes to sleep, you need to leave and go to bed early yourself.

- When Felicity first wakes up during the night, go to her and breastfeed her in her room. After the feed, you should place her back into her cot whilst she is still awake.
- Expect some more crying, but try to demonstrate a calm and positive manner. Settle her as you have done earlier in the evening and do not be disheartened, as Felicity will very soon learn to be content in her own cot. Here is a suggested regime of how to eventually withdraw. Each step should last for as many nights as you feel comfortable with.

After a brief breastfeed:

Step 1   Stroke Felicity's back, or lean right over into the cot and cuddle her. You must not rock or feed her to sleep. She needs to know where he is.

Step 2   Just sit with a hand on her back. If she wants you to stroke her, do so but cut down on the duration. As she enters sleep, do not be touching her at all.

Step 3   Sit beside the cot and just touch Felicity's hand.

Step 4   Move yourself away from her slightly. Cut down on eye contact, and avoid touching Felicity as she goes off to sleep.

Step 5   After Felicity's feed, place her in her cot and then leave. You may need to pop back in a few times to reassure her as she settles.

- It is clear that Felicity needs to have milk during the night for the following reasons:
  1 learned hunger
  2 sleep prompt.
- By cutting the duration of the feeds and not allowing her to fall asleep on the breast, you are now directly addressing both reasons for her unnecessary night feeding.
- Each time she wakes up, go through the same routine and treat anything before 6.30 a.m. as a night waking.
- Any time *after* 6.30 a.m., first open the bedroom curtains and then welcome Felicity to the day. After this, you can give her her morning breastfeed, but do not let her go back to sleep!
- Stage 1 should take between one and two weeks to complete. You should be firm and consistent but not rush Felicity too much and only move on a stage when you are both feeling comfortable.

Stage 2: dropping the night feeds

Daddy can help during the night now. Once again, commence this on a Friday night.

- Mummy to continue settling Felicity in the same way at the beginning of the night. The bedtime (7.30 p.m.) feed should be maintained but Felicity should not have another breastfeed until 6.30 a.m. at the earliest.
- Each time she wakes up in the night leave her for a moment to see if she can settle herself. If her crying becomes urgent or distressed, Mummy should go to her and reassure her. If necessary, you can stay with her, but she must remain in her cot.
- After a very few times settling without a feed, Felicity will soon lose her milk–sleep association. She has been very well prepared during the previous stage on how to fall asleep without the breast in her mouth.
- Once Felicity is no longer expecting a breastfeed during the night, you can cut down on the length of time you spend comforting her in her cot, so that she is able to re-settle without help each time she roused during the night. By this time, either one of you can go to her to settle her during the night.

The outcome

Felicity really struggled at first, breaking her normal settling pattern. She did not want to stop a breastfeed before she had gone to sleep, and she let her mother know how unhappy she was.

This was very hard for Ruth, whose natural mothering style was to feed her baby on demand. She realised, however, that in order to meet the challenge of bringing up three very little girls, she needed her baby and herself to be well rested. She stuck with it, and even in the first week, whilst she was still breastfeeding at night, she saw some very positive changes. Felicity went from feeding six times a night to just once or twice.

Over the next few days, Felicity began to eat more during the day, and actually seemed to enjoy her food, too.

By the second week, her parents were feeling confident about dropping the night breastfeeds altogether. There were a few tears, but no real distress, as they had equipped Felicity with the skills to sleep without the breast. Before the two weeks were up, she was sleeping all night in her cot.

Conclusion

By understanding the reason for Felicity's frequent night waking and excessive night feeding, the family were able to solve her sleep difficulties in a sensitive and gentle way. They particularly liked being able to tackle the problem in stages and the permission they had to take things at their own and Felicity's pace. Sleep problems are always more successfully treated if the family is able to accept and understand the reason for the solution offered.

> **Did you know?**
>
> Breast milk is very low in iron, although the iron present is much easier to absorb than in cows' milk. Full-term babies are born with their own in-built stock of iron which lasts them for the first four to six months. After this time, they need to get this essential nutrient from other sources.

There is absolutely no question at all that breast milk is the perfect food for babies up to the age of six months. They require nothing more than this. After six months, breast milk is still a highly nutritious and fabulous drink, *however* it is no longer a complete food. Your baby will need to have other food too.

Night breastfeeding to excess can sometimes lead to a baby not eating other essential food during the daytime. In some cases, babies can run the risk of developing iron deficiency: anaemia.

If your baby has a tiny appetite, you need to watch out that she is not *over*-breastfeeding and, in addition, offer her food which is rich in both iron and vitamin C (which is needed to absorb the iron that she eats).

Symptoms of anaemia are:

- pale skin
- tiredness
- fast heartbeat – but remember that a normal baby's pulse is faster than yours
- irritability
- reduced appetite
- brittle nails
- sore or swollen tongue.

A baby with mild or developing anaemia may not show these (rather vague) symptoms. If you are concerned about your baby's eating, and she shows any of the above signs, you should seek advice from your GP, paediatrician or health visitor.

Iron-rich food for breastfed babies

- Leafy dark green vegetables – especially watercress
- Lean meat – including chicken and fish
- Pulses
- Well-cooked egg yolk
- Fortified breakfast cereals
- Follow-on formula milk, either given as an additional drink or mixed with food

---

As well as being nutritionally inadvisable, night breastfeeding can sometimes prevent babies developing essential self-settling skills and can lead to daytime sleep problems too. All in all, you can run the risk of your baby becoming over-tired and over-dependent on you for all of their sleep needs. You may find yourself becoming extremely tired and run down and lacking the energy to cope with her increased mobility and need for activity and stimulation. You may also worry particularly about your baby's ability to settle if you are preparing to return to work.

It is a shame, when you have done such a great job in breastfeeding to find yourself confronted with these difficulties. You need to be clear in your own mind, however, that even if your baby does have a sleep problem related to breastfeeding that you have given her the best. Nothing can take away those early benefits, both nutritional and emotional that you have given to her by feeding her yourself.

Top tips
Dropping night breastfeeds

- Establish a familiar bedtime routine.
- Do not allow her to fall asleep on the breast at the start of the night.
- Introduce a song or story *after* the feed and before she goes into her cot. This will break the milk–sleep association.
- Keep night feeds very short, and always place her back into her cot whilst she is awake.

Remember then, that whilst breastfeeding your baby at night when she is very little is one of the best things that you can do for her, after the age of six months, unless she is unwell, night breastfeeds are no longer beneficial and can even be detrimental. Do still continue with daytime breastfeeds, however.

Dropping night bottle feeds

As with night breastfeeds, night formula feeds are almost always unnecessary once a baby gets to six months old and is on solid food. The ritual of feeding at night can become a habit that is very difficult to break. During the middle of the night, your older baby's body needs to rest. Keeping her body working by having her digest milk feeds, is not conducive to enjoying a good night's sleep.

Not only is prolonged bottle feeding at night unnecessary and bad for her digestion, it is also bad for your baby's growing teeth. Having milk pooling in your baby's mouth can lead to tooth decay. As soon as your baby's first tooth arrives you need to start a gentle teeth cleaning ritual *after* her bedtime bottle. This also gives you the opportunity to wake her and read a little story before settling her in her cot whilst she is awake.

Another very important consideration is the *safety* aspect of giving night feeds. This is particularly relevant for babies who self-feed in the cot during the night. It is so important to discourage this kind of feeding, due to the risk of choking and/or vomiting.

Five good reasons why you should not allow your older baby to bottle feed to sleep

1 She may learn to associate sleep with feeding, and may only be able to fall asleep whilst taking a bottle.

2 This may lead to unnecessary feeding at night which will impair her appetite for the food which she needs during the day.

3 Feeding during the night over-works your baby's digestive system.

4 Night bottle feeds are bad for her developing teeth, and may cause tooth decay.

5 There is a risk of choking if you leave your baby to self-feed during the night.

Case study

11-month-old baby boy waking for night bottle feeds

Billy was the second child of a part-time marketing consultant and a solicitor. His older sister, Melissa, was three years old and had no problems with her sleep. Billy slept in a cot in his own room. The family lived in a quiet commuter area of Middlesex, outside London.

Billy was born by emergency caesarian section at 38 weeks, but was healthy and had an uneventful infancy. After ten weeks of being breastfed, he had moved on to formula feeds with no problems. His weight gain and development were both excellent. His mother described his only real difficulty was that he suffered a lot from 'trapped wind', particularly during the night.

The problem

Although Billy had a great bedtime routine, he would fall asleep every night in his cot, with his mum holding his bottle and him feeding to sleep. He normally settled very quickly like this, but once he had gone to sleep, he would stir once or twice before his parents went to bed and would need to be fed back to sleep with a little more milk. This was always given to him in his cot.

At around 2 a.m., he would wake up fully and take a full 8 oz bottle. Prior to this, however, he would stir frequently and need to have his back stroked, or be sat up until he passed wind. Occasionally, Billy would take another big bottle of milk at around 5 a.m. before resettling and sleeping until morning.

It was clear that Billy was feeding as frequently as a much younger baby. His night-time milk drinking was both preventing him from enjoying sustained sleep and was interfering with his appetite for solid food during the day.

The solution

Billy is easily capable of sleeping through the night, and in order for him to do this, he needs to:

1 Fall asleep at the beginning of the night *after* and not *during* his night bottle.
2 Gently drop all of his night feeds. As he is so accustomed to taking large quantities of milk at night, the best way for him to achieve this is by having the feeds gradually diluted.

The plan

Nights 1 and 2

- Continue to follow a highly ritualized but very simple bedtime routine, using key phrases/songs/actions, etc. This will help Billy to feel safe and sleepy too.
- After his bath and pyjamas on, you should take him directly to his room and sit him *on your knee* for his bottle of milk.
- When he has had enough milk, put the bottle out of sight. After this, you should sit with him and spend a little time looking at a picture book and 'winding' him. Use the same book each night until his sleep problems have resolved. Billy will be very restless and unwilling to look at the book at first, so don't feel that you must read to him for long.
- After looking at the book, pick him up and develop a goodnight ritual of turning the lights down and closing the curtains, etc. After this, say goodnight in your usual way, and place him into his cot whilst he is still awake.
- Billy will protest at being placed into his cot without his bottle. If necessary, you can stay beside him but not lift him out of his cot. To make things easier for him, one of you can sit beside the cot with your arms around him. In time his crying will subside and he will lie down. Praise him warmly as he does this.
- To cope with the crying, remind yourselves that he is neither hungry nor frightened. He is tired and frustrated, and he *wants* to sleep. You should be positive, as this is what you are teaching him now. Spend *as much time as you need to* with him and do not be disheartened; it is worth investing this time and effort. Settle him this way for the first two nights of the sleep programme.
- Billy will only sleep through the night when he is able to settle to sleep *without either of you in the room with him*. So you need to eventually withdraw as he goes to sleep.

Nights 3 and 4

- By now, Billy will be happier with the new routine and about going in his cot without his milk. He should lie himself down after a brief cuddle but if he doesn't do this, you should encourage (but not force) him to lie down. You need to sit quietly beside him, and reduce eye contact with him. If he wants you to stroke him, you can do so but you should cut down on the duration. As he enters sleep, you should not be touching him at all.

Nights 5 and 6

- Try pottering around the room, returning to Billy every now and then if he needs you to. It is still alright to be next to him as he goes to sleep.

Night 7

- Say goodnight in your usual way, potter around for a moment or two and then leave. If Billy calls out or cries, you can go back to him, stroke his back for a minute, then leave again. If his crying is any more than a 'complaint' or 'grumble', you can keep on returning to him every five minutes or so; but you are not to go in if his cries are minor.
- Any time after midnight, if he wakes up you should lift him from his cot and offer him a bottle of milk. This milk should be normal volume but diluted as follows:

Nights 1 and 2 ³/₄ strength
Nights 3 and 4 ¹/₂ strength
Nights 5 and 6 ¹/₄ strength
Night 7 onwards Nothing, unless he is unwell and then just water.

- It is important that after this milk you remove the bottle whilst he is still awake and that he is awake when you put him back into his cot. If necessary, you can sit beside him if you had done so at the beginning of the night.
- This diluted milk can be given more than once during the night if needed.
- If he is still waking up after you have weaned him off the milk, you can go to him but do not lift him out of his cot. Reassure him and then leave him to go off to sleep alone.
- Billy should be offered a morning bottle (any time after 6 a.m.) downstairs – not in the bedroom – *and not in his cot.*
- It is vital that during the sleep training, you demonstrate a calm, confident and *resolute* attitude.

The outcome

Billy had already got a great bedtime routine, and was not in the habit of getting into his parents' bed during the night. He was having one good long nap during the day, so he was sleepy but not over-tired at bedtime. Because his parents were already doing so much right, solving Billy's sleep problem was not as difficult as they thought it might be.

The worst night was the first one. Billy was desperately upset that his normal settling routine had changed, and it took him almost two hours of on and off crying, before his sobs eventually gave way to sleep. His mother in particular found this very hard. The fact that she was sitting beside him, however, helped her to cope. She felt that not only was she supporting him, but she was going through the battle with him too. Daddy knew this was going to be hard for her, and he waited outside the room, murmuring his support and encouragement. It helped her, knowing that she was not facing this alone.

On the first night, once he had gone to sleep, Billy did not wake as usual, early in the evening. His first wake-up was for his 2 a.m. feed. He accepted his diluted bottle, but cried again for around half an hour when he was placed back into his cot whilst still awake and without the teat in his mouth. He then slept on until 6.30 a.m.

Over the coming nights, his parents continued to put him down awake and to dilute the night bottle. Each night they found that Daniel coped better than the last one.

Billy stopped waking for his night feeds before he even got on to quarter strength milk. For two or three weeks, however, he fell into a pattern of waking at the very early time of 5.30 a.m. His parents decided to give a drink of water only at this time, and stick with going in and out of his room every five minutes, and, within a month, Billy slept through until the household got up, at 7 a.m.

Each morning, his big sister, Melissa was given a sticker on her pyjamas for staying in her bed when she was woken up by Billy. This helped her to feel included in the plan and to see it as a positive thing. It also gave her parents the opportunity to recognize and praise her own good sleep behaviour.

Conclusion

Billy's sleep problem and its resolution show once again how, once you have established the *reason* for a baby's waking, you can solve it without the unnecessary trauma of simply leaving her to cry it out.

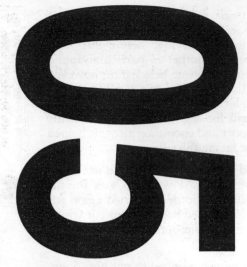

05 sleep advice for one to two year olds

Watch the techniques in action on videojug.com

In this chapter you will learn:
- how to help your older baby to consistently sleep through the night
- how to wean your baby off the dummy
- how to tackle early waking problems.

This is a truly magical age. Your baby is growing fast and is enchanting you with his funny expressions and lovely perspective on the world. He is becoming more independent and exploring all around himself. He is toddling, tumbling over, emptying cupboards and getting into mischief. You may breathe a sigh of relief that all of those early feeding and teething worries have been resolved, your confidence as a parent has grown, and even if you do make mistakes, your baby is a lot more robust.

In the second year of life, when your baby is more active than ever, his sleep requirement remains at around 12–14 hours in a 24 hour period. He may however drop one of his daytime naps and instead take just one long nap in the middle of the day. It is not at all uncommon for babies, especially when they are approaching their second year, to refuse their naps altogether. Sometimes babies who have previously been great night-time sleepers will begin to encounter problems at bedtime too.

Suddenly refusing to go to bed

If you find that at this age your baby protests about going to bed, wakes early in the morning and refuses his nap, it is most likely because he loves life so much that he doesn't want to switch off and miss anything.

Of course, sleep is still absolutely vital for his health, growth and development, and despite his objections, you need to help him to settle down and have both a decent nap and a good night's sleep.

At this age, when your baby's imagination is developing and he begins to worry about scary things, it is more important than ever that you ensure that he has a good bedtime routine. The reassurance of the familiar, repetitive run-up to bedtime will keep him feeling safe and contained. When a baby falls asleep feeling calm, safe and happy, he is more likely to sleep through the night.

When Barnaby got to 18 months, he started to protest when I put him to bed for both his daytime nap and at bedtime. Before this, he had always loved his cot, and we hadn't had any problems settling him at all. I was upset, because I knew he needed to sleep, and once I had managed to get him to sleep he slept really deeply. He was using up loads of energy during the day, eating well and was not poorly, so I couldn't understand what the problem was.

We spent a few nights bringing Barnaby back downstairs when he cried at bedtime and refused his cot. We would allow him to watch a DVD and play until he fell asleep on the sofa. Once he was fast asleep, we would put him into his cot. He would sleep well until about 5 a.m., which was far earlier than his usual 7 a.m. waking. We knew that he was still tired but there was absolutely nothing that we could do to help him re-settle. We ended up getting him up for the day. Even though he had been up so early, he refused to settle down for his nap. Having said that, he would fall deeply asleep in the car or in his pram, and by teatime, if he had not been out, he would fall asleep in his food!

After talking to other mums at his music group, I found out that some of his friends had done the same kind of thing. One of the mums told me how she managed to tackle the problem with her little girl, and I followed her advice.

We decided that even if Barnaby protested at bedtime we would not bring him back downstairs. Instead, one of us would either stay with him or keep going in and out to him, depending on how upset he was, until he settled to sleep. The first few times that we did this it took him ages to settle, but we knew that he needed to fall asleep in his cot rather than downstairs on the sofa. We also knew that we had to break the new ritual of him automatically coming downstairs after his bath. Even though it was hard, it only took him a few nights to start going to sleep in his cot again.

Once we had got the beginning of the night sorted out, the early morning waking seemed to resolve itself of its own accord. We then needed to tackle his daytime nap. I decided to set aside some time so that I could start a daytime ritual, which included lunch, teeth cleaned, face and hands washed and then his nappy changed. We followed this with a quiet period of reading a story in his room before putting him into his cot. He complained at first, and it took a long time before he settled and slept. During this time, I sat quietly beside him, reading and reassuring him when he needed it. After a week or two *(longer than it took for him to learn how to settle again at bedtime)* Barnaby began to accept having his daytime nap again. He is so much more relaxed and cheerful since he has been getting the rest that he needs.

This aversion to sleep is not at all uncommon between 12 and 24 months and beyond. It is important to be aware that it can happen and to take a firm but understanding approach to handling it. Remember how important it is for your baby, when growing into a toddler, to have as much sleep as possible. Remember, too, that if you begin to allow your baby to delay or lose sleep altogether, it can be difficult to regain his previously good sleep skills. Allowing him to get up and play after his refusal to go to sleep in his cot will only reinforce that behaviour and will very soon become a habit.

Top tips
Re-establishing good sleep skills

- Do not allow your baby to over-nap or nap too late in the day.
- Stick to a reassuringly consist bedtime routine.
- Be prepared for protest and do not give way by getting him up if he refuses or struggles to settle to sleep.
- Praise him when he is in his cot, in order for him to develop positive associations around bedtime.
- Use simple role-play techniques, using dolls and teddies to demonstrate good sleep behaviour.

The changing face of daytime naps

By the time your baby reaches 18 months, and often before this, he is likely to move from having two or three daytime naps to just one one-and-a-half to two-hour nap in the middle of the day. You need to be prepared for this to happen and to go along with the change. You may notice first of all that your baby begins to refuse his morning nap, or to sleep for just a very short period. If he does this, he is telling you that he is ready to move on to one later and longer nap. Don't be concerned; this one nap will be just as good for him, and one special benefit for you is that you will have the opportunity, whilst he is resting to catch up on your own jobs or even have a rest yourself.

The transition from two or more naps to just one is not always straightforward. Your baby's sleep needs will change gradually rather than overnight, and you may experience a confusing period when he sometimes wants a morning nap and sometimes doesn't. You may also find that he naps in the morning and then does not want to sleep again until teatime, when it is too late, and may interfere with his usual bedtime. It may be helpful for you to keep a sleep diary of his naps, including information about when he appears to be tired, when you put him to bed, whether he cries and if so for how long, how long it takes for him to go to sleep and for how long he sleeps. This will give you helpful information as to when best to schedule his nap(s). Don't worry if he is not doing the same as his peers or if he doesn't fit the textbook standard. He is an individual, and all babies progress at different rates.

My baby refuses his morning nap. What can I do?

1 Watch out for signs that he is getting tired and then put him to sleep. Try to be flexible when he is over one year and be aware that his sleep needs may be changing.

2 Be aware that he may be moving towards a more mature napping pattern of a long sleep in the middle of the day.

3 Do not force him to sleep or allow him to cry alone in his room if he is simply not tired. He may develop negative feelings about his cot, and this could have a detrimental effect on his night-time sleep.

4 Keep a sleep diary. This will help you to see how his natural sleep tendency is emerging. You can then work with this, rather than forcing him into a napping routine which is no longer appropriate for his needs.

But when am I going to feed him?

It can cause logistical difficulties when your baby wants to nap just when you usually give him his lunch. If this is the case, you have two options:

1 Give a late morning substantial snack and then follow this by a later lunch when he wakes after his nap.

2 Give an earlier lunch, and then mid-afternoon offer a snack which will keep him going until his usual tea or supper time.

Remember that in order for your baby to sleep well, he needs to be well fed but his tummy should not be over-full. By the time your baby is one year old his milk requirement will have dropped to just one pint (560 ml) a day. This is usually taken as a large morning and bedtime feed (bottle or breast), with the shortfall being made up by adding milk to breakfast cereal or other food. If your baby is used to having a lunchtime feed in addition and he is now sleeping when this feed is due, it is perfectly alright to give it either before he goes to sleep or later, when he wakes up.

My baby refuses his afternoon nap, but then falls asleep at teatime. What can I do?

- Encourage him to take his morning nap later than usual, so that he naps for a long period around the middle of the day.
- Do not try to force him to sleep at his usual time if he is simply not tired.
- Embrace his changing sleep needs, and keep a sleep diary. This will help you feel in control and in tune with his needs.
- Offer him an afternoon snack to boost his blood sugar and keep him going.
- If you absolutely cannot avoid his falling asleep at teatime, limit the nap to 20 minutes.

There is no hard and fast rule as to how long the gap should be between your baby waking up from his last daytime nap and the time you put him to bed. In babies of this age, it tends to be about three to four hours, but your baby might be different. *You know your baby best.* If you read your baby's body language, as only you can do, you will find the right bedtime for him.

The great dummy debate

This section could have easily have been included in the previous two chapters, as problems with dummy dependence can occur from anywhere between three months to five years... and beyond.

Dummies have always been the subject of often heated debate and viewpoints. There is no doubt that dummies do, in some circumstances, have their advantages.

> **Five dummy plus points**
> - Can help ease the symptoms of colic and reflux
> - Can help a 'sucky' baby to drop unnecessary feeds
> - Can provide comfort during teething
> - Can help premature, tube-fed babies to establish feeding from the breast or bottle
> - The rhythmic and natural sucking process can help to induce sleep

However, whilst a dummy may be a godsend in your baby's early weeks, the advantages are often only very short term. It is frequently the case that over time, the use of a dummy can end up working against you rather than to your advantage. This is particularly the case if your baby becomes over-dependent on his dummy and is only able to fall asleep whilst sucking.

When your baby falls asleep, his dummy is likely to fall out of his mouth. The nature of sleep is such that frequent waking up due to the sleep cycles means that he may need his dummy replacing several times.

During the first year or two of your baby's life, when he is teething or has a cold, his tiny nasal passages will become easily blocked. When this happens he will struggle to breathe through his nose. This is especially difficult for him when he is lying flat in his cot. In order to keep his dummy in place, he needs to be able to breathe freely through his nose; otherwise his dummy will fall out. For a baby who is only able to sleep with a dummy in situ, this can cause real problems.

If your baby is waking during the night due to problems with his dummy, you have two choices:

1 Get rid of the dummy altogether.
2 Teach him how to manage his dummy independently.

Case study

14-month-old baby girl: disrupted sleep because of over-dependence on her dummy

Poppy was a lively toddler who was developing beautifully despite having been born two months prematurely. She had been introduced to a dummy at an early age, in an attempt to ease the symptoms of reflux.

As all babies are, Poppy was very precious indeed to her parents, who were both teachers. The family lived in a flat in north London. Poppy's mother was early into her pregnancy with their second child and was extremely tired as a result.

The problem

Poppy had a great bedtime routine and settled independently into her cot with her dummy and 'blanky' (comfort blanket).

Despite settling all by herself, she was waking 45 minutes after going to sleep, having invariably lost her dummy, and needing one of her parents to find it for her and help her to re-settle. She subsequently woke up and needed help with settling up to four times later during the night. Her parents were afraid to take her dummy away, as they could not face their nights becoming any worse than they already were. They also felt that Poppy was vulnerable still, because of her prematurity and that that any form of sleep training would be not only detrimental to her but also traumatic for them.

After some discussion, it was clear that Poppy was over-dependent on a dummy to help her to sleep. This was particularly problematic when she had a blocked nose due to a cold or a teething episode. When she fell asleep, the dummy fell out of her mouth, and when she woke during the light phase of a sleep cycle, she felt something was missing and couldn't re-settle without it. She had also come to expect the ritual of contact with her parents when she woke in the night.

The solution

In order for Poppy to sleep through the night, she needed to do two things:

1 Learn how to sleep without her dummy.
2 To stay in her cot and overcome her expectation of cuddles and contact with her parents during the night.

The plan

• Tighten up her bedtime routine, so that it becomes a clear system of little sleep triggers.

- Include familiar phrases and a goodnight story in your routine.
- This routine and the verbal sleep triggers will very soon perform the same soothing function as her dummy – but are better for her and will promote more peaceful sleep.
- Put her to bed with her 'blanky' but without her dummy.
- Learning to sleep without her dummy should be taught at the *beginning of the night*, and then reinforced when she wakes up during the night and then during the following day.
- As Poppy learns to fall asleep without her dummy, one of you should stay beside her to minimize her stress.
- After two nights, her new bedtime routine will be established and she will have learned how to fall asleep without the dummy in her mouth.
- On the third night, you need to gently withdraw and allow Poppy to fall asleep alone again.
- Whilst working towards this objective, you need to support one another and stay calm and resolved.
- For the first two nights, each time she wakes in the night, she will need to be comforted back to sleep in her cot, with one of you beside her. This is instead of bringing her into your bed.
- She will protest at you breaking the normal ritual, but once she realises that you have not abandoned her, she will soon adapt to the change.
- From the third night, if she continues to wake up, you need to go to her and reassure her very briefly before leaving her to settle by herself.
- Once the dummy has gone and Poppy has stopped expecting to get out of her cot during the night, it is unlikely that she will wake on subsequent nights.

The outcome

On the first night of Poppy's sleep plan it took her 50 minutes to settle to sleep. As expected, she cried a lot and spent a long time standing up, rattling the bars of her cot. Even though her parents found this very difficult, they managed to remain calm and resolved. Once she had gone to sleep, she did not call out until 3 a.m. This seven-hour stretch was the longest period that she had slept since her birth! Re-settling Poppy at 3 a.m. took over an hour, but her crying was not as distressed as it had been at the beginning of the night. She woke up for the day, happily, at 7.30 a.m.

On the second night it took Poppy 20 minutes to settle alone and without her dummy. Her parents took it in turns to go to her, in order for her to realise she would receive the same calm consistent response from each of them. At 5 a.m., she briefly stirred and called out, but managed to settle back to sleep before her parents got to her.

Since then, apart from odd periods of illness, Poppy has slept through the night.

Conclusion

Poppy was introduced to a dummy for a very good reason, but by the time she was over a year old, the dummy was hindering her sleep. A gradual and supportive approach was acceptable to her loving parents and the strategy worked effectively for them all.

How to help your older baby manage his dummy himself at night:

- During bath-time, play 'race for the dummy' game, where you challenge him to beat you at picking up the dummy first and putting it in his mouth.
- Place plenty of dummies in his cot at night, so that he can find a spare if he loses one.
- If he calls out for you during the night, having lost his dummy, always give it to him into his hand rather than putting it into his mouth for him.

Of course, there may be reasons why you would prefer your baby to keep his dummy. One advantage that your older baby has, is that he can be taught how to manage it himself.

Toby was born with a foot deformity, which means that he needs to have frequent surgical operations. He gets a lot of comfort from his dummy, and we feel that it is right for him to have it for as long as he needs it. We have taught him how replace his own dummy when he loses it in the night, and we honestly have no sleep problems with him now.

If your baby is dependent upon a dummy to sleep at night, you may dread him giving it up. Remember, though, that although babies protest noisily and vigorously when presented with change, after this protest, they very quickly accept a new behaviour.

If there is no good reason for him having it, it is best to encourage him to give the dummy up. The reason for this is that there are clear health reasons why *not* having a dummy outweighs the benefits of having one.

Five dummy minus-points

- There is a link between dummy use and ear infections.
- Using a dummy during the day may delay your baby's speech development.
- There may be an increased risk of stomach and other infections.
- Dentists advise against the use of dummies (and thumb sucking) as these can lead to orthodontic problems in the future.
- Over-dependence on a dummy can impair your baby's ability to sleep through the night.

If you choose to give your baby a dummy, there are some guidelines for its safe and responsible use.

Top tips
Dummy safety

- Do not dip your baby's dummy into a sweet solution, as this will cause tooth decay.
- Always use an orthodontic teat, which has less of a tendency to push your baby's teeth forward.
- Make sure that your baby's dummy is scrupulously clean and has no cracks or tears in it.
- *Never* tie, tape or strap the dummy to keep it in your baby's mouth.
- Allow your baby to have his dummy for sleep time only. Having it during the daytime may impair his speech development.
- With very young babies, do not allow the dummy to replace milk feeds.

Babies who have good settling skills at the beginning of the night but who still wake during the night

You have a perfect bedtime routine, he naps perfectly, settles to sleep all by himself, does not have a night feed and yet he *still* wakes during the night. What is going wrong?

Babies of this age wake for a reason. Often there are physical causes of waking, such as illness or discomfort, but if he is waking consistently in the night, there is a very good chance that this is out of *habit*. The more that the habit is rewarded, then the more firmly entrenched it becomes.

Ways in which you might unwittingly reward night-time waking and cause it to become a habit include:

- bringing your baby into bed with you during the night or at dawn
- lying beside him or on his bedroom floor during the night
- offering an unnecessary night feed
- allowing your baby to get up and play or watch a video during the night.

Top tip

Ask yourself what event is happening to make it worth your baby's while waking up during the night.

Each of these night-time activities, if repeated more than a handful of times, can quickly turn into rituals – and *babies love ritual*. You may have noticed that your baby's need to follow a familiar ritual can override any other needs that he might have. This explains why, when your baby wakes up at night, even if he is very tired and wants to go to sleep, and even if he has the skills to do so, his need to go through a familiar ritual of contact with you will compel him to remain awake until that ritual has been fulfilled.

Case study

17-month-old baby boy, with good settling skills but still waking up during the night

Amir was the first child of a nurse and an accountant. He was a healthy baby, and was eating and developing well. He had walked early and was learning to speak now. His grandmother looked after Amir when his parents were working and he loved his granny.

The problem

Amir had always been a great sleeper until he suffered from an ear infection a few weeks earlier. At this time, his night-time sleep became disrupted and his parents got into the habit of bringing him into their bed to comfort him when he felt poorly. He was now fully recovered, but still woke up during the night in expectation of the transfer to his parents' bed.

Each time that they tried to leave him in his own cot, he would cry in a very distressed way, and they just didn't have the heart to leave him. As soon as he was lifted from his cot, he smiled and then once he was in their bed, he settled immediately.

His parents were concerned about the disruption both to Amir's sleep and also to their own. When Amir was in bed with them, he would wriggle all night, kicking off the covers and taking up all of the space.

The solution

It was explained that in order for Amir to sleep through the night again, he needed to overcome the expectation of the ritual transfer to their bed. His parents were reassured that because he had previously slept well through the night he would be able to do it again.

The plan

- Stick to your excellent bedtime routine.
- Put him to bed as usual and then go to bed very early yourselves. You need to be mentally prepared to be up in the night, investing time to help Amir to sleep independently again.

- When he wakes up during the night, one of you should go to him immediately and then follow the plan below.

Nights 1 and 2

- Sit quietly beside Amir's bed and do not get into conversation with him. Use the 'broken record' technique, which means repeating the same message over and over, for example, 'Ssh Amir, it's time for sleep now.'
- Expect a lot of crying, but be assured that Amir is neither frightened nor feeling abandoned, as you are right beside him. His crying is an expression of the frustration he feels because you are not following the usual ritual of letting him get into your bed.
- Eventually, he will have to give in to sleep, even though this may take an hour or longer. There is no upper time limit to how long you should sit with him. Stay with him until he has gone off to sleep if leaving him alone is too difficult at this stage.

Night 3

- Do the same as the previous two nights, but move away slightly from his cot. Cut down on eye contact and physical contact with Amir once he is calm. It is alright to remain beside him as he goes to sleep if you still need to. It is very important, however, that you do not get into the single bed next to his cot and sleep the night in his room. If you do that, you will begin another unhelpful night-time expectation and ritual.

Night 4 onwards

- By now, Amir should have stopped expecting to come into your bed during the night, and have started to consider his cot as his own safe and permanent sleeping place.
- Follow your usual bedtime routine, allowing Amir to settle independently as used to be normal for him. When he wakes up in the night, leave him for five minutes to see if he can re-settle himself. If his cries are mild and more like little moans and grumbles, you can leave Amir for longer. Provided that you are certain that he is not in an uncomfortable position or feeling unwell, you can leave him for an hour or more to resettle by himself.

- If, however, Amir becomes distressed, you need to go to him and briefly reassure him before leaving again and going in every five minutes for the period when the crying is severe. He is no longer expecting to come to your bed now, and very soon he will be sleeping happily again.
- If at any time you are aware that he is awake but quiet and content, you should not go in to him, even if he is awake for an hour or more.
- Treat any time before 7 a.m. as a night waking, and keep him in his cot, even if he is awake. Any time that he wakes up after 7 a.m., you can open his curtains in order to give a clear visual clue that it is now morning and that it is OK to get out of his cot.
- You can now bring him to your bed but do not allow him to go back to sleep there. This is important for you, as you enjoy a family cuddle, and you do not want Amir to feel rejected or unloved by your not allowing him in bed with you during the night.

The outcome

It took just four nights for Amir to stop waking during the night. Because he had already established good self-settling skills at bedtime, he was soon able to apply them when he woke up during the night. He was only able to do this, however, when his parents helped him to break out of the ritual of moving him to their bed.

Conclusion

Even babies with good self-settling skills can fall into patterns of night waking after a period of illness or change. Once you have recognized what it is that is reinforcing the waking up, it is possible to take sensitive and effective steps towards resolving the problem.

Early waking

Most babies are naturally early risers. Being up before the milkman is all part and parcel of being a parent of a young child, and to a large extent it is something that you have to accept and go along with. Early waking problems are notoriously difficult to tackle, as when your baby has had a long block of sleep (even if it is not enough) he will find it very difficult to re-settle. This is especially true in the one- to two-year age group, when babies are only too aware of the delights of the coming day.

Putting your baby to bed later in the evening rarely makes any difference to the time that he wakes in the morning. This is because he is often 'programmed' by both internal and external wake up triggers.

Parents vary in the opinions about what constitutes an acceptable getting-up time for their baby, but generally, any time between 6 a.m. and 8 a.m. can be considered a normal wake-up time for a baby.

When might early waking be a problem?

- If your baby wakes before 6 a.m. and is crying and still looking tired
- If your baby has a ritual of a dawn waking, followed by a milk feed or transfer to your bed – and then back to sleep
- If your baby is tired and grumpy on waking and then takes an early, lengthy nap

---

If any of the early-waking situations listed in the box sound familiar to you, then it is well worth considering applying some gentle sleep training in the early mornings to extend your baby's sleep. Before you start, though, you need to take an honest look at your baby's overall sleep ability. If early waking is part of a picture of generally poor settling and night waking, you need to address these issues first of all. You will get nowhere with morning sleep training if you do not have good bedtime settling practices.

If your baby's early waking is part of his generally poor sleeping skills, you should concentrate on teaching him to fall asleep independently at the start of the night and on removing any incentives for night-time waking. You should then treat the early waking as if it were a night waking, offering the same consistent response as you did at settling and night waking times. If you approach it in this way, you have a great chance of successfully stopping the early waking without having to resort to specific measures.

Case study
20-month-old baby boy waking at 5 a.m. every morning

Jack was the first baby of a full-time mother and a father who worked unsociable hours in the music industry. The family were expecting their second child in a few weeks time. They lived in a large flat in North London, and Jack slept in a cot in his own bedroom.

The problem

Jack had always been a fragile sleeper. He was used to having his mother or father beside him as he went to sleep at night, but once he had gone off to sleep, he usually slept through the night until around 7 a.m., when he would get up and start the day. Recently, however, he had been waking up at 5.30 a.m., full of tears, looking very tired but unable to go back to sleep. His mother and father tried giving him a bottle, bringing him into their bed and even putting a video on in his room. He was not, however, able to go back to sleep.

Jack was then taking a two-hour nap at around 8 a.m. After this nap, he was happy for the day, but became very tired and grumpy at around 4 p.m. He would either fall asleep at this time and then struggle to get off to sleep at bedtime or his mother would keep him going until bedtime, when he would fall asleep over his night-time bottle.

The solution

It was explained to his parents that in order for Jack to sleep longer in the morning, he needed to:

1 improve his night-time settling skills, which could then be used to get himself back off to sleep when he woke up at dawn
2 reschedule his daytime napping to prevent him from being either over-tired or not tired enough at bedtime.

The plan

- During the day, limit his two-hour morning nap to one hour. Offer a second nap after his lunch. This nap can last for up to two hours if necessary. This daytime schedule will discourage him from becoming over-tired at teatime, and prevent him from falling asleep over his bedtime bottle.

- As his early morning waking improves, encourage Jack to drop the morning nap all together and just offer him one long sleep over the lunchtime period.
- You already have a good bedtime routine. Stick with it, but make sure that Jack does not fall asleep on his last bottle.
- Before putting him into his cot, introduce a picture book to look at for a few moments before saying goodnight. The book needs to be the same one each night, so that it becomes a sleep signal for him.
- Draw the bedroom curtains together and place Jack into his cot whilst he is still awake.
- Sit beside the cot for a few moments and then start to potter quietly around the room, returning to him from time to time if he needs you to.
- As he becomes tired, extend your pottering, so that you are coming in and out of the room every few minutes. If he cries you can briefly reassure him, but keep on leaving him and remain calm and cheerful.
- As he goes off to sleep you should not be in the room with him.
- Treat any time before 7.00 a.m. as a night waking. If he wakes and cries before this time, go to him, but keep him in his cot, and be prepared to stay with him if he is very upset. Do not offer him a bottle of milk – even if he struggles to go back to sleep.
- It is hard for babies to get back to sleep at dawn, even though they need more sleep, so you need to be very patient.
- If he is still awake and showing no signs of going back to sleep when it gets to 7.00 a.m., you should open his curtains to show him that it is now daytime and say, 'Good morning!' Then you can get him up for the day.
- If he manages to go back to sleep before 7 a.m., you should allow him to sleep on freely and then wake naturally. Once again, you should open the curtains and say, 'Good morning!' before getting him up.
- Once Jack has learned some robust self-settling skills at the beginning of the night and has overcome the expectation that he will be lifted from his cot as soon as he wakes up and cries, he will begin to sleep in for longer.
- The change in his daytime napping schedule will help this process along.

The outcome

Jack struggled at first with going to sleep without having his mother beside him, but after two or three nights, he began to feel more relaxed and was able to fall asleep quickly and all by himself. It took about a week for the early waking to resolve, but he was soon sleeping from 7.30 p.m. to 7 a.m. and having a one-and-a-half to two-hour nap over the lunchtime period.

Conclusion

His parents were surprised when it was suggested to them that in order to solve the early waking, they needed to address what was happening at the *beginning* of the night. They stuck with the plan, however, and were delighted that they had good results so quickly.

Early waking and crying

If your child wakes early, is crying, rubbing his eyes and still looking very tired, it is clear that he needs to sleep on for longer. It is not a good idea to leave him alone for a long period to cry before going in to him, as you will teach him that in order for the day to begin he has to cry for you. This is not good start to the day for either him or you. It is better to go to him before he becomes upset and tell him that it is still sleep time. Then either remain beside him or keep popping in and out to him until you reach an acceptable getting-up time. When you reach this time, you should open his curtains (even if it is still dark outside) *before getting him out of his cot*, just to give him a visual prompt that it is now getting up time. He will soon come to realise that when the curtains are closed it means that it is sleep time. If at the beginning of the night, you incorporate closing his curtains before he goes into his cot as a part of his settling routine, you will further reinforce this message. These visual clues and routines are very important for babies, who obviously are not yet able to tell the time.

Climbing out of the cot

For some very active children, as they approach their second birthday, there is a danger that they might climb out of their cot first thing in the morning and hurt themselves. Sometimes, lowering the mattress to the bottom setting can be enough to prevent this happening. There are some very resourceful babies, however, that will simply use toys or a cot bumper to lever themselves up to the top of the cot bar and hurl themselves out.

If your baby is like this, you will need to move him into a small bed, and to consider placing a stair gate in his bedroom doorway, to keep him safe. Even then at this young age, you will need to place the bed against a wall and place a soft removable cot side under the mattress and against the open side of the bed to prevent him rolling out as he moves around in his sleep.

Did you know?

Your baby does not sleep badly on purpose. If he is not sleeping well, you need to teach the skills of how to sleep. The best way to do this is by getting to the root cause of his waking and then to gently and systematically change it.

06

family life

In this chapter you will learn:
- how to manage the differing sleep needs of more than one child in the family – including twins and triplets
- how to feel more confident about caring for the needs of an adopted child
- how to accept childcare help with confidence and without detriment to your baby's sleep.

Bringing up a family is both a privilege and one of the greatest challenges that any of us will ever face. Is it any wonder, given a task so important, so daunting and so *exhausting* that at times we question our ability to rise to the task?

When our children are small, we worry about their eating, their development and, perhaps most of all, their sleeping. As parents, we need our babies to sleep well, not only for their own sakes but for our sakes too.

Well rested children are more likely to be content, secure and better able to play and learn. Well rested parents are more likely to enjoy their children and have the energy to maintain other important relationships and interests.

Brothers and sisters

Having more than one young child to put to bed at night can present logistic difficulties: one child needs help with homework, another needs a story, a chat and a cuddle and the other needs a nappy change and a milk feed. Of course, it helps if the children have their own rooms, and your partner is home in time to help with bedtime; but for many of us, this is not possible. At the end of a tiring day, when everyone's energy and sense of humour levels are low, bedtime can become a time to dread rather than to enjoy.

> *I love my children more than words can say, but at one point, when they were small, I used to live in fear of bedtime. The fact was that I needed the two of them to go to sleep by 7.30 p.m., so that I could have some time to myself. Bedtime was always a stressful, unhappy time and looking back, I think that they sensed my desperation and they felt rushed and pressured into sleep. I wish that I had taken the time to make bedtime a happier time for them and for me too.*

Of course, finding the energy to create a good bedtime routine to meet more than one child's needs is always going to be a challenge. If you are able to just give that tiny bit extra at the end of the day, however, it will repay you generously.

The first thing that you need to do is take some time to think about what you want bedtime to be like and then take some practical steps towards achieving this.

First, you need to establish a bedtime routine that is both consistent and will also meet your children's individual needs. From the age of six months, if not before, your baby can be bathed together with her older sibling(s).

It is perfectly alright to run a bath for your toddler and whilst supervising him in the bath, you can 'dip' your little one into the water for her bath too. You can then put her into her new nappy and night clothes, on a clean towel on the floor, while you chat to and watch your older child in the bath. There is no need to have a separate baby bath or bath-time for your little one.

After this, you can go to your children's bedroom, your own bedroom or, if your older child has a room of his own, to his room. Whilst feeding your baby, you can read to your older one. We have seen already how it is wise to avoid allowing babies to fall asleep over their bedtime feed, so when your baby is fed but still awake, you should encourage a kiss goodnight ritual and then take your baby to her cot. If this is in her own room, you should ask your older child to wait in bed for you to come back for your final kiss goodnight and cuddle.

Following the advice given in the previous chapters, you should settle your baby to sleep in a way that is appropriate for her age and then return to your older one(s) for a very brief but affectionate parting ritual.

It is important, wherever possible, for your older child to have some exclusive, loving time with you, however brief that might be. It can be hard for an older child to accept that you are giving the attention that was previously all hers to a new baby. Try to make the time just before sleep a time of reassurance and special intimacy. You will feel so good about this and so will she. If you somehow miss this time of comfort, your older child may not only fall asleep feeling unhappy, but she will look for this attention from you in other ways. It is very important when you leave your children for the night that you go on good terms.

There is no right or wrong way when it comes to whether it is best for brothers and sisters to share a bedroom. One advantage of sharing is that children often settle better and feel more secure at night in the close company of a sibling. Another lovely thing about siblings sharing a room is that they have a chance to develop their relationship in a natural way, often in the absence of their parents. They learn about sharing space, respecting privacy and belongings and about sharing secrets too. Often, because of limited space, there is no other option than for children to share with one another. If this is the case, then they might just be the lucky ones. Sharing a bedroom is a great preparation for life in nursery, school and of course, in later life.

There are, of course, some drawbacks too. The most obvious one being that if one child is a poor sleeper, then there is a risk that she might wake the other one up during the night or early morning. This is especially common in babyhood and, in particular, with twins, or with older babies and children when they are unwell. Later on, with toddlers and young children there is the issue of running amok after bath-time and being too giddy and playful to settle down. Older children who share a room will inevitably experience conflicts over space and personal possessions from time to time.

Case study

Brother and sister who are both poor sleepers preparing to improve their sleep skills and share a bedroom

Nicolas (26 months) and Jenny (12 months) were the children of a fashion designer and a banker. The couple came from America, and were living in a large, three bedroom rented flat in South-west London. Jenny had her cot in her parents' room, whilst Jack had a small toddler bed in his own large bedroom. The third bedroom was needed as a guest room for the frequent visits of both sets of grandparents.

Both children were healthy and had no developmental difficulties, but their sleep and bedtime management were proving to be problematic.

The problem

1 Nicolas needed to have his mother beside him every night as he fell asleep. As a consequence of this, he would wake later and need her to come and sit or lie beside him again in order to settle back to sleep. Inevitably, he would end up, at some stage during the night, in his parents' bed.

2 Jenny was only able to settle if she was breastfed to the point of sleep each night. She subsequently woke up several times

in the night and needed more feeds to help her re-settle. Like her brother, she ended up at some point in bed with her parents during the night.

3 Their mother usually managed the bedtime routine alone and was finding meeting both children's needs very difficult. She wanted them both to share a room but was worried that one child might wake the other, and that their nights would be even worse.

The solution

1 Both children needed to fall asleep at the beginning of the night without their mother beside them.

2 They needed to find a bedtime routine that was less stressful and much more enjoyable.

3 Both children needed to feel safe and secure in their own beds and not need to transfer to their parents' bed during the night.

4 They would both benefit from sharing a bedroom together.

The plan

• Move both children into the same room. Place the cot parallel to Nicholas' toddler bed, position a chair in the middle, so that you can comfort both children if they cry. This will be a little disruptive in the short term, but long term they will each benefit from the company. It will be logistically far easier for you to manage, too.

• Explain in simple and cheerful terms to Nicolas that he is going to have baby Jenny to sleep in his bedroom. During the day, move her cot into his room, and encourage the children to do a little role-play game where they play at going to sleep or putting their toys to sleep. This should be kept very light-hearted.

• Bath them both together every night. Jack needs to get in first, whilst Jenny is being undressed on the bathroom floor. Hold her and bathe her in the shared water and sing a familiar bath-time song.

• After this, put Jenny's pyjamas on, whilst still in the bathroom and give her a toy to play with whilst you get Nicholas out of the bath.

• Go directly to the children's room. Nicholas is to have his nappy and pyjamas on whilst Jenny plays on the floor. After this he can choose a book as the bedtime story.

- During the story, the three of you should sit on Nicholas' bed, and Jenny can have a breastfeed. It is important that she doesn't feed to the point of sleep. Following this feed, encourage the children to kiss each other goodnight and then put Jenny into her cot. Nicholas should be tucked into bed at about the same time. Turn the light right down and keep the room in soft semi-darkness. It is important at this stage that both babies are awake.
- This routine will be easier for you, you will no longer need to run from room to room comforting each of them.

Nights 1 and 2

- Remain in the room comforting each child if they cry or are unable to go to sleep. Stay calm during this process. You are allowed to stroke and pat Jenny, for whom the change is greatest and even lean right into her cot and put yourself close beside her. It is very important though, that you keep her in her cot. Eventually Jenny will begin to give in to sleep. When she goes to sleep in her own cot, even if she has cried and even if you have been beside her, that is marvellous progress and she is well on the way to sleeping through the night.
- As she enters sleep, you need to withdraw the amount of her physical contact, so that you are just quietly sitting by her cot.
- During this process, you should keep Nicholas in his little bed next to the cot, and reassure him constantly, gently praising him and explaining what you are doing and that you are teaching Jenny how to sleep.
- If Nicholas is still awake once Jenny has settled, you need to remain beside him still until he feels relaxed and tired enough to go to sleep.
- As Nicolas settles to sleep, you should just sit in a chair between the cot and his bed. Even if he cries and disturbs Jenny after she has settled, you still need to help him to go to sleep in his own bed.
- When Jenny first wakes up during the night, you should go to her and breastfeed her for a very few moments only. Do not allow her to fall asleep on the breast. After the shortened feed, place her back into her cot whilst she is still awake. Expect some crying, but try to demonstrate a calm and positive manner. Settle her in her cot as you did earlier in the evening, and do not bring her into your bed. Although this might be a hard habit to break, try not to be disheartened, as

Jenny will very soon learn to be content in her own cot. If she wakes Nicolas, he should be reassured but kept in his bed.

- Repeat this each time Jenny wakes up. By not allowing her to fall asleep at the breast, you are breaking the suck–sleep dependence. By keeping her in her own cot, you are showing her that it is a safe and permanent space. She will very quickly overcome the expectation that she will be moving to your bed.
- If Nicolas wakes independently of Jenny, you should go to him as you usually do. If you need to stay with him, you can sit quietly as you did at the beginning of the night. It is most important, however, that he does not come into your bed, or he will lose the sense of safety in his *own* bed.
- In the morning, after first opening their bedroom curtains to show that it is now daytime, you should warmly welcome both Nicolas and Jenny into your bed. Give them both a sticker on their pyjamas, as a reward for sharing a bedroom.
- After two or three nights of doing this, you will have already taught them new habits and you will be able to move on to the next stage.

Nights 3–7

- Keep up the new bedtime and settling routine, but move out of the chair between the children's cot and bed. At first you need to potter around in the room and then gradually extend this pottering until you are moving very briefly out of, then back, into the bedroom.
- Once again, do not worry if one disturbs the other – this will only happen whilst they are learning new sleep habits. Be warned that you may have to pop back in to them several times before they go to sleep. Eventually, they will both settle to sleep without you in the room… You are nearly there now!
- During the night, if Jenny wakes for a feed, you can go to her and settle her by patting, etc. You should *not offer her a night feed from now on*. She doesn't need it and the expectation of a feed has been hampering her ability to settle and sleep really well.
- By Night 7, go through their normal routine and after kissing the children goodnight you need to leave them and try not to go back in. You will have to listen out for them on the landing in case they become upset. By now, though, they will be used to settling with less help from you, and will be getting used to their new sleep set-up. If they cry, it will be in mild

protest and last for a relatively short period. If necessary, go in every 5 minutes and stay for only 30 seconds.

- By this point, Jenny should have dropped her night feeds and be moving towards sleeping through the night.

The outcome

Nicholas and Jenny very soon grew to love sleeping in the same room together. It took about a week for them to get over the change in their bedtime routine and to settle to sleep in the same room. Their mother found the whole bedtime routine much easier to manage and she felt much more in control. Both children stopped waking in the night once she had managed to leave them to settle without her and had dropped Jenny's night feeds.

Soon, not only bedtime improved, however; before long, they were sleeping later in the morning, and when they woke up they would play rather than cry to be brought into bed with Mummy and Daddy. When they *were* brought into their parents' bed, they were very welcome guests, and the parents started the day feeling well rested and delighted to see their two lovely children.

Conclusion

When there is more than one child in the family, it can be a help to have them in the same room, provided they are taught good settling skills. From a parent's point of view, if the children are of a similar age, having them share a bedtime routine and a bedroom makes it easier to establish a happier settling process.

Bringing your baby up alone

Bringing up your child or children by yourself can bring its advantages as far as sleep is concerned at least. You are able to focus more fully on your child's and your own needs and are free from the concern of caring for another adult. Having your baby in bed with you is less likely to be problematic, as is choosing to go to bed at the same time as your baby. There is no doubt that you alone have to cope when your baby wakes during the night, but the upside is that you do not have the additional stress or worry of her disturbing a partner.

When you have the responsibility of bringing up one or more children on your own, your friends and your family are very important. You should not be afraid to ask for help when you need it. Caring for a child, however much you love her, day in and day out is completely demanding. If you are in paid work in addition to looking after your baby, you will know only too well how little time you have to yourself. Sometimes you need someone to hold her for just half an hour whilst you have a bath, or make a telephone call. Whilst this might not be possible to organize on an ongoing basis, it is good to ask for support as regularly as you can.

The middle of the night presents its own special challenges, and if you are on your own with a crying baby, this time can feel very lonely and scary sometimes. Please follow the guidelines in this book to ensure that your baby is sleeping the best that she can for the age that she is. However, whether she is a good sleeper or not, it is important that you have a night off from time to time. One bad night's sleep will do no harm to your best friend, sister or your mother, and yet one good night's sleep will do *you* so much good.

Babies who sleep badly at home with their parents often sleep like a dream when staying at grandma's house. If this is the case with your baby, try not to feel undermined. It does not mean that you are a hopeless parent; it is merely that your baby has a different set of sleep associations in a different environment, and this can mean that she sleeps well during her 'sleep over'.

Twins and triplets

So far, we have considered the sleep needs of babies of various ages and habits. All of them present their own challenges but nothing compares to the challenge of parenting twins, triplets or more. If you are to really enjoy your babies' miraculous infancy, it is important that both you and they get as much sleep as possible.

It is perhaps useful to follow the story of the first year of one couple, Julia and James, as they learned how to be parents to twins, Amelia and (baby) James.

> *Julia describes the first few days after coming home from hospital with her babies as 'a nightmare!' She found it difficult to establish any kind of a routine, and felt that she was constantly having to leave one baby out whilst she dealt with the needs of the other one. Fortunately she was well supported by her husband, James, and together they muddled through this exhausting but amazing time.*

After about eight weeks they had introduced a bedtime routine, and both babies were sleeping for most of the night. They felt much more relaxed, in control and the babies were well rested and contented.

The secret of their success was as follows:

1 The early introduction of a highly repetitive bedtime routine. Julia made good use of simple sleep clues such as songs, repeated phrases and a familiar sleep environment.

2 After a milk feed at around 7 p.m., both babies would be put down *awake*. When they first did this, the babies would take some time lying awake, cooing, kicking and sometimes 'grizzling'. In a very short time this wakeful period got gradually shorter and both babies began to fall asleep quickly and easily.

3 Before the babies were taking solids, Julia and James would wake them at around 10 p.m. for a second milk feed, and once again put them back in their cot, making sure that they were well winded and sleepy, but awake.

4 One of the babies was a better sleeper than the other. Despite being in the same cot, however, he was rarely disturbed by his more wakeful sister. This was because he was very accustomed to her presence and her sounds. Julia heartily recommends having baby twins sleep close to one another. She feels that it prevents them from feeling lonely in the middle of the night, and that the comfort that they gain from being near to each other means that they are less likely to need their parents.

5 At first, they put the babies in a Moses basket each, placed 'top to tail' in the same large cot. They slept like this until they were 15 weeks old and then they were each given a separate cot, placed in parallel and very close to each other.

6 After the 10 p.m. feed, they did not change nappies in the night unless they were soiled.

One of the major difficulties with managing twins' sleep is how to cope with early waking.

As Julia and James found, at the beginning of the night, one twin is unlikely to disturb the other one with her wakefulness. This is because sleep is deeper in the early part of the night, and the sleeping twin is tired enough to ignore the familiar disruption going on around him.

However, at 5 a.m. in the morning, sleep is lighter and one wakeful twin really can disturb the other sleepy one.

Many parents find the best solution is to bring the awake baby into their bed. Sadly, this often has negative repercussions, with the wakeful baby often rising earlier and earlier in anticipation of the move into the big bed. Some babies will even fail to settle at all in their own cots, feeling that they are merely in a temporary space that is not their 'real' bed.

For Julia and James, this was the beginning of a difficult period, which took several months to resolve itself.

The best solution to this tricky situation is to keep both twins in their own cot/s, despite the disruption, your own sleep deprivation and the despair of your neighbours. You may find that, initially, you need to stay close by until the babies either go back to sleep or it is time for the day to begin.

Babies under six months or not yet taking solid food three times a day, will sometimes require a milk feed at dawn. After this feed, it is important to put them back into their cot awake and encourage them to stay there until getting up time. (Ideally at least 11 hours after their initial bedtime.)

If you repeatedly allow your baby/babies to get up at dawn, they will never have the opportunity to learn to settle back off to sleep. You may need to sit quietly with them without playing or talking, but soothing them through the inevitable crying, until they eventually go back off to sleep.

During this difficult period, it is important to go to bed early yourself, and be mentally prepared to get up at dawn when they wake, and invest this time with your babies. It makes sense that if you have a supportive partner, you are able to share the burden of getting up early. Julia and James would alternate their 'dawn duty' and this prevented them from becoming exhausted.

Just after Amelia and James reached the age of one year, they were sleeping through the night from 7 p.m. to 7 a.m.

According to their mother, 'One of the most wonderful things about twins is that they have each other. Unlike, single babies, they do not suffer the loneliness of being left alone to sleep through the night.'

Try not to worry too much about one twin or triplet being disturbed by the other(s). This is a transient period and babies are amazingly resilient. If you are able to demonstrate a calm manner and to feel in control of the situation, your babies will feel calm and safe too and their distress will be minimal. They will soon benefit from a longer night's sleep.

Guidelines for good sleep for baby twins and triplets

- Let them sleep close to each other.
- Follow a highly familiar bedtime routine.
- Always put them in their cot/s awake.
- Do not allow fears of one disturbing the other lead you into a complicated night-time scenario of 'musical beds'.
- Help them to feel safe by your loving, confident and consistent manner.

Adopted babies

If your first experience of parenting is with your adopted baby, you may feel daunted by the responsibility. It is very important for you to realise that *all* new parents feel the same way. One of your difficulties, however, is that you might have limited information about your baby's birth history or her family health history.

The really important information that you need, however, in order to help your baby sleep well is right in front of your eyes. When you are managing your baby's sleep, you need to respond to the signs and cues that she gives you. Your interpretation of these cues and your response to them is no less valid than if you were her birth parent.

When your new baby or toddler comes into your home you need to gather as much information about her sleep as you can.

Does she have a dummy?
Does she have a night feed? If so, at what time does she have this?
Does she have a comfort blanket or toy?
Does she sleep with the light on?
Does she like to be rocked to sleep?
Does she settle all by herself?

You may want to change some of her sleep rituals, and this is fine. You need to know what she is used to, however, before you go ahead.

Case study

Two-year-old boy, recently adopted: learning good sleep skills

Brett was adopted by Frankie and Sue when he was 18 months old. Before adoption he had been in foster care from the age of three months. His new parents knew very little about his birth and early history; only that his birth mother was very young and had problems with drug abuse. He had had developmental delay until the age of a year, but now he was reaching his milestones along with his peers.

The problem

Although his foster mother reported that Brett had always been a good sleeper with her, he had never slept through the night since coming to his new home.

Frankie and Sue had blamed this on his anxiety at the change and had taken care to offer him lots of reassurance, especially around bedtime. It had become a pattern that at bedtime, after his stories and milk, he would be held in his mother's arms until he went to sleep and then placed into his cot. He would wake later, crying and looking for her. It took up to an hour to re-settle him and this happened sometimes more than once in the night.

Quite understandably, Frankie and Sue put Brett's night-time behaviour down to anxiety caused by his early life experience, which he was unable to express in any other way.

This may have been the case to some extent, but the waking and crying was also typical of any two-year-old child who is rocked to sleep only to wake up later and find himself alone.

The solution

It was decided that Frankie and Sue would teach Brett how to settle to sleep at night without either of them beside him. This was a very worrying prospect for them, as they felt that he needed lots of reassurance in order to sleep. It was explained that it was, in fact, more traumatic for him to wake up and find himself alone, than it would be for him to fall asleep without either of them there in the first place. This was providing that they withdraw their presence in a sensitive and gradual way. The family was receiving counselling and support which was arranged through their adoption agency and Brett was expressing his feelings very well through his (rather beautiful) drawings. The signs were that he was a happy and well balanced little boy.

The plan

- During the day, Frankie and Sue were asked to role-play with Brett putting his toys into his bed, tucking them up and then leaving. They were all to praise the toys for going to sleep all by themselves.

- Also during the day they were to tell him that he would be going to go to sleep in his own bed all by himself like a big boy. They needed to be positive when they told him this and to meet any protest with good humour.

- After his usual bath-time ritual, either Frankie or Sue was to read a maximum of three stories to Brett, with him cuddled up on their knee. They needed to keep the final story book the same each night. This familiar ritual would help to create a feeling of security.

- When it was time to leave him, they were to use a little verbal ritual like 'Rock you for a minute now'. Either of them could then rock him for a moment or two and then gently place him into his cot, whilst he was still awake.

- After that they were asked to stay beside him as he fell asleep in his cot. They were warned that he would stand up and cry, as he sought the familiar ritual of being held in arms as he fell asleep. This was bound to pull on their heartstrings, but they needed to be aware that his need to be rocked to sleep was habitual rather than emotional. After an hour or so, Brett would fall asleep in his cot, and they were asked to remain close beside him as he did this.

- For three nights they were to settle him in this way before beginning to move away. Once he was accustomed to falling asleep in his cot, this would not be as difficult as they imagined it might be.

- For the next four nights they were asked to move a little further away from the cot each night, so that by night 7 they were sitting by the door as he fell asleep.

- On the following week they were asked to position a chair just outside his door after following their new bedtime routine and saying goodnight to him. Each time he called for them they could either briefly return to him or simply call back, 'I'm just here, Brett.'

- It was very important that when they returned to him, they did not allow themselves to be drawn into negotiations about position of toys, another story/cuddle, etc. It is really difficult to refuse a cuddle, so they were asked to give the briefest hug and then say, 'Big cuddles in the morning!'
- After many times of being reassured, Brett would eventually go to sleep. When he did this, it was essential that they were not in the room with him.
- If Brett woke up during the night, they were to go to him immediately and reassure him. They were to be positive in their response to him and tell him he was a clever boy for staying in his own cot. They should leave him then to settle back to sleep without either of them in the room, returning to reassure him every 5 minutes if needed.
- In the morning, they were to first of all open his curtains before getting him out of his cot and then heap praise on him for going to sleep by himself. They were advised to give him a sticker on his pyjamas or a little treat or toy with breakfast and to have these rewards already prepared, as it was vital that he received this positive reinforcement as soon as possible.

The outcome

Frankie and Sue were very reluctant to begin what they regarded as a harsh solution to Brett's sleep difficulties. Once they decided to implement the plan however, they were determined to see it through.

After one night of quite severe protest, Brett began to learn the skills of settling to sleep by himself. Within ten days, he was settling alone and had stopped waking during the night. He was better tempered during the day, and seemed less 'clingy' too.

Conclusion

Even if your baby's sleep difficulty has arisen from an emotional, medical or situational issue, using a sensitive sleep technique which addresses the presenting behaviour will still work to solve the problem.

Provided that you have other measures in place to address any potentially emotional or psychological issues, it is safe and sensible to use a 'behavioural' approach to help solve your child's sleep problem. This is the case, whether it is your adopted child or your birth child.

When it comes to caring for the sleep needs of your baby, just like any new parent, you will need to gather information from books, family, friends and professionals about how to care for her. Armed with this information, you can then start the fabulous process of 'learning on the job'.

Don't be frightened of the fact that she is not your birth child. You are her parent now. You wanted her very much and are getting to know her more each day. Because you are a loving adult and you have her very best interests at heart, you can safely follow your instincts when planning her care. Parenting is a learning process and this is the case for both adoptive *and* birth parents.

A guide for grandparents ... and sisters, aunts and best friends

You owe it both to your child and to yourself to allow a trusted grandparent, to care for her from time to time. It is lovely for your parents to have a baby to care for, and provided they are fit, coming to it fresh the chances are that they will have the energy to cope with her needs, even if she is not a good sleeper. Allowing your baby to develop close relationships with them will be a real benefit and a life-enriching experience both of them. Not only this, but allowing a trusted grandparent to look after your baby will give you a well-earned break when you need it. Don't forget that enabling your child to feel comfortable with other adults in the family will provide you with a reassuring back-up in case you are ever ill or need to be away from her for other reasons.

When you hand over the care of your baby for baby-sitting in your home or an overnight stay in theirs it takes planning and the confidence to step aside. You are leaving them in charge of the most precious thing in the world to you, so you need to trust them completely. It will make their task easier and help your baby to feel more secure if you are able to provide enough *essential* information, so that the needs on both sides can be met. You also need to accept that a grandparent, with all of the years of experience, may have their *own* ways of settling your child. Provided that their values and methods are broadly in line with your own, this really should not cause any problems. Babies from a very young age are able to differentiate and to understand, for example, that whilst Grandpa might rock her to sleep, Daddy reads a story and puts her in her cot whilst she is awake.

Top tips
Sleepover success

- Make certain that your parents are clear about your baby's normal bedtime and the routine leading up to it.
- Send along some familiar items which your baby associates with sleep. These might include her usual bedding, a familiar toy or bedtime story book.
- If your baby still has night feeds be sure that you provide plenty of milk. It is better to give more than she normally needs, just in case you are held up, or she needs extra feeds to settle.
- Have her milk safely and conveniently stored to cut down on bottle preparation time. Ready-made formula feed in cartons or frozen expressed breast milk is easier to prepare than powdered milk.
- In preparation for the visit, if possible allow your baby to spend time alone with her grandparents during the daytime.
- The first time you leave your baby at night, stay fairly local, so that you can be home quickly if needed. Your parents will need to feel completely confident that they can care for your baby before you go away for the weekend, for example.
- Leave a number of ways that you can be contacted whilst you are out. This isn't a sign of mistrust, but a sensible precaution that increases everyone's confidence.
- Show your parents that you have confidence in them. Tell them how much your baby loves them and how you trust them.
- Come back at the time that you said you would – not earlier and not later. This will help to build trust on both sides too.

Where do nannies, nurseries and childminders fit into the picture?

Most of us at some point in our baby's life will rely on some form of paid childcare. As more and more families have both parents working and as we increasingly live away from our close families, nannies, au pairs, nurseries, childminders and babysitters have become a normal part of our support network.

Frustratingly, babies who will not sleep well for their parents will often sleep well at nursery or with their childminder or nanny. Carers *and* parents need to be absolutely clear that this is not because the parents are doing things wrong, but simply that the baby has a different set of expectations, routines and rituals with her carer than she does with her parents; and this often results in different sleep behaviour.

The reasons why babies tend to sleep better in a formal childcare setting include:

- other babies and children 'modelling' good sleep behaviour
- a more formal and structured day, which allows babies to anticipate when sleep time is coming, and to become sleepy as a result
- less rocking or handling by a caregiver around sleep time.

For similar reasons, babies often settle to sleep easier when put to bed at night by a nanny than with you. With a nanny, there may be less expectation of extended cuddles and parting rituals, and a tendency on the baby's part to fall asleep more quickly and easily.

When you come home after work, the time with your baby in the evening is very precious to both of you, and you may want to cuddle or feed her to sleep at night. In addition, you may be less likely to be able to tolerate her 'grizzling' or crying before she goes off to sleep. If this is the case, you need to accept that your methods of settling your baby are different to those of your nanny, and that her sleep may differ as a result.

It is not harmful or confusing for your child to experience different settling practices with different people, but be aware that after the first few weeks or months of her life, she will expect a consistent approach from the person who is settling her to sleep and will respond accordingly. So whilst she may settle happily to sleep with just a brief cuddle from her nanny, she may protest if you settle her in the same way, if that is not what she is used to from you.

For this reason, it is usually unhelpful to ask a nanny or night nurse to teach your baby to sleep at night for you and to not be involved in the process yourself. What is likely to happen is that your baby will respond to the sleep training initiated by the helper but as soon as she leaves and you take over, your baby will be as unsettled as ever. She might have learned to sleep well, but not necessarily for *you*.

For sleep training to be successful, it needs to be carried out by the person who most often puts the baby to bed and attends to her during the night.

> *I was still breastfeeding Helena during the night at 18 months, and I was newly pregnant with our second child. Both my husband and I were working and I was becoming exhausted, especially with all the night feeds. We decided to get help from a night nursing agency, who sent a lovely nanny to us who would sleep-train Helena. It took her just over a week to get Helena to settle to sleep at night without the breast, and to drop all her night feeds.*

> *We were delighted, but as soon as I tried to settle Helena in the same way as the night nanny had done, she started to search furiously for my breast, and ended up settling to sleep as she had previously done, and then waking up during the night for more!*

> *I realised that if any one was going to help Helena to sleep well at night, it had to be me. It was very hard, but I followed the instructions that the night nanny had given me, and with lots of resolve (and tears) I managed to get there in the end. She now has a feed, a story, a cuddle from either myself or my husband and then goes into her cot awake and sleeps through the night.*

> *Having a night nanny was brilliant in that we had a whole week of unbroken sleep, but in the end I still had to sleep train her.*

In order that the relationship between care giver and parent works well to promote good sleep for your baby, you need to *communicate* with each other. One of the best ways of doing this is by asking the care giver to keep a simple daily diary. The information in this should include details about:

- naps – times, duration and where the nap was taken
- meals and snacks – times, what food was given and the amounts taken
- nappy changes and when your baby has a bowel movement
- outings and activities.

You need to be very clear about what is happening around daytime naps. Often, because a baby sleeps so well for her childminder or nanny during the day, she may not be tired enough to settle happily to sleep at night. If you know how long or late she has slept during the day, you can time her bedtime accordingly. This is just one of the instances of how your baby will benefit from honest and open communication between you and her care giver.

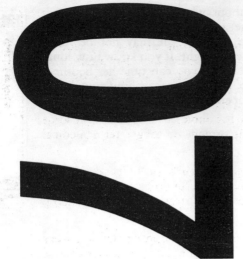

07

special babies

In this chapter you will learn:
- how to manage your child's sleep when he is unwell
- how to find an appropriate settling routine if your child has special needs
- how to minimize the impact on your baby's sleep of a longer term medical problem.

There are times when babies are particularly fragile and need extra care, especially at night. For many, this time of fragility and extra need is very temporary, lasting through a period of minor illness or a bout of teething for instance. For others, this period may last for a few weeks or months, as is the case with babies who have reflux or certain forms of infantile eczema. Some babies will need special care at night for much of their early childhood, as is the case for babies with Downs and some other syndromes, sensory impairment or longer term medical conditions.

For all of these babies, a good night's sleep is particularly important. They need to be well rested in order to cope with the challenges with which their condition presents them. Good sleep is important for *you* too – for the very same reasons.

Sleep training a fragile baby needs to be approached in a very thoughtful and sensitive way. It is completely unacceptable as well as counterproductive to leave a child who is in discomfort to cry alone in his cot. Sleeping difficulties need to be addressed in gentle, gradual steps and combined with any recommended medical treatments.

When your baby is unwell or in pain, treating his discomfort must take priority above teaching him how to sleep through the night.

Teething

Although a natural process and not an illness, teething can cause pain and general discomfort. Babies typically cut their first tooth at around six months old, but for some this might not happen until much later. Some babies cut their teeth earlier than this, and some are even born with some teeth.

Teething troubles: what are the symptoms?

- Red and sore-looking gums
- Baby wanting to chew on everything
- Excess drooling
- Red cheeks
- Loose bowel motions
- Baby pulling at his ears
- General irritability

Not all babies suffer during teething, but many do, and the discomfort of teething is invariably much worse during the night.

Important: some of the symptoms of teething can be indicators of more serious illnesses. If your baby has a temperature (above 39°C) or seems very unwell, you should always seek medical advice.

Very often teething is responsible for the development or worsening of sleep problems in babies. If your baby is teething, there are measures which you can take which will ensure that as soon as the acute phase of teething is over, you and your baby can enjoy a good night's sleep.

- During the day, make sure that he has lots of opportunity to bite and chew.
- Encourage him with finger foods, provided that he is old enough, choosing crusty bread, bagel and toast which has been allowed to cool and go soft but tough.
- Because the cold has a numbing effect, keep his teething ring as well as whole peeled or scrubbed carrots in the fridge for him to chew on.
- *Never* put his teething aids in the freezer.

When babies are teething they tend to drool and this often leads to the skin around the chin and neck becoming very chapped and sore. To help with this:

- Change bibs frequently or use soft, dry muslin cloths or even bright cotton neckerchiefs to co-ordinate with his clothes.
- After meals and drinks, use warm water and soft dry cotton cloths to clean him rather than wipes that may sting.
- Don't forget to clean and dry him in the soft skin folds under his chin, where food and moisture can easily become trapped.
- A gentle barrier cream here will protect him even further.

Another feature of teething can be frequent loose bowel movements. This can often lead to the skin on his bottom becoming sore. To prevent problems in this area:

- Check and change his nappy frequently.
- Be aware that if his bottom is sore, it will sting when he does a wee.
- Allow your baby to kick around without a nappy, sitting or laying on a towel.
- Once again, when you clean him, avoid using harsh wipes. It is better to stick to warm water and cotton wool.

- Use a barrier cream and watch out for signs that his skin may be becoming red and shiny.
- If you have been treating your baby's nappy rash for 48 hours and there is no sign of improvement, you will need to visit your doctor to check for signs of Candida (thrush). If this is the case, it will require an antifungal cream.
- Thrush infections in the nappy area are just as common in boys as in girls. They have tendency to crop up in warm, damp areas – like nappies and under the chins of teething babies.

If you notice that your baby is pulling at his ears, this is often a sign of discomfort and can indicate inflammation within the ear. This is common during teething, but to be safe, you will need to visit your GP who will establish the cause of the pain and then recommend a suitable painkiller. If the pain is cause by bacterial infection and not just teething, he may be prescribed an antibiotic.

Jonathan was always a happy, smiling baby who had always had a good bedtime routine and slept well during the night. During the day, he was full of smiles and only ever cried if he was tired or hungry. When he began teething at six months, it was as if he had a personality change! He seemed to cry constantly and I found it very difficult to comfort him. His mouth was clearly very uncomfortable and his gums were swollen. The constant drooling made his skin chapped and sore. He also suffered from diarrhoea and soon developed a nappy rash, which made matters even worse.

During the day, he found relief by biting on his teething ring (and anything else he could put in his mouth). Night-time was a different matter, however. He would frequently wake up crying and was very difficult to comfort. He was usually very snuffly and had problems breathing through his little nose. We went to our GP, who was very helpful, and seemed to understand that teething can be more than just a minor ailment. She gave us Paracetamol medicine for bedtime and rash cream for his sore bottom. She also advised us to tilt the head of the bed to help his night-time breathing.

Fortunately the first bout of teething was the worse and passed fairly quickly. We are more confident now about how to handle it when it happens, including how to manage any discomfort during the night. When he is not actively teething, his sleep is good. I think that this is because we have never comforted him by bringing him into bed with us or by re-introducing a night-time bottle.

Colic

Colic is a form of very severe tummy ache, occurring mainly during the late afternoon and evening. Babies who have colic tend to be very difficult to console during an episode; feeding does not help, and the only thing that tends to have any kind of positive effect is carrying your baby around in your arms. This is very hard on all of you, and having to constantly hold and rock your baby in the evening can lead to future settling and sleep problems.

Infantile colic is a common condition in very young babies and although it can be really dreadful to manage, babies tend to grow out of it by the age of three or four months.

The crying which comes from colic can be alarming – especially when it first happens. *It is essential that colic is diagnosed only after other more serious conditions have been ruled out. If you are in any doubt at all, you should seek medical advice.*

Signs and symptoms of colic

- All the threes:
  1 crying for more than three hours per day
  2 for more than three days per week
  3 for longer than a three-week period.
- Typically starts at around two to four weeks old.
- Baby cries often at the same time each day – usually in the evening.
- Sometimes you can hear or even see your child's stomach rumbling.
- Sometimes excessive 'wind' is produced.
- Baby tends to pull his knees up towards his tummy and strains whilst he cries.

Once you have a diagnosis of colic, you will need to go about managing it as best as you can. There is no recognized medical treatment for this condition, although there are steps that you can take both to minimize your baby's discomfort and to help you cope.

Top ten colic management tips

1   If you can anticipate when your baby is going to have a colicky episode, arrange if possible for a friend, family member or your partner to be around to help you.

2   Get a good quality sling, and hold your baby in this as you walk around with him. It will be far less tiring on your arms, and he will benefit from being upright and close to you.

3   If there is a history of cow's milk intolerance in your family and you are breastfeeding, try eliminating cow's milk protein from your diet for a while.

4   If you are breastfeeding, watch out for signs of colic that are triggered by certain foods that you eat. You may need to cut out spicy and acidic foods, certain strong vegetables or dairy products.

5   If your baby is formula-fed, discuss with your health visitor or GP changing to a different milk.

6   Always wind your baby well after his feeds. Slow strong circular strokes to the base of his back are more effective than little taps on his upper back.

7   If you are using bottles, consider using an anti-colic system. This involves using a collapsible bag inside the bottle and limits the amount of air that your baby swallows.

8   Use the right sized teat for your baby to make sure that the milk flow is neither too fast nor too slow – both of which may cause him to swallow excess air.

9   By all means try homeopathy or some of the over-the-counter colic remedies that are available from your pharmacy.

10 Sometimes a warm bath will help to comfort your baby when he has tummy pain.

Colic and sleep

Many colicky babies, after a period of intense crying in the evening, tend to settle and sleep well for the early part of the night. Partly this is because crying is extremely tiring and he is, quite simply, worn out.

It is not unusual, however, for a colicky baby to wake some time later, either for his feed or before his feed is due and need to be re-settled for an extended period. This is not necessarily because he has tummy ache; it is more likely that it is because he has become used to falling asleep in your arms and knows no other way to settle himself.

Given that colic rarely lasts beyond four months, it is advisable that you give your baby the contact he needs during these early weeks, despite this not being conducive to good sleeping. He really does need to be held close to you during an evening colic episode, and if you rock him to sleep at the beginning of the night only to refuse to do so later, you will only cause him to feel confused.

There is no doubt that babies who have suffered from colic in the early weeks tend to develop sleep problems later, but there is little that you can do about that at the time. It is better to be aware that when he has grown out of the colic, you will need to make some changes to his night-time settling routine. Don't worry – he will still be young enough to learn how to sleep beautifully.

When Antonia was about two weeks old she developed evening colic. It was a really tough time for all of us, as she was so difficult to comfort. I felt exhausted and demoralised, as I was so helpless to ease her pain. We spent weeks just pacing up and down the living room with her, and it was impossible to ever put her down, even for a moment. It said in all the baby books that I should be putting her into her cot whilst she was still awake, but this was impossible for us. I worried that we were creating 'a rod for our own backs', but there was absolutely no other option.

The colic began to improve when she was about three months old. We were so relieved about this, but we realised that she was still difficult to settle to sleep and she woke up constantly during the night for cuddles. Once we were confident that she was not in pain, and she was waking merely out of habit, we set about teaching her to go to sleep more independently at bedtime. This involved starting a very structured bedtime routine and then rocking her for a few moments until she was sleepy, but not actually asleep.

We would then put her into her cot and pat her until she went to sleep. She would protest at first, but she soon got the hang of it. For a time she continued to wake during the night – even when she was not due for a feed and we needed to pat her again. As, however, we began to withdraw our contact with her as she went to sleep at bedtime, she then began to sleep through the night. We now have a very content and well-rested baby, and those 'Colic Days' feel like ancient history.

129

special babies

07

Reflux

What we commonly call 'reflux' is known in medical terms as 'gastro oesophageal reflux'. It is condition that, thankfully, is being increasingly recognized and treated. It is most common in the first six months to one year of life. The vast majority of babies naturally grow out of their reflux and suffer no future digestive problems.

What happens in reflux is that the contents of a baby's stomach leak back into the oesophagus (food pipe or gullet) and cause posseting, vomiting and/or a burning pain (heartburn) due to the acidity of the stomach's contents. This is because the action of the valve (pyloric sphincter) between the oesophagus and the stomach is often not yet fully working in babies. With maturity the valve becomes more efficient, although this may take up to a year, and sometimes a little longer.

Sometimes reflux (especially 'silent reflux', where there is no significant vomiting) can be confused with colic, as many of the symptoms are similar, including the age of onset – two to four weeks. Unlike colic however, reflux, although more serious, *can* be treated.

Signs and symptoms of reflux

- Poor feeding: your baby may refuse feeds, as feeding may cause discomfort
- Poor weight gain: as a result of poor feeding
- Vomiting and posseting (very demoralizing if you have struggled to get your baby to take a feed)
- Crying, drawing his knees up and arching his back after feeds
- Coughing
- Difficulty settling to sleep

If you suspect that your baby has reflux, you must seek medical advice and a proper diagnosis. Although the reflux cannot be cured, it can be controlled. Your baby's symptoms can be improved, which is very important so that he can enjoy his food and his sleep.

Your doctor may recommend agents to thicken his feeds or to control the acid production in his stomach. She may even feel that the reflux is linked to a cow's milk allergy and suggest that you try a different feed. Whilst you take the medical advice that is offered to you, you can employ some simple comfort strategies of your own.

Top tips
Reflux management

1 Hold your baby in an upright position during his feed and for at least half an hour after it.

2 Try not to rush your baby's feeds. Take things at his own pace and be prepared to feed him little and often if that's what he wants.

3 Allow him to have a dummy or to suck his thumb. Swallowing may help ease his discomfort.

4 Keep him 'feet to foot' (see Chapter 2, page 19), tilt the top of his cot, so that his tummy and chest are higher than his feet. This will help to prevent his stomach contents spilling upwards.

5 Lying flat makes the pain of reflux worse, so, as with the cot, make sure that his pram is also tilted downwards.

6 During the day, allow him to sit semi-upright in a baby chair.

7 Invest in a good quality, well-fitting baby carrier (sling) so that when your baby is unsettled and has pain, you can keep him upright and close to you.

8 Accept any offers of help from trusted family or friends. Caring for a baby with reflux can be a real challenge and you need a break from time to time.

9 When you start to introduce solid food, ask for specific advice from your health visitor or doctor. Avoid acidic foods for obvious reasons, and take heart that once solid food is established, the symptoms of reflux often improve.

10 Try not to get down-hearted. Your baby is more than likely to grow out of this condition very soon.

Reflux and sleep

As with colic, if your baby is in pain at bedtime you may need to hold him until he is comfortable enough to go to sleep. As reflux tends to last for longer than colic does, and to some extent can be helped with positioning, sensitive feeding and medication, there is a little more that you can do to prevent future sleep problems from developing.

As with all babies, you need to observe the principles of promoting good sleep, such as a consistent bedtime routine, a comfortable and quiet sleep environment and a cosy cot. In addition to this, you need to schedule your baby's bedtime feed so that it has time to settle before you put him into his cot. You also need to take into account how long it takes for any medication to work. For this reason, it may be necessary to have a slightly earlier bedtime routine and to take longer over it, too.

Sasha was diagnosed with reflux at about 16 weeks old. Before that, we were told that she had colic and would grow out of it. She didn't grow out of it, however, and we were relieved finally when our doctor gave us an explanation as to why she was so unsettled. I think that as she was not a typical 'sicky' baby, no one thought that her problems might be caused by reflux. This resulted in a delay in her reflux being identified. I was frantic that she had not gained enough weight and had found feeding her to be really upsetting, as she seemed to hate her milk. Once she was diagnosed and given the medicines, I noticed the difference in her almost immediately. She became much more settled and content. We were given advice on how to position her slightly upright in her cot to ease her discomfort and how we should hold her erect after feeding her.

Once her treatment was established, she began to sleep much better at night. I think that this was partly as a result of her feeding better during the day, and partly because we able to put her into her cot to go to sleep rather than holding her in our arms. I would urge all parents with babies who are not feeding well and crying a lot to seek medical help. I wish that we had identified the reasons for Sasha's feeding and settling problems earlier.

Once your baby's treatment for reflux is established, you need to make sure that he is placed in her cot at the beginning of the night whilst he is awake and then comforted there. After any night feeds, you need to hold him upright to allow the feed to go down and then place him back into his tilted cot (with a dummy if necessary) and allow him to self-settle if he possibly can.

Head banging

Many babies bang their head against the cot as a prelude to sleep. Alarming as it might appear, head banging is rarely a sign of emotional distress and is usually a simple self-settling device that babies use. Believe it or not, head banging is similar to rocking, and the rhythmic nature of the banging provides a similar comfort to being rocked in arms or pushed back and forth in the pram. Most babies grow out of this behaviour between the ages of two to four years.

Head banging can often occur when a baby is teething or has an ear infection – perhaps to distract him from the discomfort that he feels.

Although head banging can be associated with sensory problems such visual or auditory impairment, and with learning problems, such as autism, it is *not* the major signal of these conditions and is very common among physically and mentally healthy babies.

Sometimes, a baby who bangs his head and causes anxiety to his parents can learn that head banging leads to a predictable and rewarding outcome, such as being lifted from the cot, given a feed or being brought into his parent's bed.

Whilst the initial point of the head banging might not have been to seek this kind of outcome, the head banging can soon become a means to an end in seeking a certain reaction from his parents. It must be stressed that this is in no way a manipulative act on the part of the baby, but merely a learned response and a seeking of the familiar.

Case study
22-month-old baby girl banging her head at bedtime

Tatiana had recently become a big sister. She lived in London with her mother, Della, a pharmacist who was now at home full-time and her father, a property developer. Her baby brother, Jonathan, was just a few weeks old. Apart from some feeding issues when she was a baby, Tatiana had a trouble-free babyhood. She was a bright, happy and well-developed toddler and had recently settled well into part-time nursery. Her parents were sensitive to her emotional needs and were aware of the changes going on in her life; as was her live-in nanny, who had been with her since she was a young baby.

The problem

Tatiana had recently begun to bang her head against her cot when she was about to go to sleep. This had caused considerable alarm to her family, partly because it was a new behaviour and partly because they were afraid that she would seriously hurt herself. They were reassured that it was extremely unusual for such a small child to cause herself any significant injury, and were advised to continue with her excellent bedtime routine and to ignore the behaviour. They accepted this advice, but, one night, Tatiana was seen on the video monitor to hit her head very hard indeed. When her mother rushed to her, she found that she had a very large swelling on her head and some serious bruising. Della's concern was so great that she needed to seek a medical assessment. Although the injury was visible and the incident was extremely worrying, thankfully, no long-term damage had been sustained.

The family needed the head banging to stop, and could no longer ignore it and hope that it would go away. To this end, one of them would stay with Tatiana as she fell asleep in her cot or bring her to sleep in their bed. Each time they turned away from them for a moment, Tatiana would bang her head very hard, and they would lift her from the cot.

The solution

Given that this head banging could not be ignored, Tatiana's parents decided to employ behavioural techniques to stop her head banging. This approach often involves ignoring the unwanted behaviour and rewarding the good. In their case, however, the undesirable behaviour could not be ignored. A system was introduced where under close supervision, a mild disincentive was introduced each time Tatiana tried to bang her head.

The plan

- Tatiana's cot bars were covered with the kind of foam that plumbers use to lag pipes. This was as a safeguard in case she banged her head before she could be stopped.
- After following her normal bedtime routine, Tatiana was to be placed in her cot as normal and the lights were to be turned down, so her room was dark (as it usually was).
- After saying goodnight, her parent was to leave the room but wait out of sight and in silence by the door.
- If Tatiana banged her head, the parent was to return to her quickly and silently and lift her from the cot. She was to sit on the floor rather than be held in her parent's arms.
- One of them could remain in the room with her, but offer no conversation or cuddles. At first, Tatiana tried to bang her head on the bedroom floor, but her father said a firm, 'No!' and gently restrained her from doing it again if she tried. Once she had stopped attempting to bang her head, they were advised to place her back into the cot.
- Each time she banged her head, she was to be lifted out again, and spend five minutes sitting quietly on the carpeted floor. As the room was very dark, it was not possible for her to play with her toys.
- Eventually, on one of the occasions that she was placed back into her cot, she would go to sleep without banging her head. This might take time, but they were advised to remain calm and to stick with it.
- As Tatiana learned that the outcome of banging her head was not as good as when she didn't bang it, she would soon learn that head banging was not a good idea.

The outcome

It was Tatiana's father who implemented the sleep plan initially, as her mother found the whole thing too emotionally charged and stressful. Once the plan was put into practice in a consistent and confident way, it only took Tatiana a night or two to realise that being in her cot was cosier than sitting on her bedroom floor. She very soon understood that being in her cot meant that she was not allowed to hurt herself. Once she had done this, her head banging in the cot soon stopped completely.

Conclusion

Although head banging is mostly harmless, it can on occasions cause real concern. Tatiana's parents were very worried about Tatiana's physical and mental well-being, especially with all the changes that had happened in her life recently (new baby, new nursery). By supervising and monitoring her head banging very closely and by neither ignoring nor rewarding it, the family were able to eliminate it altogether. They are aware that the head banging may possibly be associated with emotional issues and are working closely with her nursery to monitor her happiness and well-being. She still uses a rhythmic element as a sleep prompt, but now this involves singing and moving her legs up and down.

Vomiting

Babies and toddlers have a very fragile vomit reflex. It very often happens during coughing or crying. Some babies have more of a tendency to vomit than others and if you are teaching your baby how to sleep independently, his tendency to vomit when left may well put you off leaving him to cry.

Vomiting in babies can be a sign of illness, such as a tummy bug, food intolerance/allergy, reflux, asthma, an ear infection or raised temperature. If your baby is otherwise well, however, vomiting only when left at bedtime is usually a learned behaviour.

> *Nathalie was never really a 'sicky' baby, but the first time that we left her to cry herself to sleep at bedtime, she was sick so violently that we gave up at once, feeling terribly guilty and vowing that we would never do that to her again.*

A common scenario when sleep training is that the baby vomits, is taken out of the cot, cleaned, soothed and fed again and then allowed to fall asleep either over her second feed or in her parent's arms after it. Whilst this is an utterly natural response on the part of parents, it needs to be said that from the baby's point of view, vomiting that is rewarded in this way, soon becomes a learned response to being left alone.

It is hard to do, but if your baby is sick during sleep training, a better response is to gently but quickly clean her, change the bedding and then place her back into her cot without offering another feed or cuddling her to sleep and then carry on where you left off. It is safe to do this if your baby is otherwise healthy and is over six months old.

Case study
13-month-old baby girl who vomits when left alone at bedtime

The problem

Georgina was the first child of a teacher and a carpenter. The family lived in a house in central London, and Georgina had a cot in her own room. She had been breastfed to sleep until the age of eight months. She moved onto formula after this and at bedtime, after her feed, her mother would climb into the cot with her (not as uncommon as you might think!) and cuddle her until she went to sleep.

Later on, Georgina would wake up and cry until her mother got back into the cot with her.

Neither parent was happy with this arrangement, but they were afraid to do anything else. The reason was that they had tried 'controlled crying' once, and Georgina had got so upset that she had vomited. Taking this as a sign of real emotional distress, they had vowed never to leave her to cry again.

The solution

Georgina's parents needed to understand that Georgina's vomiting had been a mechanical response, triggered by her crying. They needed to teach her how to go to sleep by herself.

They had to be prepared for her to vomit; and to respond in a confident and helpful way, so that vomiting didn't become a learned response to being left alone.

The plan

- Give Georgina a beaker of milk (approx 6 oz) with her supper.
- After this, allow her to play for at least half an hour before her bath.
- Go directly to her room after her bath and then give a small (3 oz) bottle of milk.
- Just one of you should then read her story/stories *after* her milk. The final story should be the same one each night.
- Meet any resistance to the new routine with confidence and humour.
- Throughout the bedtime routine, consciously use key phrases/songs, etc., as these will become part of her system of sleep clues.

Nights 1–3

- After the story, develop a little kiss goodnight phrase or ritual; place her in her cot and be prepared to stay beside her until she settles to sleep. When she cries you can give her as much physical contact as she needs. Eventually, her crying will subside and she will lie down. Praise her as she does this.
- If she vomits:
  - Just one of you should deal with her.
  - Be as calm as possible, as you quickly change her bedding. Do not bath her again, but bring a warm flannel and just wipe her hands, face and hair if necessary.
  - Offer her a small drink of water – but do not give her another bottle.
  - Throughout this process, you should keep the bedroom lights down low.
  - As soon as she is clean and you have changed her sheets, you should place her back in her cot and leave her to settle off to sleep with one of you still beside her but not in the cot with her.
  - Remember that the vomiting is not a sign of illness, and you are probably a lot more distressed about it than she is. You need to try not to reward her behaviour with lots of attention.

- Once she has gone to sleep, go to bed early and be prepared to be up with her during the night.
- When she wakes you should settle her in the same way as you did at the beginning of the night. Remain calm and resolute.

Nights 4 and 5

- By now, Georgina will have overcome her expectation that you will lie down beside her until she goes to sleep, and will have learned that any vomiting is not going to lead to another feed and you getting into the cot with her. You can now begin to reduce the contact that she has from you as she goes to sleep.
- Lie her down when she goes into her cot and then potter around the room, tidying up, etc. It is OK to return to her if she needs you to, but you must reduce any physical contact.
- If she wakes during the night, you can go to her and after you have settled her down, sit beside the cot as you have done earlier, but with reduced physical contact.

Night 6 onwards

- Keep up with the new bedtime routine, then extend the 'pottering' so that you leave the room for a moment or two. At first, you should leave for a very few seconds and return to the room whether she is crying or not. Georgina needs to feel reassured that you are close by.
- Any vomiting should be treated in the same matter-of-fact manner as earlier.
- As the nights progress you are to leave the room for longer periods. Georgina may grumble or complain, but by now, with all the groundwork that you have done, these complaints are less likely to lead to vomiting, and will be not anywhere near as distressing as the 'controlled crying' had been.
- Once she has learned to fall asleep at the beginning of the night without having you in her cot with her, she will find it much easier to sleep through the night.

The outcome

On the first night of the new gentle sleep training programme, Georgina vomited twice at the beginning of the night and once during the night. It was very difficult for her parents to stick with the sleep plan, but they supported one another, and feeling confident that she was not unwell, or feeling abandoned and frightened, they were able to remain on task.

On the second night, she did not vomit at all, even though she still cried a little. From then on, they felt increasingly confident about implementing the sleep plan. It took two weeks before they felt able to leave Georgina alone in her room to settle, but they managed to do it in the end. As soon as they were able to leave her to self-settle, Georgina slept the whole way through the night.

Conclusion

Babies who vomit when left to cry, benefit from gentle and gradual withdrawal techniques. Parents should not be afraid of the vomiting, because if it is treated calmly and left unrewarded, it will usually resolve itself.

Top tips
Vomiting at bedtime

- Do not panic, or this will alarm your baby.
- Just one of you clean up the mess.
- Keep the lights low and your voice calm.
- Do not take him out of the room.
- Offer a small drink of water but no more milk.
- As soon as your baby and his cot are clean, place him back into his cot.
- Do not treat the vomiting as a sign of illness if he is otherwise well.

Very rarely there are babies whose vomiting behaviour is so severe that, if left, there is a danger that they will carry on until they are dehydrated. If your baby vomits more than four or five times when left alone, you need to:

1 Seek a medical opinion to rule out any underlying physical cause.
2 Withdraw your presence in an even more gradual way than outlined in the case study above.
3 Still respond in a calm manner to the vomiting.

Eczema

The most common kind of eczema in young babies is the *seborrhoeic type*. This is also known as 'cradle cap', although it can extend from the scalp to the eyebrows and face. It might look unpleasant, but this type of eczema is not usually itchy and most babies grow out of it in the first few months of life. It is rarely the cause of sleeping problems.

The other kind of eczema is called *atopic type* and this *is* itchy and uncomfortable. This eczema is linked to allergies: usually to substances in the environment coming into contact with baby's skin, but sometimes to food as well. Eczema is more common in babies than in adults, and this means that the majority of babies will outgrow their condition before they reach adulthood.

If your baby has atopic eczema, there is a chance that at some time his sleep is going to be affected by it. The most disruptive aspect of eczema on sleep is the constant itching, and desire to scratch. As a parent of a baby with eczema, you will know that if your baby has spent the night awake and scratching, his skin is likely to be much worse in the morning. For this reason, it is natural that when you know your baby is awake, you will do anything to help him stop and to soothe him back to sleep.

Although baby eczema can only be controlled rather than cured, there are some measures that you can take to minimize the disruption to your baby's sleep of this common condition.

Top tips
Managing eczema and sleep

- Use pure cotton clothing and bedding.
- Use a non-biological washing powder and avoid fabric conditioner. Machine wash your baby's clothing. At the end of the wash, use an extra rinse cycle.
- Unless you have been advised not to by your specialist, bath your baby *every night* in not too hot water that is well moisturized.
- After the bath, whilst his skin is still warm and receptive, use a thick emollient cream on his skin.
- Keep his room and his bedding cool. Use light cotton layers as bedding.

- Vacuum his room each day and steer clear of heavily upholstered furniture, drapes, etc.
- Let your baby sleep on a hypoallergenic mattress.
- Place cotton mittens on your baby's hands and keep his fingernails short to reduce the damage caused by scratching.

Babies with longer term medical conditions

One of the most difficult aspects of helping a baby who has a longer term medical condition to sleep through the night is deciding whether the sleeplessness is caused by the illness or is merely habitual. Of course, with a vulnerable child, who may be in pain or other discomfort, it is wiser and kinder to err on the side of caution and blame the illness. *However*, if you feel that your baby is suffering from a lack of sleep, and that his medical condition is more difficult for him to cope with as a result of this, it makes sense to do your best to maximize his sleeping potential. Not only this, but as a parent of a child with an illness or disability, you need to get as much rest as *you* can in order to care for him to the best of your ability. As we have already seen, sleep training need not be harsh, and it is invariably more successful if the *reason* for your baby's sleeplessness is taken fully into account and sensitively addressed.

Pain

Sadly, some babies suffer from chronic pain, caused by a variety of conditions and medical treatments. It is absolutely vital that pain is treated effectively and that you discuss all possible options with your doctor or specialist. Treatment for pain need not always be with drugs (although if drugs are recommended, you ought to follow your doctor's advice). Often, treatments such as massage, positioning, warm baths and complementary therapies can be very useful in the treatment of painful conditions, and these should be explored.

Once you are confident that your child's pain is under control, you need to teach him to sleep independently. If his sleep skills are robust, he is more likely to be able to sleep through any minor pain that he experiences during the night.

As always, it is sensible to teach your child how to go to sleep alone at the *beginning* of the night. After a warm bath, a dose of any necessary medication and a milk feed, he is likely to be in his optimum state of comfort, and this is the right time to teach him how to go to sleep alone in his cot. 'Controlled crying' techniques are not usually appropriate for babies who are susceptible to pain. For one thing, as his parent, your resolve may not be strong enough if you feel that his crying is due to pain rather than habit. For this reason, it is more acceptable and sensible to use one of the gradual withdrawal techniques that have been previously illustrated and will be discussed further in the next chapter.

Difficulty in breathing

Some longer term medical conditions that babies can suffer from will cause difficulty in breathing. These difficulties are likely to worsen during the night, when your child is lying down. Coughing also has an adverse impact on a baby's ability to sleep through the night. As with pain control, it is important that your baby receives the best possible treatment to control his symptoms, whether this be with drugs or by other means. Some of the medicines used to treat breathing difficulties can have a stimulating effect and therefore cause further sleep problems. You will need to discuss with your doctor the possible effects of your baby's medication and its administration.

If your baby has difficulty in breathing, or has a tendency to cough during the night, there are certain practical steps that you can take to keep him comfortable.

Top tips – helping your baby to breathe at night

- First and absolutely foremost is that you avoid him coming into contact with cigarette smoke, both during the day and at night. *Do not allow anyone to smoke in your home* even if they are downstairs and he is upstairs.
- Tilt the top of his cot, by placing thick books such as telephone directories under the feet of his cot. Make sure that he is positioned 'feet to foot', however, (see page 19) to prevent his slipping down and suffocating under his bed clothes.
- Invest in a humidifier for his room. If this is not possible, boil a kettle in there for several minutes before he goes to bed.
- If your baby is over three months old, you can use preparations of menthol or eucalyptus impregnated onto a handkerchief and

placed near to the cot, or used in conjunction with a steamer device.

- Have a drink of cool boiled water close to hand, to ease any coughing during the night.

In common with babies who suffer from painful conditions, it is important to teach babies with breathing difficulties how to go to sleep independently at the beginning of the night. If you are able to do this, it will strengthen his ability to settle if he wakes up during the night. After attending to your baby after a coughing or wheezing episode during the night, you will both be very tired. It is important that your baby is able to re-settle himself once he is comfortable again, and that he doesn't rely on being rocked back to sleep in your arms, for instance.

Limited mobility

For some babies, limited mobility can be a serious cause of sleeping difficulties. This is not usually the case with babies who are *born* with a mobility difficulty, as these infants are amazingly proficient at adapting as they grow.

Babies who are most likely to have problems with restricted movement are those who find their movements *suddenly* limited: after a broken bone or a period of correctional orthopaedic treatment, for example. During this kind of treatment, you are faced with not only restriction in your baby's movements, but also possible pain and sometimes itchiness caused by a plaster cast.

To some extent, you need to go with this problem and to treat the symptoms with medication, massage and positioning. If you are able to soothe your baby prior to sleep and not *to the point of sleep*, you will avoid any sleep problems from continuing once your baby is mobile again. Be aware that comforting your baby with unecessary night feeds will cause future problems.

Hospital admissions

The disruption of frequent hospital admissions can have a negative impact on your baby's ability to sleep. Often his sleep will be disturbed by a constant level of light, which limits his body's ability to recognize daytime and night-time clues. He may be frequently woken up for medical observation of his vital signs or for the administration of drugs or other treatments.

Your normal bedtime routine will be disrupted, and he will lose the benefit of the familiar environmental clues that tell him that it is time for sleep.

Whilst you are in hospital with your baby, the most important thing is that you help both him and yourself to be as comfortable as possible. Take as many familiar items from home as possible into the hospital with you if you can; especially those things with a night-time association, which you can use for bedtime, such as a familiar teddy, mobile or night-time book. If you are able to bath your baby, do this before bed and use as many familiar verbal sleep triggers from your home bedtime routine as you can. These include the familiar bath-time song that you sing to him, goodnight phrases and so on.

Take heart in the fact that babies even from a very young age are able to recognize that there are different settling 'rules' when away from home to the normal ones. Babies who usually sleep well and settle without problems at home, will often settle back into their usual sleep routine and settling habits once they are back in their own familiar environment.

Babies with learning disabilities or special needs

If your baby has a physical or mental handicap, you may find managing his sleep especially difficult. Partly this comes from fear of the unknown: is he waking at night because of neurological factors or is he just in the habit of waking? In the first two years of his life, it can be unclear what the exact impact of his disability has on his capacity for sleep. It is true that babies who have certain syndromes or conditions such as visual impairment may have a tendency to poor sleep. What is important, though, is that if your child has sleep problems, you do not simply accept this as an inevitable part of his condition. The two may very well not be linked at all.

All babies benefit from a clearly laid out system of sleep clues leading up to bedtime (a bedtime routine). For babies who have learning or physical difficulties, it is even more important that this routine is to be utterly consistent as well as *multi-sensory*. If your baby is presented with a variety of physical sleep cues leading up to bedtime, he is more likely to understand and learn that sleep is coming soon.

For many babies with a learning disability, it can take longer for a bedtime routine to become meaningful. If you can make the bedtime routine as rich and as consistent as possible, you will definitely speed up the learning process for him.

Bedtime routine – a multi-sensory approach

Sight   Use visual sleep prompts, such as dimming the lights and following a familiar pattern of actions (a song in the bath accompanied with actions, closing the curtains, etc.). These are very helpful sleep triggers for all children except those with profound blindness.

Hearing   Use the same phrases and songs at each step of your bedtime routine. These verbal sleep prompts will help to reinforce the familiarity of a bedtime routine and are useful to all children except those with a serious hearing impairment.

Touch   A warm bath, a gentle massage, changing into a soft sleeping suit and a loving cuddle. These are all examples of how the sense of touch will tell your baby that sleep is coming soon.

Smell   Use familiar bathing products, massage lotions and skin creams in preparation for bedtime. Try to keep these for night-time only and use other products for daytime cleansing and nappy changes. Lavender has been recognized for many years as having a calming effect.

Taste   The familiar taste of toothpaste, for instance, and night-time medication and warmed milk will all act as sleep triggers if they are experienced in the same order each night.

Night-time sleep training should be gentle with *any* baby, but especially so with babies who have special needs. You should aim to be as consistent and predictable as possible both in settling your baby and in responding to his night-time waking. This will help him to feel safe. If you are planning to drop night feeds, or to teach your baby how to settle by himself in his cot, you should always plan to make the changes with gradual and gentle steps.

During meetings with your baby's doctor, you should discuss his sleeping if you are having problems. Sleep is highly important to any baby's growth and development, but is particularly significant for babies who have a special need. It may be that a medication he is taking is having an impact on his sleep, for example, and your doctor will be able to advise you about this. You may even be advised to use a medicine specifically designed to help him sleep. Your doctor will also be able to tell you what is safe or unsafe for your child in terms of sleep training.

Sadly, there are some babies who at times will need 'round the clock' care to keep them safe and comfortable. If your baby needs this, you should seek out all the help you can get. This includes statutory services from health or social care organisations as well as help from trusted family, friends and voluntary groups. If you are able to get some rest yourself, you will be better able to enjoy your child and to meet his needs.

Except in the case of a very severe physical difficulty, chronic sleepless nights need not always go with the territory of having a child with a learning disability.

getting ready for change

In this chapter you will learn:
- how to identify the reason for your baby's sleep problem
- how to set a realistic goal as to what you want to achieve
- how to prepare yourself for tackling your baby's sleep.

Keeping a sleep diary

One of the most difficult aspects of helping your baby to sleep better at night is contemplating the seemingly overwhelming changes that you need to make. It is difficult enough, coping with your baby's constantly changing needs during the day, in terms of feeding, playing and so on. By the time it gets to bedtime, most parents, quite understandably are tempted to take the line of least resistance. If your nights with your baby are bad, then the prospect of them getting worse can be an unbearable thought.

Remember, though, that if your nights are already difficult, you have little to lose.

> Successful sleep training is about using the time that you would have spent being up in the night anyway in a more positive way.

Before commencing sleep training of any kind, it is advisable that you first of all record a diary of your baby's sleep. Ideally, you should do this for at least one week before you begin. The diary need not be complicated but it should be completed honestly and be written up *at the time*. You may not feel like completing a diary in the middle of the night, but the fact is, that writing events up on the morning after may mean that your information is not accurate. If both you and your partner take it in turns to attend to your baby during the night, you *both* need to fill in the diary.

What a sleep diary will show you

Sleep diaries reveal:
- a realistic overview of your baby's sleep
- the times at which your baby naturally wants to sleep at
- whether there is a relationship between certain foods/ activities and her sleep
- under what conditions she is likely to sleep best
- what (if any) her sleep triggers are.

Sometimes the mere action of keeping a diary will help you. The record may show you that her sleep is in fact usual for her age, and provide you with the reassurance that she is 'normal'.

Keeping the diary may highlight an obvious cause of her poor sleep, for example over-napping during the day leading to settling problems at bedtime. If this is the case, the solution is easy – you just need to adjust her daytime nap. No formal sleep training will be necessary.

It is not at all unusual for the very action of keeping a diary to have a direct and positive influence on the way you address your baby's sleep needs. By adopting a more organized approach, you may find that you solve your baby's sleep problem without even knowing that you are doing it.

Your diary should be tailored to meet your child's and family's needs. For example, if night-time sleep is not a problem, you only need to document daytime events. Feel free to design the layout and content of your personal sleep plan, but here is an example that you might like to use.

Sample sleep diary

Morning wake-up time Where did she wake?	Monday 6.30 a.m. in our bed.
Morning Food taken. What time? Time, length and place of nap/s. How did you settle her? How long did it take?	6.30 a.m. breast. 7 a.m. porridge – not interested – 2 tsp. 8.30 a.m. nap. Breastfed to sleep then placed in her cot. Slept 45 min. Woke up crying. 11 a.m. long breastfeed. She dozed during the feed, but would not let me unlatch her and put her into her cot.
Afternoon Food taken. What time? Time, length and place of nap/s. How did you settle her? How long did it take?	12.30 – vegetable casserole + pear puree. Enjoyed it. Ate two 'ice cubes'-worth. 2 p.m. – nap in the pram when out shopping. Slept 2 ½ hours. Woke happy. Breastfed when she woke up. 5 p.m. sweet potato and chicken + yogurt. Ate well

Evening routine	
Time started. Time she went into her cot. How did you settle her?	Bath 6 p.m. Breastfed on my bed. Fell asleep at the breast.
Was she asleep or awake when placed into the cot? Evening awakenings?	Asleep when put into her cot at 6.45.
	Woke 7.15, crying. Settled her in her cot by patting her. Took 15 min.
During the night	
Times and length of waking.	Woke 11 p.m. Breastfed 5 min. Fell asleep. Back into the cot. Same at 1am.
What did you do to re-settle her?	At 2.30 a.m. brought her to our bed. Fell asleep feeding. Fed again (in her sleep) 3.45 a.m. and 5 a.m. At 6.15 woke and unable to re-settle with a feed. Got up for the day.

What kind of a sleep problem does your baby have ... and why?

Having kept a sleep diary, you may now have an inkling not only of the type of sleep problem that your baby has, but perhaps *why* she has it. As we have already seen; there is *always* a reason why a baby does not sleep well. In a newborn baby it may be that her body clock has not yet adjusted into a mature pattern of more sleep being taken at night, or that she still needs very frequent feeds.

In an older baby however, a long-term sleep problem is likely to be down to behavioural or environmental factors. Remember, though, that all babies have occasional periods of poor sleep caused by teething pain, illness and so on.

It is useful at this point to look at some of the most common sleep problems and their possible causes.

Take a very honest look at what is happening around your baby's sleep. You may have a fantastic bedtime routine; you may have avoided ever bringing her into your bed; you may have never given her a dummy and so forth. There may be *just one tiny thing* going wrong for you. (Continuing dawn feed? Rocking her to sleep at the start of the night? Lying beside her cot if she wakes during the night?) Unwittingly one of these small factors may be causing the misery of your broken nights. It can be very hard, when you are a loving, sensible and conscientious parent to admit that there is something that you might be doing wrong around your baby's sleep, but you need to look very carefully at all of your routines.

There is no doubt at all that some babies are better sleepers than others. You might be a mother of more than one child, and have never had problems with your older ones. Your bedtime routine with your sleepless baby may be just the same as with the others, so why do you have a problem? The fact is that all babies are individual and whereas, for example, falling asleep over a night-time bottle will not cause later waking problems for some babies, for others it is a recipe for night-time disaster.

You are about to change the way that you approach the bedtime practices with your sleepless baby; but this does not mean that what you have been doing previously has been wrong. It is just that it is *wrong for your baby right now*.

Don't forget, either, that some of the habits that you established to settle your newborn baby, which were appropriate at the time, may now be working against you. The prime example of this is continuing with night feeds when they are no longer nutritionally necessary.

The problem	The possible reasons
My baby will not settle to sleep in her cot at night.	• Too much or too little sleep during the day • Doesn't like you to leave her alone • Lack of a meaningful bedtime routine • Is in the habit of falling asleep on the sofa/pram/your bed

The problem	The possible reasons
My baby wakes during the night.	• It is normal for babies to wake in the night: her problem is that she can't re-settle without help. • She is too hot/cold/uncomfortable. • She is hungry or thirsty. • She is alarmed to wake and find herself in a different place to where she originally fell asleep. • She is unable to re-settle without you feeding or rocking her back to sleep. • She has lost her dummy. • She is expecting the ritual transfer to your bed.
My baby wakes very early in the morning.	• The room is too light. Traffic and/or other morning noises are disturbing her. • Her sleep skills are fragile and this is the most difficult time for her to re-settle alone. • She is accustomed to having a dawn feed.
My baby feeds frequently during the night.	• She is hungry or thirsty. • She is feeding as a sleep trigger.
My baby will not settle for her daytime naps.	• She has failed to establish good sleep skills. • The naps are scheduled at the wrong times.

Aiming for a goal

Once you have established the exact nature of your baby's sleep problem you need to set a goal as to what you want her sleep to be like. This is when you need to be realistic. Whilst it is perfectly reasonable to expect your healthy six-month-old to settle by herself at the beginning of the night and sleep through for a solid 11–12 hours, expecting her to lie in until 9 a.m. on a weekend morning is clearly over-optimistic. Similarly, expecting your three-month-old baby to sleep through the night without a feed may be unrealistic too.

When deciding what you would like to achieve for your baby's sleep it may be useful for you to set some 'SMART' targets. These are targets that are:

- Specific – i.e. clear and unambiguous
- Measurable – i.e. you will know when you have reached it
- Achievable – i.e. you have the resources to reach your target
- Realistic – i.e. you will be able to carry them out
- Time related – i.e. you are aiming for a specific deadline.

Here is an example:

- *Specific* I want my baby to sleep without her dummy.
- *Measurable* I will know that I have taught her this when she sleeps through the night without it.
- *Achievable* I have the patience, resolve and knowledge to do this.
- *Realistic* I know that her dependence on her dummy is merely a habit, and I can help her to lose this.
- *Time related* I will start at the weekend and give myself a week to achieve this target.

Based on what you have learned so far, you might find it helpful to write a clear overview of your baby's sleep problem and what you would like to achieve. Use the overview as a guide.

An overview of my baby's sleep	
My baby's typical night's sleep is like this:	She takes a long time to fall asleep at the beginning of the night. She will not go into her cot and needs to fall asleep on my bed with me close by. When she is asleep I put her in her own cot, but she wakes up later, screaming. The only way to settle her is for her to come into my bed. She then sleeps all night with me, but she wriggles and kicks the covers off.

An overview of my baby's sleep	
The reasons that my baby is not sleeping through the night are that:	1 She can only fall asleep with me lying with her on my bed at the beginning of the night. 2 When she stirs later, she needs to come to my bed and for me to lie with her again.
What I want is:	1 For her to be happy to fall asleep in her own cot at bedtime. 2 To sleep through the night in her cot.
In order to achieve this I need to:	1 Teach her how to go to sleep happily in her cot at the start of the night. 2 Help her to learn that her cot is a safe and permanent place to sleep. 3 Break the ritual of her getting into my bed during the night.
I will know I have succeeded when:	1 She is happy to go to sleep in her cot by herself. 2 She sleeps through the night.

Getting motivated

By now you may have established the exact nature of your baby's sleep problem and you may be clear about your goal. You should also have a strong idea about how you intend to achieve that goal. The trouble is, though, that you are already exhausted and you feel a bit demoralised that despite all your previous efforts in caring for your baby, you have a sleep problem on your hands.

In these circumstances, it can be very difficult to summon up the confidence and motivation needed for change.

You may find it useful to try the following exercises:

1 Name three good things that will arise from improving your baby's sleep.
2 Name three things that you have achieved over the past year.

For example

The three good things that will come from my baby sleeping through the night are:

1 She will be better tempered during the day.
2 I will be able to join an evening yoga class.
3 My partner and I will have more time for one another.

Three things that I have achieved over the last year are:

1 I have had a baby.
2 I have decorated the spare bedroom.
3 I have given up smoking.

If you are still feeling unsure about tackling your sleep problem, you should take an honest look at what is preventing you from starting. Once more, make a little list.

The things that are holding me back from teaching my baby from sleeping through the night are:

1 I am scared of her crying. I don't believe that it is right.
2 I like the contact with her during the night.
3 I am worried that I might be too exhausted to carry it through.
4 Having my baby in bed with me means that I can avoid having sex with my partner.

Once you have been honest with yourself about what might be holding you back from teaching your baby to sleep, you will better placed to make a choice about whether you really want to sleep train your baby and, if so, which method to choose.

If you decide to postpone tackling your baby's sleep plan or if you plan to leave things as they are for the long term, then at least you can be sure in your own mind that *you* have made the decision. This in itself can be very helpful, as for many people, the feeling that they are out of control with their baby or the vague feeling that they *ought* to be addressing their baby's sleep behaviour, can be more unsettling than the sleep problem itself.

If you have decided that you really do want to commence sleep training, you need to start preparing to make the necessary changes.

Taking care of the practicalities ... and caring for yourself

Before you begin sleep training you need to do some simple forward planning.

1 If your baby is currently sleeping in bed with you, take some time to adjust mentally to fact that she will soon be sleeping in her own cot. However positive you might feel about the move, you may find that you have a small sense of regret too. Make the most of your last few nights together, and check out your feelings. It may be that you *can't wait* for her to move out but equally, despite the fact that her sleep and your own is disrupted, you fear that you will miss having her there. Remember that even when she is sleeping in her own space, she will still be welcomed into your bed in the morning for a loving cuddle.

2 You will need to prepare any older brothers and sisters for the changes that you plan to make. Even the most gentle sleep training will involve some crying at night, and if older siblings are not used to hearing this, they may worry. Reassure them that you are teaching the little one how to sleep through the night. Explain that when they hear her cries you are awake and dealing with her. Older siblings may be disturbed by more than just night-time crying. Sometimes it is necessary to leave an older child to his own devices as you tackle the settling problems of the younger one. Once again, you need to give as full an explanation as he can understand. After you have managed to settle the little one, you should turn your attention to your older one(s). Any sacrifices that they have made in terms of the loss of your attention or being disturbed during the night, should be rewarded by your generous praise, and perhaps formalized with a reward sticker or little gift. This is especially important if your sleepless baby is sharing a room with an older sibling.

3 Similarly, if you have close neighbours, you should inform them that you are about to teach your baby to sleep. They will appreciate the courtesy, and are more likely to support you. Many times, sleep plans have had to be abandoned when parents fear disturbing or upsetting their neighbours. As with older children, if they are not used to hearing your child cry excessively at night, they may fear that something has happened to her or to you. If they understand the reason for your baby's cries, they are more likely to be able to ignore them.

4 Choose a period of relative quiet and stability in which to start sleep training. You are less likely to be able to stick with it, if things are especially demanding at work or if you are preparing for a family holiday, for instance. Although this might mean that you have to postpone changing your baby's sleep habits, it is better that you start later and achieve success. Even if just one of you is going to be largely responsible for the sleep training, you should check out what your partner's schedule is going to be like. Choose a time when your partner's support is more likely to be forthcoming. For most people, commencing a sleep training plan at the start of the weekend is an ideal time.

5 Getting support from your partner is so important when you start to change your baby's sleep behaviour. If you have a traditional set-up at home where one of you looks after the baby and the other one goes out to work, you may worry that your baby's crying will disturb your partner's sleep and make work the next day extremely difficult. Your partner may have a low tolerance of your baby's cries and see it as your responsibility to get up and stop the crying, regardless of the long-term implications of this. If your partner is like this, it might be helpful to suggest that they sleep in another room, if that is possible, for a short period. You also need to help them see that helping your baby to sleep will ultimately benefit all of you.

6 If you are in paid work, you should consider informing your boss and colleagues about what you are planning to do. They may not be able to decrease your workload, but they may be a little more understanding if you seem tired at work. Sharing information about home (especially if it is about a baby) can often lead to warmer working relationships. Over the few nights of sleep training, you may value your colleagues' interest in how you are doing, as well as their advice and understanding.

7 Most important of all, you need to prepare *yourself* for the impact of sleep training your baby. Get as much support lined up as you can from friends, family and work colleagues. Asking a friend or your mother to take the baby for a walk in the pram for a couple of hours during the day means that you can catch up on some precious missed sleep and will allow you to maintain your resolve for the coming night. Before you start, you need to get as much rest as you possibly can. Although the time in the evenings, after your baby has gone to bed may be the only time that you can make phone calls or watch TV, you need to go to bed early for a few nights. Even if you can't get to sleep, your body will still be resting, and you *need* to stock up on this rest.

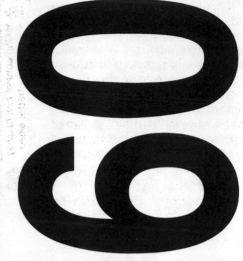

09

taking control and helping your baby to better sleep

In this chapter you will learn:
- how to take control of your baby's sleep problem, and no longer allow yourself to be helpless
- how to design a personal sleep plan which will successfully tackle your baby's sleep needs
- how to choose a sleep training routine which will actually work for you, as it suits your child's individual needs and your own values.

Now that you are armed with all the necessary information that you need about your baby's sleep and you have made all the possible preparations for change, it is time for you to take control and help him to sleep better. You may have been feeling a little out of control for a while, as you have struggled at night and at nap times. This feeling can be utterly demoralizing, especially if you are by nature an organized kind of person. For lots of people, who have been used to having control in their work and personal lives, the experience of becoming a parent can be a real shock. Parenthood may not always fit the mental picture that you had in mind, and babies are not always the docile, smiling little beings that you might have imagined. You *can* take control over the many aspects of his sleep, however, and what is more, your baby needs you to. Not just in sleep, but in a world where he is vulnerable, your baby very much needs the security of knowing that Mummy or Daddy is in charge. Remember that he will not be able to improve his sleep without your help.

> Once you have successfully tackled your baby's sleep problem, you will feel more in control in all aspects of his care. With your confidence restored, you will find parenting much more enjoyable.

Choosing the method which will work for you

There are two main approaches which you should consider when sleep training your baby. Both of them, *if consistently applied*, will help your baby to sleep better.

These two *basic* sleep training methods are:

1 *Controlled crying* Leave your baby to cry himself to sleep from night one; returning to reassure him briefly at specified intervals.
2 *Gradual withdrawal* Remain with your baby as he learns to settle to sleep alone, and then gradually move away from him.

Controlled crying

Suitable for healthy babies of six months or more, and for parents who are able to allow their baby to cry it out. It is an especially useful method for families needing a very quick solution to their baby's sleep problem.

May not be suitable for babies who are under five months old, are unwell, or have special needs. It is not an acceptable method for parents who cannot bear to leave their baby to cry for long periods.

Gradual withdrawal

Suitable for babies of all ages. This method is especially good for babies with ongoing medical or developmental difficulties. It will suit parents who cannot or will not allow their babies to cry excessively.

May not be suitable for parents in need of a speedy solution, or for parents who are unable to commit to the demands of sitting beside their baby for lengthy periods during the night.

There are so many books available on babies' sleep, each one often claiming to have a new and failsafe solution to all of your problems. The truth is that all sleep training methods are *variations* on the two approaches above. It is very well worthwhile checking out a variety of techniques to find one which you think might work for you. You may find, though, that once you understand how babies' sleep works, you can design a personal sleep plan just for him.

It may be unrealistic to expect that one single method of sleep training will solve the problems of all babies. What works best for all babies is to *identify the reason for waking* and address this within the context of either of the two approaches.

Example

Your baby is in the habit of feeding himself to sleep at the beginning of the night. Because of this, he wakes several times during the night needing shorter feeds to re-settle. He no longer needs night feeds for nutritional purposes, but instead, is feeding as a sleep cue.

Prepare

1 Introduce a consistent bedtime routine which will familiarize him with other sleep cues other than just feeding.
2 Feed him after his bath, but do not allow him to fall asleep over the feed.
3 Before placing him into his cot briefly look at a picture book together or have a spoken kiss-goodnight ritual. This will both ensure that he is awake when he goes down and will also break the close feed–sleep connection.
4 Choose your sleep training method.

1 Controlled crying

- *Night 1* After placing your awake baby into his cot, kiss him goodnight and then leave the room. Leave him to cry for five minutes before returning briefly to him to pat, reassure and help to re-settle him again. Spend no more than a minute with him and then leave him again, even if he cries.
- Leave it for ten minutes this time before returning to him and settling very briefly again.
- Extend the period of your absence to 15 minutes. Return to him if he is still crying and settle him briefly as before.
- From then on, go in every 15 minutes until he has gone to sleep. Make sure that you are not in the room with him as he does this.
- *Night 2* After placing him into his cot awake, leave him and go in after ten minutes, then at five minute intervals up to a maximum of 20 minutes. If he is still awake and crying, go in to him and settle him in the same consistent manner every 20 minutes.
- *Night 3* Initially leave your baby for 15 minutes, then at five-minute intervals to a maximum of 25 minutes. After tonight, he should be sleeping through the night.

> **Top tip**
>
> If your baby is merely fussing, or his cries are softer and have a rhythmic, tuneful quality, you should not go in to him, even if you are due to. He is getting himself off to sleep now, and your going in will only interfere with the process.

2 Gradual withdrawal method

- *Step 1* (approximately two nights) Place your baby into his cot whilst he is awake and remain beside him until he has gone to sleep. You can give as much physical contact as he needs to settle – leaning right into his cot if necessary, but you must not get him out of the cot or feed him again. He will cry because he is used to being fed to sleep, but don't worry, you are constantly beside him to reassure him and to make sure that he comes to no harm.

- *Step 2* (approximately two nights) Once your baby becomes comfortable about falling asleep in his cot and is no longer dependent on sucking or being rocked to sleep, you need to withdraw some of your physical contact, but not leave him alone yet. Remain beside his cot, cut down on eye contact with him and make sure that as he enters sleep, you are not touching him.

- *Step 3* (can take up to two weeks) Move your chair a little further away from your baby's cot each night until you are outside his room. Do this in tiny stages, so that your baby has time to get used to the change.

Top tip

Do you want a gentle solution that works within a week?

There is no reason why you can't combine the two methods. Start of with the first two stages of the gradual withdrawal method and then move on to night 1 of the controlled crying method.

Important points:

1 Sleep training should *always* commence when you first put your baby to sleep at night. Allowing him to fall asleep in your arms or over a feed at the beginning of the night and then starting it when he first wakes up is too confusing and difficult for him.

2 When you re-settle your baby during the night, use the same approach as you did at the beginning of the night, e.g. going in at five-minute intervals if you are using the controlled crying method or returning to sit beside him if you are using the gradual withdrawal method.

Throughout this book, we have tended to look at the gradual withdrawal approach, as this is safe for all and effective, provided that it is carried out in a consistent manner and followed through to its conclusion, i.e. ultimately you have to leave your child to settle to sleep alone.

Whether you decide on a 'controlled crying' technique or a 'gradual withdrawal' technique will depend upon your values as a parent, your family circumstances and your level of desperation. Remember that the decision is yours, and whatever choice you make, your success with it will depend upon how consistent you are and your ability to see it through. So make sure that you choose an approach with which you feel not only confident but comfortable.

Designing your baby's sleep plan

Now that you have identified the *reason* for your baby's sleep difficulties, and chosen a *method* of sleep training with which you feel happy, have decided upon a *time* when you are able to start, and have *informed* those people who are likely to be affected by it, it is time to get on and design your sleep plan.

It is best to have something written down, as this will remind you of what you are meant to be doing. Writing your plan will give it clarity and help to focus your thoughts. Remember that simple is best. You might like to design your own sleep plan or try something like the 'sleep action plan' here.

Sleep Action Plan (nights 1 and 2)

At the start of the night

- Introduce a very consistent bedtime routine, when I know that he is beginning to get sleepy, but is not over-tired.
- Take him directly to his room after his bath and prepare him for bed.
- Give him milk sitting in the armchair and then read a story book with him. If he protests about any of these changes, I need to remain calm and in control.
- After the story, put him into the cot whilst he is awake. I know that he is going to cry, so I will stay beside him for as long it takes until he falls asleep. This way, although he might be angry and frustrated, I know that he will not be afraid.
- When he is asleep I will go to bed early, so that I can respond consistently and calmly to him when he wakes later.

Night 1

What happened

He liked the new bedtime routine but was very lively when I put him into his cot. It took him 55 minutes from cot to sleep. Not much crying at first. More playful really.

Fell asleep at 8.25.

Woke at 9.15. Settled very easily and quickly by me patting him in his cot.

Night 2

What happened

When I put him into the cot, he was playful again. I pottered in and out of the room until he started 'fussing' and was ready to sleep. Then sat beside him like last night. Took 20 minutes for him to go to sleep. Not much crying.

During the night	*Night 1*	*Night 2*
• When he wakes up during the night, sit beside him again until he goes back to sleep. I know that this will take some time, and there will be more crying, and I will be prepared for this to happen.	**What happened**	**What happened**
	Woke at 12.30. Very difficult to re-settle. Awake on and off until 2.20.	*Woke at 12.45. Settled within 15 minutes of me patting him.*
• No matter how many times he wakes up, or how long he is awake for, I am resolved to keep him in his cot.	*I felt very desperate but stuck with it.*	
	Woke again at 4.15. Took approx half an hour to re-settle.	

Early in the morning		
• Keep him in his cot until 7 a.m., even if he wakes earlier than this. If I bring him into my bed at dawn and allow him to go back to sleep, it will make all that we have achieved earlier meaningless.	*Woke again at 6.15. Would normally have got him up at this time, but stayed with him until he fell back to sleep at 6.50.*	*Didn't wake again until 6.30! He was completely wide awake and smiling, as he had had such a good night, I decided to get him up for the day.*
	Woke again at 7.20 and got him up for the day.	

During the day		
I am going to aim for two naps and let him fall asleep in what ever way is most comfortable for him. Once he has learned good night-time sleep skills, I will help him to improve his daytime sleep skills too.	*9.45 a.m. he looked tired, so I put him in his cot. Screamed for half an hour before eventually settling. Slept for 30 min. Woke up still looking tired – couldn't bear to let him cry again so got him up.*	*Waited until 10 a.m. before putting him into his cot for a nap. Screamed again, like yesterday for half an hour – even though I was next to him. Slept for 1$\frac{1}{2}$ hours, though, and woke up happy. Enjoyed his lunch.*
	1.45 p.m. looking tired again. Went out in the pushchair and he slept for two hours. Woke up happy.	*45 min. at 3 p.m. this afternoon in his pushchair.*

Sleep Action Plan (nights 3–7)

At the start of the night	Night 3	Night 4	Night 5	Night 6	Night 7
		What happened			
As before, but begin to move away from him as he goes to sleep.	Sat next to the cot but no patting. Fell asleep in 15 minutes.	Moved my chair further away from the cot. Closed my eyes and did some Yoga breathing – so wasn't watching him – 10 min. to settle.	Chair even further away. Took him 15 min. to settle. No crying.	Chair positioned almost at his door. Took him 5 min. to settle. No crying.	Left the room to wash my hands, and when I came back he was asleep!
During the night Leave him for a few moments before going to him, to see if he can settle himself.	Woke 1 a.m. Went to settle him but he was already asleep.	Think I heard him stir a couple of times, but no need to get up to him.	Didn't wake during the night.	Didn't wake during the night.	Didn't wake during the night.
Early in the morning As above	Woke 4 a.m. Took 1/2 hour to re-settle him. Woke 6 a.m. Too tired to get up to him again. By time I'd summoned the energy he'd gone back to sleep.	Woke 7.10 a.m.!	Woke 6.45 a.m. Got him up for the day.	Woke 6.30 a.m. Heard him chatting to himself so didn't go in. Eventually he called for me at 7.15 a.m.	As yesterday.

During the day	Night 3	Night 4	Night 5	Night 6	Night 7
We are both finding these hard. I will aim for one nap in his cot and one in his pushchair.	*What happened*				
	Put him into his cot at 9.15. Stayed with him. Cried for 20 min. Slept 1½ hours. Afternoon nap (45 min.) in pushchair.	*Into his cot at 9.30. Stayed with him. Cried for 10 min. Slept 1 hour 15 min. Afternoon nap (1 hour) in pushchair.*	*Put in cot at 9.20. Left him as needed to answer the phone. Cried for 5 min. Slept 1½ hours. Afternoon nap (45 min.) in pushchair.*	Cot at 9.15. Left him. Cried 10 min but not too severe. Slept 1½ hours. Cot again for afternoon nap. Left him as this morning. Slept 1 hour.	Cot: 9.30 – 11 a.m. Cot: 2.30 – 3.30 p.m. Both times, put in his cot and left to settle alone.

Once you have designed your sleep plan it is advisable for you to show it to a person that you trust. This is so that they know what you are planning to do and will be better able to support you during the process. Another person will also be able to tell you if there any obvious errors in your plan.

Making it work

By now, you know why your child is not sleeping through the night, what you need to do to solve his sleep problem and how to do it.

Once you have made the decision to start changing your baby's sleep habits, you need demonstrate the three Cs:

- consistency
- calmness
- confidence.

These three qualities will make the process easier for both you and your baby. There may be times when your resolve weakens and you need to be prepared for these.

Sleep training stumbling blocks

The problem	The solution
After crying for a period, my baby vomits	Quickly and calmly clean him up, and then place him back into the cot with no further feed and carry on sleep training. If necessary, stay beside him but do not pick him out of his cot unless he is sick again.
He wakes his older sibling(s) with his cries	Explain to them (if they are old enough to understand) that he is learning how to sleep at night, and you are awake and looking after him. Be aware that the disruption to other family members' sleep is short-term and that if you stick with it, all of you will benefit. Remain calm and confident.
He cries for much longer than I expected/his crying is very severe.	Don't be frightened of his crying. So long as you are close beside him or returning to him periodically, he will know that he has not been abandoned. He is crying out of frustration at the change in your usual response to him.
Part way through the sleep training, he has developed a cold, bout of teething, etc.	Take care of his physical discomfort by lifting him from the cot, but keeping him in his room. Give a drink of water and a dose of painkiller if needed. Hold him in your arms if necessary for around 20 min., until the painkiller has worked and he feels more settled. Then place him back into his cot and carry on where you left off.

If you possibly can, you should seek out someone to support you during this process. Practical help, such as taking your baby for a long walk during the day to allow you to catch up on some rest is absolutely invaluable and will keep you going. If you have been up for hours in the middle of the night, things will not look so bleak if you know that you will get the chance for a two-hour nap the following day.

Sometimes, all you need is some moral support: someone telling you that you are doing a good job and who will listen to you when you describe how the sleep training is going.

This help doesn't have to come from a partner. It can come from a friend, mother or sister for instance. Your health visitor should be able to offer you some advice and moral support as well as putting you in touch with other parents who might share the same issues. It helps if you are living in an area where there are other parents of babies around and you are able to support one another. If you are alone in your area with a baby or young family and have access to the internet, there are many parenting websites offering chat room facilities whereby parents from all over the world are able to establish a supportive network.

How long will it take?

During most forms of sleep training, you can expect things to be worse than ever for up to a week before they begin to improve. If you plan for the worst it will be easier to cope when things are difficult.

- Try to avoid planning any special events when you know that you are going to be sleep training your baby.
- Stock up the freezer and cupboards with easy meals for both the family and your baby a week or so before you begin.
- Abandon all unnecessary housework. Let the ironing pile up and cope with it when you have more energy to do so.
- Learn how to 'power nap' – i.e. always rest if you can, when your baby is sleeping during the day.
- Try not to spend all day in the house alone with your baby. Even though you are tired, it will do you both good to go out for a walk or to an organized baby activity at least once a day.
- If you are working, try to take a couple of days annual leave, but still sending your child to his usual day care provider… and don't feel guilty about spending that time resting.

A word about naps and timing

If your baby tends to sleep a lot during the evening or late afternoon, and has a very late bedtime you should aim to bring his bedtime forward in gradual stages of around 15 minutes each night before you begin sleep training. This is so that his body clock has time to adjust to an earlier bedtime. You will, of course, need to address the timing of his daytime naps for this. It may be that you can abandon a late afternoon or teatime nap altogether and then simply introduce an earlier bedtime. If it is impossible to drop that late nap, you may find that you have to cut the duration of it by ten minutes or so each day and then systematically bring his bedtime forward by the same amount. Suddenly bringing his bedtime forward from 11 p.m. to 7 p.m. will cause you real difficulties and make sleep training particularly tough for him, as his body may simply not be ready for sleep at a much earlier time.

Another thing about naps is that for many babies the old adage that 'sleep begets sleep' holds true. The better rested your baby is at bedtime, the less likely he is to struggle to sleep through over-tiredness at bedtime. It is typically from around 18 months old that babies' over-napping during the day can cause settling difficulties at night.

Evaluating your success and getting the support you need

Once you have started sleep training, you may find it helpful to evaluate your progress as you go. Sometimes, if things seem to be dragging on, it can be useful to check out how far you have come and what you are still aiming for. This will show you what improvements you have made and help you to keep motivated. It will also help you identify what, if anything, might be going wrong.

Every morning ask yourself the following questions:

1 What was good about his sleep last night?
2 What was bad about his sleep last night?
3 How far did I stick to the sleep plan?
4 What am I going to do tonight?

An example

1 What was good about his sleep last night?

He went to sleep in his own cot without me rocking or feeding him to sleep.

He didn't wake up during the evening, as he usually does.

2 What was bad about last night?

He woke up at 2 a.m. and took an hour to re-settle. Normally he would have gone straight back to sleep if I'd brought him into bed with me.

3 How far did I stick to the sleep plan?

I stuck to it completely!

4 What am I going to do tonight?

I am going to continue to teach him that his cot is a safe and permanent place. The more I reinforce this, the more the message will get home to him, and he will soon stop waking during the night.

When you evaluate your progress you will need to keep your original goal in the forefront of your mind. Remind yourself of the advantages of what his good sleep will bring, not only for him, but for you and the rest of the family too.

Top tip

You should try to stick with your sleep plan for at least three nights. If at the end of this time you have made no progress at all then you should consider adopting a different approach.

What if your sleep plan hasn't worked

You might have started a sleep plan with utter resolve and confidence. Your goals may have been clear and your plan utterly watertight, but somehow your baby just didn't respond as he was meant to and you are left exhausted, asking yourself, 'Where did I go wrong?'

If sleep training has not worked/is not working for you, it is down to one or more of the following reasons:

- *The method is at odds with your natural, instinctive parenting style*
  This means that your heart isn't really in it, and you need to consider the following:
  1 whether to try a different, gentler or tougher approach
  2 whether a part of you enjoys and allows contact with your baby during the night – if so, that's OK. Give yourself permission to enjoy the closeness with him during the night.

- *You have lost heart when progress has not been quick enough*
  If this is the case, then you should consider speeding up the process by allowing your baby to cry it out. After a period of preparation such as establishing a consistent bedtime routine and teaching him how to go to sleep aware that he is in his cot, this method will be less traumatic than if you had started it from scratch. It should be quicker too.

- *Your baby has been distressed by the process of sleep training*
  You should not give up, but switch to a gentler method. 'OK, I can't leave him alone to cry, but I can at least teach him how to go to sleep in his own bed.' Remaining close beside him as he makes changes to his sleep behaviour and then withdrawing in small gradual steps will work better for you.

- *Circumstances such as an illness, holiday or house move have broken the consistency that has been needed for success*
  These events of family life are usually outside of our control and can have a real impact on our baby's sleep. The best that you can do is to put sleep training 'on ice' and try not to lose any ground that you might have gained. For instance, if you have been making progress and your baby suddenly goes through a bad phase of teething, there is no reason to reintroduce night feeds or bring him into your bed again. It is better to comfort him in his room, with a cuddle, a drink of water and a dose of infant painkiller. Once he is calm and comfortable, you should re-settle him in his cot. This kind of approach will give him the attention and contact that he needs when he is unwell, whilst not allowing him to slip back into bad sleep habits.

- *You have been criticized by others for your approach*
  Whilst up to a point it is good to listen to others' advice and to appreciate their concern for you and your baby, it is ultimately your choice as his parent to care for him as you see fit. You know your own baby better than anyone else and you

also know your own limitations and capabilities. Thank them for their advice, tell them that your baby's needs are your top priority and that you feel you are meeting them in the best possible way. Of course this is particularly difficult if the criticism is coming from your partner (baby's father or mother). If this is the case then you need to take the time to discuss what approach will not only benefit your baby, but be acceptable to both of you.

- *You have suddenly brought his bedtime forward by several hours before his body has had time to adjust*

  If your baby is used to a late bedtime, suddenly to change this will inevitably bring problems, as he may simply not be 'programmed' to sleep at an earlier time. You can tackle this by gradually bringing his bedtime forward by ten minutes each evening before or even during sleep training. Another alternative is that if your baby takes a late nap, at say 6 p.m., you start his bedtime routine at this time and put him down for the night after this. In other words, you substitute his nap time for his bedtime. Provided that you observe the golden rule of his being awake when he is placed in his cot, you should subsequently be able to re-settle him there if he stirs. A word of warning though: be prepared for him to wake up earlier in the morning if he has gone to bed early the night before. When you first start sleep training, success means having your baby sleep for a 10–11-hour night-time stretch.

- *You have not followed the method to its conclusion*

  It is not at all uncommon to commence sleep training, achieve a degree of success and then get stuck. This is particularly the case with the more gentle methods. What tends to happen is that you teach your baby to fall asleep in his cot with you sitting beside him. This may work very well at first, but when you come to try and leave the room, you may encounter some problems. This is because he has cottoned on to the fact that when he wakes up he will find that you are no longer beside him. This leads to his developing the sleep of what can be described as that of a 'guard dog', i.e. he is reluctant to settle to sleep and will delay giving in to sleep for as long as he can. He may also resist settling into deep sleep and be fitful and easily roused especially during the evening. In order to make progress, you may have to force the pace rather, and withdraw from the room before he has gone to sleep. There will, of course, be protest and/or crying, in which case, you will need to return at intervals to reassure him. You need, though, to make sure that when he does eventually give in to sleep, you are not beside him. If you can do this, you will improve his chances of sleeping the whole way through the night.

- *You have started following the sleep plan at the first or subsequent waking rather than at the beginning of the night*
  It is absolutely vital that when you decide to start sleep training, you concentrate first and foremost on how he settles at the beginning of the night. If you allow your baby to fall asleep over his feed, in your arms, downstairs on the sofa, or in your bed, only to later transfer him into his cot, he will naturally wake up later, feeling alarmed. He will need you to recreate the circumstances under which he originally fell asleep at the start of the night. Not only this, but having had the equivalent of a 'power nap' he will find it especially difficult to fall asleep again without your help. Try to capitalize on the fact that at the very start of the night he is surrounded by night-time sleep prompts and is sleepy.

Sometimes, if you are failing to make progress with sleep training, you may need to have a rethink and change your approach. Whilst a consistent approach is usually recommended during sleep training, if things are really not going well, you may have to switch tactics.

When Polly was eight months old we found that her night-time sleeping was getting worse instead of better. We decided that we needed to take action and sleep train her. Neither of us liked the idea of her crying herself to sleep, so we decided to use a more gradual approach.

We decided that first of all, we would help her to go to sleep without me breastfeeding her. First of all, I would feed her and then take her off the breast whilst she was still awake and then rock her in my arms until she had gone to sleep. After this, I was going to cut down on the amount of rocking and place her in the cot whilst she was awake and comfort her there until she went to sleep. We were going to start with just the beginning of the night first and continue to feed her to sleep and bring her into bed with us when she woke up in the middle of the night. Once she was settling well at the start of the night we were going to tackle her waking up during the night.

We were very positive when we started and she did make some progress. She woke much later in the night, for instance. To be honest, though, we never really got beyond square one, as the commitment of all that sitting beside the cot was just too much for us. I think it might have been confusing for Polly too. I know that we needed to move on to addressing the night feeds, but we were shattered and the whole thing was dragging on for too long.

After sitting down and taking an honest look at what we were doing, we decided that it was in all our interests to implement a shorter and more clearly structured sleep plan. We decided to do the thing that we both were originally against – to let her cry it out.

The work that we had done in establishing a good bedtime routine and helping her to settle in her cot at the start of the night was not wasted. She was happy to settle in her cot, but now we had to put her into her cot and go!

We returned to her after five then ten then 15 minutes and went in every 15 minutes after that to reassure her (and ourselves) that everything was alright. It took her 45 minutes the first time we did it. She woke up just once towards dawn and this time it took her 25 minutes to resettle. She then woke up at 7.30 a.m. I was almost afraid to get her out of her cot as I thought she would hate me. She was fine though, full of smiles and totally her normal self.

On the second night she cried for just ten minutes and then slept through until 5 a.m. I heard her cry and was getting ready to go and reassure her, but found when I got to her room that she had gone back to sleep by herself.

By the third night, she went to her cot and 'fussed' for a few minutes before settling herself to sleep. We didn't need to go back to her at all. She then slept through the night and we woke up to her 'chatting' at 7.15 the next morning.

Letting her cry it out turned out to be the best solution for us in the end, even though we had been against it originally. It was not easy to listen to her crying and I'm glad that we started off with a gentler approach as I think this helped with the process. All in all, I think that sleep training was one of the best things that we have done for her.

Sometimes things work out in the opposite way, and illustrates that on *some* occasions, sticking to the plan for three nights may not be a sensible option:

Jonah was a year old when we decided that we needed to do something about his frequent night waking. There was no reason that we could think of why he was waking up so often during the night, except that it was habit and he was used to one of us rocking him to sleep at the start of the night and then repeating this again during the night, sometimes as many as four times! He was a strong, healthy boy and we were advised that the best way to teach him how to sleep was to do 'controlled crying'. This method had worked for lots of my friends, and I presumed it was the one and only way to teach him how to sleep through. I'll be honest that I wasn't looking forward to it much, but I thought that it would really benefit him, and it would be quick.

The first night we tried it was absolutely awful. We planned to return to him every five, ten and then at 15 minute intervals, but after 20 minutes he was sick all over his clothes and his cot. We were told that this might happen, so we changed him as best as we could and then put him back into his cot. He was sick again after another ten minutes or so, and we cleaned him again. At this time, it was very difficult for us to remain resolved, but somehow we managed to stick with it, and he eventually fell asleep sobbing after nearly two hours.

To be fair, he did sleep better than he had ever done before on that night, but I think this was because he was completely exhausted. I couldn't sleep at all because I felt so guilty.

On the following night, Jonah was sick as I moved to put him into his cot. As far as I was concerned enough was enough. This was clearly not the right approach for him.

We abandoned the whole thing and went back to our previous settling techniques of rocking him to sleep. Even this began to take longer than it used to do. He was still waking during the night and needing to be rocked again.

After a while, we sought help from a sleep specialist who recommended a more gradual transition from being rocked to sleep to settling in his cot alone. It involved us placing him into his cot and then staying close beside him but not rocking him to sleep. We were to withdraw a little further from him at night-time only when he was comfortable. We felt that this was a better solution for Jonah, even though it demanded more in terms of time commitment from us.

Gradually withdrawing from Jonah at the start of the night took three weeks rather than three nights, but we got there in the end. He now sleeps the whole way through the night. He did not vomit during this second kind of sleep training, and although we were very tired during it, we felt it was the best thing for him.

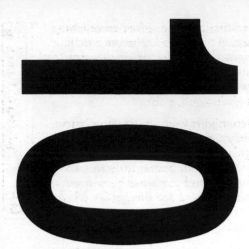

10

keeping on the right track

In this chapter you will learn:
- how to avoid your baby slipping back into poor sleep when she is unwell, going on holiday or moving house
- make the most of your success
- address your own sleeping difficulties.

Once you have invested so much time and effort in teaching your baby to sleep through the night you need to make sure that you do not let things slip back again. You really don't want to go through the tears and the endless sitting in your baby's room or outside on the landing again, do you? What's more, your baby doesn't want to go through it again, either.

Most babies will need just a few nights of sleep training before their problem is solved and they never look back, sleeping 12 hours a night and taking regular restorative daytime naps as necessary for the rest of their babyhood. Some, however, have more fragile sleep skills than others, and for these babies, sleep will always be a little problematic. These are the babies whose sleep goes awry at the slightest changes, such as holidays, illnesses, house moves and so on.

If your child is one of these, then you need to be extra attentive to her sleep needs and be very wary of allowing bad habits to develop again.

All babies will have the odd bad night, and it is unrealistic to expect that once you have taught her how to sleep through the night, you will *never* be up with her in the small hours again. You need to be aware that when she is genuinely unwell, it will do no harm to comfort her in your arms for as long as she needs you to during the night. As soon as she is better, however, you need to allow her to carry on sleeping as she did before the illness.

Did you know?

It usually takes two or three consecutive nights of her coming into your bed, being given a night feed again or being rocked to sleep, for instance, for this behaviour to become a habit again.

Going on holiday

It is a real shame that many parents dread the thought of going away on holiday, in case it disrupts their baby's sleep, or causes problems on returning home. No one feels comfortable about letting their baby cry it out whilst they are staying in a hotel, tent, caravan or holiday cottage. Not only is this disruptive for the family, but it can also upset other nearby holiday makers.

It is far better, when you are away, to be a little flexible with your baby's sleep routines. She is likely to sleep for longer during the daytime if she is out in the open air in her pram or being carried around in a back pack. If this is the case, allow her to go to bed much later. If she wants to stay up with you while you have dinner, this is absolutely alright and it is not at all necessary to keep to her normal bedtime if this doesn't suit you on holiday.

When you do put her to bed for the night, however, try to use some of her familiar sleep triggers which she is used to at home. These include the same songs that you sing around bedtime, her goodnight story book, her familiar sleep suit and her usual teddy/blanket/comforter. It might not be possible to bath her every night, but you can still use your same bath-time song as you wash her hands, face and bottom, and clean her teeth.

Even if her cot is very close to your bed, it is better that you continue to settle her there rather than under the covers with you. Not only will this prevent resistance to going into her cot when she returns home, but will also enable you all to have better nights' sleep when you are on holiday too.

Travelling

Babies' sleep is often seriously disrupted by travelling – especially long distances. If your baby is like most and tends to be lulled to sleep with motion, then she will tend to sleep on and off during any journey. Of course, if you have travelled during the day, this excessive sleep can affect her ability to settle down and sleep at night once you have reached your destination. Her settling can of course be further affected by the fact that she will be sleeping in a different environment to home.

There are two possible solutions to this one:

1 Travel during the night.
2 If you travel during the day and she has slept a lot on the way, put her to bed much later than usual, and only then when she is showing signs of tiredness. She is far less likely to struggle to settle if you do this and you will avoid all the negative sleep associations and habits which can occasionally develop in relation to a holiday cot.

Plane journeys

If you are intending to travel by plane or if you are going to a country which has a significant time difference, it is worth planning ahead, so that you can minimize any disruption to your baby's (and your) sleep.

Outbound

In preparation for the flight:

1 Reserve a bassinet for your baby to sleep in during the journey, or find out the policy on taking baby car seats on board.

2 If necessary, get a doctor's note giving you permission to take an infant painkiller on board, in case she needs it for earache on take-off or, especially, descent.

3 If you do take a painkiller – fresh, unopened sachets are easier to use and have the advantage of being pre-measured.

4 If your baby is old enough, buy some dried organic apple rings. Hook one onto her thumb and allow her to suck and chew it if she gets bored. This will also help with her ear pressure. Alternatively, use a dummy or, if you are allowed to, offer a breastfeed.

5 Dress your baby in a simple one-piece soft suit with popper fastenings and take two or three more with you for the journey. These should double up as pyjamas.

6 Try not to check in her pram until you are about to board. This way she should be able to nap in it if she needs to as you wait for the flight.

7 Check in as early as you can, and don't be afraid to ask if there are any spare seats. They may give you an extra one so that you have more space for your baby and your stuff. Remember that it is in the airline's own interest you make sure that you are comfortable. That way, fewer passengers will be disturbed.

8 As soon as you can after take-off, offer your baby a drink. This will help to ease any pressure in her ears, as well as preventing dehydration.

9 Allow your baby to sleep as much as she likes on the plane. The motion may help her sleep for longer than normal, and you should encourage this.

10 Regardless of the time difference, feed her at her usual times as far as possible. If you need a bottle to be warmed, ask well in advance. The stewardess might be busy or she might make the bottle too hot, in which case you will have to wait for it to cool down.

11 When she is awake, entertain her by walking her up and down, showing her the in-flight film and allowing her to

play with a few safe objects. Don't bother packing too many toys. She'll soon get bored with them.

12 Once at your destination, if she is awake, allow her time to familiarize herself with her new surroundings. Then when she is looking tired, use all your familiar verbal sleep clues in your preparation for bed.

13 Do not allow another (especially unfamiliar) family member to put her to bed on her first night – no matter how tempting that might be.

14 Try to go to bed at the same time as your baby, and if you are travelling with your partner, you might like to organize yourselves into shifts to deal with the night or very early morning waking which is so common when you change time zones.

15 It is likely that your baby will adjust to the time change quicker than you will. To encourage this, allow her to sleep freely during the early part of the following day, but then restrict afternoon and tea-time naps, so that she is tired at her new evening bedtime. If you need to put your baby to bed later than usual, you should do so, rather than putting her to bed at a time when she is simply not tired and possibly creating a negative sleep association with the new cot.

Moving house

Moving house can be exciting and stressful; it is also absolutely exhausting, especially if you are caring for a baby as well. It is easy to overlook your baby's sleep needs when you are busy ferrying furniture to and fro and sorting rooms out. Here are some simple tips to help you cope.

- Try and sort out the place where your baby will be sleeping first, so that you have somewhere to settle her for a nap when she needs it.

- Take a few familiar objects from her old room, so that she feels a sense of security.

- If she has napped a lot during the day, be prepared to put her to bed later than usual, so that she finds it easier to sleep. It would be a shame if her first experience of her new sleeping environment was laying awake and struggling to settle.

- Keep as many elements from her usual bedtime routine as possible. If you are used to using verbal sleep prompts such as songs and stories as part of your routine, this should be easy for you as these elements are utterly portable.

- Do not bring her into bed with you even if you are very tired and needing sleep. If you do this, she will get the message that in the new home, she sleeps with Mummy and Daddy!

A new baby in the family

When you are expecting another baby, it pays to make sure that your older toddler is sleeping through the night in her own cot or bed. The last thing that you want to do is to evict your precious older one from the big bedroom to make room for the little one. Presuming that you have already done this you need to make sure that you maintain her independence, whilst continuing to reassure her that she is still your special girl. The following suggestions might help you achieve this.

- A few days before your new baby is born, have the Moses basket ready, next to your bed, so that your toddler is able to understand that that is where her new brother or sister will be sleeping. This way, it will not come as quite such a surprise when the baby comes home.
- When she first sees the new baby, whether in the hospital or at home, make sure that your arms are free for *her*. Allow her to look into the crib in her own time and as well as seeing the new baby, have a special gift in the crib just for her.
- When you first come home, you need to follow your older baby's normal routine as much as possible. Newborn babies are pretty flexible (certainly more so than toddlers) and if you need to put the little one down for a moment in order to attend to your big girl, he will come to no harm.
- Always make sure that you continue to put your toddler to bed as usual. You might need to do this with a baby in your arms, but the main focus of attention should be on the older one.
- It is not possible to tell your toddler too much just how much you love her. She really needs to hear this when a little one has just come into her life.
- Try not to worry about your new baby crying and waking your older one. Toddlers are surprisingly good at ignoring night-time cries. Part of the reason for this is that they know it is not their problem.

Your own sleep needs

Many parents are shocked to find that after training their baby to sleep through the night, they have somehow lost the ability to sleep themselves.

This is not surprising, as after several weeks or months of deeply disturbed sleep, it can be difficult to regain a good sleep pattern. If you cast your mind back to how the sleep cycles work, you will recall that babies tend to wake up as they are coming into a light sleep phase. Their waking is natural and therefore not too damaging. You, on the other hand, may have been used to being woken during the deep phase of a sleep cycle, and after a time this disturbance can be very debilitating. You may have responded by not allowing yourself to fully relax into sleep knowing that you are soon going to be woken up... and so *you* now have a sleep problem. Don't worry, if you were a good sleeper before you had children, there is every chance that you can be a good sleeper again.

1 Start a relaxing, repetitive bedtime routine for yourself. Seriously, you will benefit from the sleep cues just as much as your baby has.

2 Go to bed at a reasonable time, i.e. do not allow yourself to become over-tired.

3 Avoid caffeine-containing drinks in the afternoon and evening.

4 If you can't relax and go to sleep, read a book. You may not be asleep but your body is still resting.

5 If, when you turn the light off, you struggle to go to sleep, close your eyes and make an alphabetical list of, for instance
   • countries
   • authors
   • birds
   • parts of the body, etc.
   This might sound silly, but these mental exercises prevent your mind from wandering, excessive planning or worrying. They provide a focus and yet are sufficiently unimportant as to not prevent you from sleeping. If you do these regularly, they will begin to act as a sleep prompt for you.

6 If you do have something that is on your mind allow yourself 15 minutes of planning or 'worry time'. This is all you need, as after this time, your thoughts will end up just going around in circles. After this time, you should either get back to doing

your lists or get up; have a warm drink and then return to bed once you are feeling tired.

7 Be reassured that good sleep *will* come back if you relax and give it time.

Enjoying the fruits of your success

If you have successfully treated your baby's sleep problem, you should give yourself a massive pat on the back. You alone know that although it can be a straightforward process, it is certainly not easy. Take a moment to think of your unique skills and qualities and what you have achieved.

- You have cared enough about her to want to help her.
- You have watched and assessed her in a way that only you could have done.
- You have read and listened to information in order to equip you with the tools to help her.
- You have taken that information and designed (whether formally or not) a treatment plan for her.
- You have put that plan into practice – even though it might have been easier to give in at times.
- You have shown patience and compassion whilst she has struggled to learn how to sleep.
- You have allowed her to learn independent sleep skills, even when you have wanted to run to her and cuddle her to sleep.
- You have taught your baby a vital life-skill: the ability to enjoy sleep and all its benefits.
- *You* have given your baby a most precious gift.

Well done.

taking it further

Action for Sick Children
A charity which offers support and advice to parents of sick children. Works with health care agencies to promote high standards of care.
Website: **www.actionforsickchildren.org**
Tel: +44 (0)207 8436 444

Association of Breastfeeding Mothers
Voluntary organization providing support from mother to mother. Telephone and email counselling.
Website: **www.abm.me.uk**
Email: info@abm.me.uk
Tel: +44 (0)870 401 7711

La Leche League
Advice and information on breastfeeding, plus local group meetings.
Website: **www.laleche.org.uk**
Email: books@laleche.org.uk
Tel: +44 (0)845 120 2918

Childcare Directory
Resource to help parents find childcare and other child related facilities in their area.
Website: **www.childcaredirectory.co.uk**
Email: info@childcaredirectory.co.uk
Tel: +44 (0)1379 898 535

Cry-Sis Helpline
Cry-sis offers support for families with excessively crying, sleepless and demanding babies.
Website: **www.cry-sis.org.uk**
Tel: 08451 228 669

NCT: National Childbirth Trust
Childbirth and parenting charity. Information on pregnancy, childbirth, breastfeeding, and parenthood.
Website: **www.nct.org.uk**

Post Adoption Centre
Offers advice and support with all aspects of adoption.
Website: **www.postadoptioncentre.org.uk**
Email: advice@postadoptioncentre.org.uk
Tel: 020 7284 0555
Advice line: 0870 777 2197

TAMBA: Twins and multiple birth association
Tamba provides information, a confidential helpline, and mutual support networks for families of twins, triplets and more.
Website: **www.tamba.org.uk**
Email: enquiries@tamba.org.uk
Tel: +44 (0)870 770 3305
Advice line: +44 (0)800 138 0509 Mon–Fri 9.30a.m.–4p.m.

index

teach yourself®

From Advanced Sudoku to Zulu, you'll find everything you need in the **teach yourself** range, in books, on CD and on DVD.

Visit **www.teachyourself.co.uk** for more details.

Advanced Sudoku and Kakuro
Afrikaans
Alexander Technique
Algebra
Ancient Greek
Applied Psychology
Arabic
Aromatherapy
Art History
Astrology
Astronomy
AutoCAD 2004
AutoCAD 2007
Ayurveda
Baby Massage and Yoga
Baby Signing
Baby Sleep
Bach Flower Remedies
Backgammon
Ballroom Dancing
Basic Accounting
Basic Computer Skills
Basic Mathematics
Beauty
Beekeeping
Beginner's Arabic Script
Beginner's Chinese Script
Beginner's Dutch

Beginner's French
Beginner's German
Beginner's Greek
Beginner's Greek Script
Beginner's Hindi
Beginner's Italian
Beginner's Japanese
Beginner's Japanese Script
Beginner's Latin
Beginner's Mandarin Chinese
Beginner's Portuguese
Beginner's Russian
Beginner's Russian Script
Beginner's Spanish
Beginner's Turkish
Beginner's Urdu Script
Bengali
Better Bridge
Better Chess
Better Driving
Better Handwriting
Biblical Hebrew
Biology
Birdwatching
Blogging
Body Language
Book Keeping
Brazilian Portuguese

Bridge
British Empire, The
British Monarchy from Henry VIII, The
Buddhism
Bulgarian
Business Chinese
Business French
Business Japanese
Business Plans
Business Spanish
Business Studies
Buying a Home in France
Buying a Home in Italy
Buying a Home in Portugal
Buying a Home in Spain
C++
Calculus
Calligraphy
Cantonese
Car Buying and Maintenance
Card Games
Catalan
Chess
Chi Kung
Chinese Medicine
Christianity
Classical Music
Coaching
Cold War, The
Collecting
Computing for the Over 50s
Consulting
Copywriting
Correct English
Counselling
Creative Writing
Cricket
Croatian
Crystal Healing
CVs
Czech
Danish
Decluttering
Desktop Publishing
Detox

Digital Home Movie Making
Digital Photography
Dog Training
Drawing
Dream Interpretation
Dutch
Dutch Conversation
Dutch Dictionary
Dutch Grammar
Eastern Philosophy
Electronics
English as a Foreign Language
English for International Business
English Grammar
English Grammar as a Foreign Language
English Vocabulary
Entrepreneurship
Estonian
Ethics
Excel 2003
Feng Shui
Film Making
Film Studies
Finance for Non-Financial Managers
Finnish
First World War, The
Fitness
Flash 8
Flash MX
Flexible Working
Flirting
Flower Arranging
Franchising
French
French Conversation
French Dictionary
French Grammar
French Phrasebook
French Starter Kit
French Verbs
French Vocabulary
Freud
Gaelic

Gardening
Genetics
Geology
German
German Conversation
German Grammar
German Phrasebook
German Verbs
German Vocabulary
Globalization
Go
Golf
Good Study Skills
Great Sex
Greek
Greek Conversation
Greek Phrasebook
Growing Your Business
Guitar
Gulf Arabic
Hand Reflexology
Hausa
Herbal Medicine
Hieroglyphics
Hindi
Hindi Conversation
Hinduism
History of Ireland, The
Home PC Maintenance and
   Networking
How to DJ
How to Run a Marathon
How to Win at Casino Games
How to Win at Horse Racing
How to Win at Online Gambling
How to Win at Poker
How to Write a Blockbuster
Human Anatomy & Physiology
Hungarian
Icelandic
Improve Your French
Improve Your German
Improve Your Italian
Improve Your Spanish
Improving Your Employability

Indian Head Massage
Indonesian
Instant French
Instant German
Instant Greek
Instant Italian
Instant Japanese
Instant Portuguese
Instant Russian
Instant Spanish
Internet, The
Irish
Irish Conversation
Irish Grammar
Islam
Italian
Italian Conversation
Italian Grammar
Italian Phrasebook
Italian Starter Kit
Italian Verbs
Italian Vocabulary
Japanese
Japanese Conversation
Java
JavaScript
Jazz
Jewellery Making
Judaism
Jung
Kama Sutra, The
Keeping Aquarium Fish
Keeping Pigs
Keeping Poultry
Keeping a Rabbit
Knitting
Korean
Latin
Latin American Spanish
Latin Dictionary
Latin Grammar
Latvian
Letter Writing Skills
Life at 50: For Men
Life at 50: For Women

Russian Grammar
Sage Line 50
Sanskrit
Screenwriting
Second World War, The
Serbian
Setting Up a Small Business
Shorthand Pitman 2000
Sikhism
Singing
Slovene
Small Business Accounting
Small Business Health Check
Songwriting
Spanish
Spanish Conversation
Spanish Dictionary
Spanish Grammar
Spanish Phrasebook
Spanish Starter Kit
Spanish Verbs
Spanish Vocabulary
Speaking On Special Occasions
Speed Reading
Stalin's Russia
Stand Up Comedy
Statistics
Stop Smoking
Sudoku
Swahili
Swahili Dictionary
Swedish
Swedish Conversation
Tagalog
Tai Chi
Tantric Sex
Tap Dancing
Teaching English as a Foreign
    Language
Teams & Team Working
Thai
Theatre
Time Management
Tracing Your Family History
Training

Travel Writing
Trigonometry
Turkish
Turkish Conversation
Twentieth Century USA
Typing
Ukrainian
Understanding Tax for Small
    Businesses
Understanding Terrorism
Urdu
Vietnamese
Visual Basic
Volcanoes
Watercolour Painting
Weight Control through Diet &
    Exercise
Welsh
Welsh Dictionary
Welsh Grammar
Wills & Probate
Windows XP
Wine Tasting
Winning at Job Interviews
Word 2003
World Cultures: China
World Cultures: England
World Cultures: Germany
World Cultures: Italy
World Cultures: Japan
World Cultures: Portugal
World Cultures: Russia
World Cultures: Spain
World Cultures: Wales
World Faiths
Writing Crime Fiction
Writing for Children
Writing for Magazines
Writing a Novel
Writing Poetry
Xhosa
Yiddish
Yoga
Zen
Zulu

teach yourself

baby massage and yoga
anita epple and pauline carpenter

- Would you like to improve your baby's wellbeing?
- Do you want to deepen your parent–child bond?
- Do you need basic instructions for gentle massage and yoga exercises?

Baby Massage and Yoga will introduce you and your child to the benefits of massage and to some simple yoga stretches. The sensible, step-by-step advice and techniques are designed to help you deepen both your bond and your child's development at every level.

Anita Epple and **Pauline Carpenter** are fully qualified infant Massage Teachers, and the co-directors of Touch-Learn, a training organisation that trains infant Massage Teachers.

green parenting
lynoa cattanach

- Do you want advice on natural pregnancy and birth?
- Do you want to be an environmentally aware parent?
- Would you like a happy, healthy and balanced family?

Green Parenting is a practical guide to making informed, ethically aware choices for your family. It covers all elements of domestic life, from children and nappies to travel and toys, offering step-by-step advice and useful suggestions for every level of interest and commitment.

Lynoa Cattanach is a director of BabyGROE, a charity promoting a parent-friendly approach to a greener life through its magazines and website.

teach yourself	**pilates** matthew aldrich

- Would you like to know more about Pilates and its benefits?
- Are you interested in improving your fitness and toning up?
- Do you want to find out why Pilates is so popular?

Pilates is an easy-to-follow introduction for everybody who wants to know more about the origins, theory and practice of this popular technique. Packed with useful exercises suitable for both newcomers and those already practising, this guide will ensure you benefit from all the health advantages that Pilates offers. This new edition is fully updated with a comprehensive introduction to abdominal exercises and the latest classes and resources.

Matthew Aldrich has been teaching and working within the health industry for over 17 years. The aim of this book and his work is to help you to get the most out of your body and your life.

massage
denise whichello brown

- Are you interested in the benefits of massage?
- Do you want to learn a variety of techniques?
- Would you like to know about oils and different kinds of massage?

Massage introduces both the practical skills and the spiritual principles behind an ancient and highly influential practice. Follow this illustrated guide to learn about everything from stress relief, treating sports injuries and self-massage, to using massage in relationships and while pregnant. This new edition includes even more practical advice and medical background, as well as fully updated resources and information.

Denise Whichello Brown is a highly acclaimed practitioner, lecturer and author of international repute, with over 20 years' experience in complementary medicine.

THE NON-DIRECTIVE APPROACH
IN GROUP AND COMMUNITY
WORK

Other books by the same author:

Communities and their Development
School and Community in the Tropics
Training for Community Development
The Human Factor in Community Work
The Human Factor in Youth Work
Problems of African Development

THE NON-DIRECTIVE
APPROACH IN GROUP
AND
COMMUNITY WORK

T. R. BATTEN
with the collaboration of
MADGE BATTEN

LONDON
OXFORD UNIVERSITY PRESS

Oxford University Press, Ely House, London W.1

GLASGOW NEW YORK TORONTO MELBOURNE WELLINGTON
CAPE TOWN SALISBURY IBADAN NAIROBI DAR ES SALAAM LUSAKA ADDIS ABABA
BOMBAY CALCUTTA MADRAS KARACHI LAHORE DACCA
KUALA LUMPUR SINGAPORE HONG KONG TOKYO

SBN 19 215429 X

First published 1967
Second impression 1971

PRINTED IN GREAT BRITAIN

Preface

NOWADAYS both governments and voluntary organizations employ a great many workers in order to influence people's behaviour in some way for the better. Such workers are nearly always better educated than the people with whom they work and most of them also have some professional or technical knowledge or skill. It is natural therefore that they, and their employers, should see their role as one of leading, guiding, and persuading people to do what the worker (or his organization) thinks they ought to do, whether this is to plant a new crop, adopt a new method of cultivation, bring up their children differently, practise birth control or, in the case of young people, behave acceptably according to the norms of the adult society in which they live.

In practice, however, many people reject the advice such a worker gives them, either because they suspect his motives in giving it or because they think it inapplicable or impracticable for them. This is especially true of people who appear to be most in need of help. On the whole, the poorer a person is, the more ignorant he is, or the more deprived or under-privileged he is, the harder it is for the worker to get him to do what the worker wants him to do.

Realizing this problem, many organizations in 'developing' countries have experimented during recent years with a quite different approach. This approach is now usually called the community development or *non-directive* approach. Workers who adopt this approach no longer try to guide or persuade. They stimulate people to think about their needs, feed in information about possible ways of meeting them, and encourage them to decide for themselves what they will do to meet them. The theory underlying this approach is that people are far more likely to act on what they themselves have freely decided to do than on what a worker has tried to convince them they ought to do.

At first this approach was mainly used in 'developing' countries, but it is now increasingly used by group and community workers in 'developed' countries also. However, because it is still relatively new, the specific role and the positive functions of the worker who uses it are still not very clearly defined, and while these remain unclear the appropriate role and functions of the trainer who trains such a worker also remain unclear.

During the last eighteen years we have been working with all the many experienced administrators, trainers, and field workers from 'developing' and 'developed' countries who have attended our courses either in England or overseas to get the *positive* roles and functions of non-directive workers and trainers specific and clear. In this book we present the conclusions which we and they have reached, in the hope that these will stimulate further thought and be of some practical help to all the many workers and trainers now experimenting in this field.

T. R. Batten

University of London
Institute of Education
1967

Preface to the Second Impression

The printing of this new impression has provided an opportunity of bringing the text up to date by incorporating in it some minor changes in the training methods detailed in Parts Three and Four. The main changes will be found in the appendices to Chapter Eleven and in the Observer's Checklist on p. 123.

Contents

PART FOUR

TRAINING TRAINERS

DIAGRAMS AND CHECKLISTS

PART ONE

APPROACHES

Introduction

COMMUNITY workers work for the betterment of people. But 'betterment' is a very vague and general term which every person will interpret for himself according to his own ideas of what is good. Thus what the worker regards as betterment for the people with whom he works they may not regard as betterment for themselves. If this should happen, what then should the worker do? Should he try to direct, lead, guide, or persuade people to accept his judgement of what is good? If he does, how can he be sure that he is right? Or should he try to help them think out for themselves what they themselves want? If so, and if the people decide on something that conflicts with his own ideas of what is good, what then becomes of his purpose of promoting betterment for them?

How a community worker answers these questions will govern his choice of basic approach. He will choose a *directive* approach if he feels that he must be the ultimate judge for people of what is good for them; or a *non-directive* approach if he feels that he ought to help them judge this for themselves.

A clear distinction also needs to be made between an 'approach' and a 'method'. It is particularly important to get this clear since so many people tend to equate the lecture method with a directive approach and the discussion method with a non-directive approach. In fact, both methods can be used, and are used, by workers adopting either approach. Thus a worker can use a lecture either directively as a means of persuading people to accept his conclusions as good for themselves; or non-directively in order to stimulate people to think out their own conclusions for themselves. Similarly, a worker may value discussion either as a valuable means of 'implanting' in people his own pre-fixed ideas for them, or as a means of stimulating people to think, express their own ideas, and make their own decisions for themselves.

3

CHAPTER ONE

The Directive Approach

IN this book we are using the term *community work* in the very broadest sense to include almost anything that anyone may do to influence people's values, ideas, attitudes, relationships, or behaviour for the better; the term *community worker* to denote anyone who does this kind of work, whole-time or part-time, paid or unpaid, for a social, educational, or religious agency, or as an individual working on his own; and the term *community agency* to include all those who decide on policy or supervise and support the activities of its workers in the field.

The basic problem of determining and achieving 'betterment'

Community work, as we have defined it, includes both social work and informal education; work with young people, with the aged, and with delinquents; and work with people in various kinds of special need. The common element in all these different kinds of community work is that they involve working with people for the betterment of the people, and this is why all community workers have certain problems in common. Thus in order to promote betterment they need first to define it, and then achieve it: but this is by no means easy in view of all the many complex factors inherent in some of the situations in which they work. Different people have different ideas about what constitutes betterment, and the mere fact that the worker wants to influence people for the better, as he sees it, suggests that his ideas about what is good are different from theirs. How then can he be sure that his ideas are better than theirs, not only for him but for them also? And if he is sure, how can he most effectively get people to accept his ideas if they already have their own quite different ideas about what is good for them? These are real problems, and if the judgement of the agency or

4

its workers in dealing with them is anywhere at fault, not only may they fail to do good, they may actually do harm. This has obvious implications for those of us who presume to try to influence others in relation to what we see as good. Good intentions are not enough. We can only really justify our presumption, to ourselves and to others, by continually reviewing our purposes and the assumptions on which they are based, and by continually evaluating the efficacy of the approaches and methods we employ.

Although our definition of community work includes a very wide variety of purposes and programmes, they are all implemented through only two basic approaches: the one, which is directive in character; and the other which, for want of a better name, is usually called non-directive. Of these two approaches the directive approach is by far the more common. The non-directive approach is relatively new. It is still not very well understood and applied by most community workers, many of whom doubt its value.

The directive approach: planning and providing FOR people

The directive approach, as its name implies, means that the agency which adopts it itself decides, more or less specifically, whatever it thinks people need or ought to value or ought to do for their own good, and sometimes even how they ought to behave. These decisions become the agency's betterment goals *for* people. The agency will then provide whatever staff, equipment, premises, and programme it thinks are needed to meet the needs or interests of the people it wishes to help, in the hope that they will avail themselves of the services or activities it provides. This will bring them into contact with the agency's workers, who will then try to influence people in relation to the agency's ideas of betterment for them. It is the essence of this approach that the agency and its workers think, decide, plan, organize, administer, and provide *for* people. Always the main initiative, and the final say, remains with them.

This is the essence of the directive approach, but it is not always obvious as such to the superficial observer. This is

because an agency, as a prior condition to achieving its betterment goals, must be able to attract people to its programme
and, having attracted them, keep them attracted for long
enough to have a chance of exerting its influence over them.
Thus however directive in intention an agency may be, it may
still ask people what they want and then provide it, unless it is
something of which it disapproves. Similarly, an agency
worker may allow, or even encourage people to decide some
things for themselves, but he will still be using a directive
approach if he attempts to persuade them to decide according
to what he thinks is good for them; or if he retains the power,
however seldom he uses it, to veto any decision with which he
fundamentally disagrees; or if he imposes any conditions, such
as compulsory participation in some 'worthwhile' activity, as
the price of participation in other more popular activities.

Those who respond to this approach, and very many do, do
so in order to satisfy some need or interest of their own. They
will join an Evening Institute, for instance, to pursue a hobby
or interest under the guidance of a qualified instructor and to
meet other people with a similar interest; or because they are
lonely and want to extend their circle of friends; or because they
live in a cold cheerless room and feel that joining a class is as
good a way as any of spending an evening in comparative
warmth and comfort. Young people join youth clubs for much
the same reasons. Many of them like the directive approach
because it frees them from all real responsibility; and even those
who do not like it will accept it and conform to it as long as the
advantages it offers outweigh for them the disadvantages of
having to conform. The fact that they conform, however, does
not necessarily mean that they have accepted or will accept the
agency's ideas of what is betterment for them. All that can certainly be said is that while they stay with the agency's programme, the worker has continuing opportunities of influencing
them in situations of his own contriving.

Leading or guiding people

So far we have mainly described the directive approach in terms of agency planning and provision, but it is also applied in the relationship that the worker establishes with people, especially with young people and with adults in certain categories of special need. The worker's initial aim is to get himself accepted as a friendly, trustworthy, and competent person whose advice is worth having and opinions worth listening to. Once he has achieved this he will have many opportunities of guiding the thinking and the attitudes and behaviour of the people with whom he works, both as a leader of groups and as the counsellor of those who approach him individually with their problems.

The directive approach evaluated

Although the directive approach is very widely used, some people dislike it and criticize it. They query the agencies' assumption that they know better than the people what is good for them, and they dislike the worker–client, superior–inferior relationship that this implies. They also believe that many of the agencies' potential clients dislike it too, and that this reduces the effectiveness of these agencies' work.

This may well be true, at least to some considerable extent, but is it not also true that those who control the agencies' policies, and the workers who implement their programmes, are, for the most part, more strongly motivated by feelings of social responsibility and more competent through education, training, and experience than the generality of the people they try to serve? And does this not justify them, if they feel they have something worthwhile to give and want to give it, in deciding for themselves what they will give and in what way they will give it?

Its achievements

In fact, few if any of the critics of the directive approach would deny that the agencies which use it have achieved and are still achieving a tremendous amount of good. No one can

B

seriously argue, for instance, that they have not enriched the cultural, recreational, and social life of millions of people, quite apart from the massive help and support they have given to many categories of people in special need.

Its limitations

However, it is also true that agencies find the directive approach less effective for some purposes than others, and in some situations than in others. Although it has proved very effective as a way of providing people with whatever kinds of help and services they already want, it is by no means as effective a way of getting them to change or modify any of their strongly established ideas, attitudes, or patterns of behaviour. Thus the Reverend Henry Solly who saw the need for working-men's clubs and was the founder of their Club and Institute Union was, in the words of the Union's official history, 'both the propeller and the brake of the movement; he got it going, but his objects were typically those of a Victorian parson'. He not only aimed to make the clubs centres of adult education but was also intent on keeping them teetotal and that 'was probably why they failed, for the emphasis in those early years was not upon giving the members what they wanted, but upon deciding what was good for them ... even smoking was heartily discouraged'.[1]

It was not until after the Union's members assumed control that the restriction on beer-drinking was relaxed and that the movement really began to flourish. Today it has more than 2,500,000 members. Indeed, people are quick to sense, and to resent and resist, any direct attempt to influence them, and all too often its only effect is the reverse of what the agencies intend. This difficulty is least with those people whose ideas are already close to the agencies' idea of what is good for them—and who presumably are therefore least in need of 'direction'; and greatest with those who, in the agencies' opinion, most need to be influenced for the 'better'. Most young people in youth clubs are already reasonably well behaved. One major problem of

[1] George Tremlett, *The First Hundred Years*, London, 1962, pp. 11-12.

the Youth Service and one which many youth workers regard as *the* major problem, is how to reach and influence the more delinquent types who will not come in or who, if they do, will not conform.

Faced with this kind of problem an agency has a difficult choice to make. On the one hand, it can decide to persist with its directive approach which implies that it will fail to influence those who need its influence most. On the other, it can decide to abandon its attempts at 'direction', accept people as they are, and try to help them in some other (i.e. non-directive) way.

While the directive approach is therefore relatively ineffective as a means of influencing all the very many people who for one reason or another dislike it and resist it, it does at any rate bring the worker into personal contact with all those who are attracted to his programme. Many of these may not only not resent, but even welcome, direct advice and guidance from someone they have learned to like, respect, and accept as their 'leader'. It is with this kind of person that the worker can do his most effective work.

But effective for what? Most effective, one might think, in meeting people's short-term needs, and least effective for the long-term goal of helping them to realize their full potentialities as persons. This is because the more effectively the worker succeeds in leading, guiding, and persuading them to accept the *results of his thinking* for them, and the more he provides for them, the less they need to think, decide, and provide for themselves. Thus he deprives them of many potentially valuable learning experiences and tends to make them more dependent on himself. This is a major weakness of the directive approach for agencies that aim to increase people's capacity for responsible and effective self-directed action.

Community work in its modern sense in Britain was begun in the nineteenth century by upper- and middle-class idealists and reformers who sought to ameliorate the often appalling conditions under which working-class people lived in the new industrial towns. Such people's material needs at that time were obvious and specific, and many of them were too poor, too ignorant, and too disorganized to do very much to help themselves. In this context the newly-formed social agencies necessarily took the initiative in planning and providing *for* people, and this directive approach was undoubtedly the most effective way of providing help.

Conditions today, however, are very different. Fewer people are really poor, and the main emphasis in community work has shifted from providing for people's material needs to helping them in relation to what, broadly speaking, one might call their psychological needs. Such needs may be stated in a variety of different ways: to find a real purpose in life; to control their emotional impulses; to think more objectively; to establish more rewarding relationships with others and thus acquire status with others; to make some more satisfying use of their increasing hours of leisure; or to learn how to choose from an ever-widening and often worrying range of choices those most likely to produce the greatest satisfaction to themselves. Experience has shown that the traditional directive type of approach has limitations as a means of helping people in relation to such needs, for reasons that have already been explained: and this is why many agencies are now experimenting with the non-directive approach. This is the subject of the next chapter.

CHAPTER TWO

The Non-Directive Approach

DURING the last twenty years or so many agencies have experimented with one form or another of non-directive approach, but many of their workers still do not understand it very well and some actively mistrust it. This is unfortunate but not altogether surprising. The idea of 'non-direction' is not in itself very appealing. It is far too negative to satisfy the really conscientious and committed worker who has a strong sense of purpose, and of direction derived from that purpose. Such people are willing to work hard but they also aim to get results. They want to do more than merely 'non-direct'! Thus before they will commit themselves to using this approach they need to be quite clear about what the change will mean for them— just how it can help them better to achieve their purposes, and just what it implies in terms of what they *positively* need to do in order to achieve them.

The non-directive approach

The worker who uses the non-directive approach does not attempt to decide for people, or to lead, guide, or persuade them to accept any of his own specific conclusions about what is good for them. He tries to get them to decide for themselves what their needs are: what, if anything, they are willing to do to meet them; and how they can best organize, plan, and act to carry their project through. Thus he aims at stimulating a process of self-determination and self-help, and he values it for all the potential learning experiences which participation in this process provides. He aims to encourage people to develop themselves, and it is by thinking and acting for themselves, he believes, that they are most likely to do so. Moreover, the outcome will usually be a project designed to produce some change for the better in the people's lives. Thus two kinds of betterment result, and change in people and change in their environment go hand in hand.

At least, that is the theory, but stated thus briefly it leaves a mass of relevant questions unanswered. For instance, even if the worker succeeds in getting people to consider meeting some of their needs themselves, how can he be sure that they will agree on what these are? or if they do agree, that they will decide on what is really best for them? or even on what is practicable for them? And if, for whatever reason, their project fails, as it well may do since the worker is in no sense in control, how then does betterment of any kind result?

Conditions necessary for self-directed action

To answer these questions we need to look much more closely at the worker's role. First, let us note that people do quite often agree on a need, decide on a project to meet it, and carry it through successfully without any outsider's help. They may establish their own recreational or cultural or interest group, and decide on a programme quite independently for themselves; they may form a protest group to demand a playground or a safe road crossing for their children; or they may form a service group to help other people in need.

While this is true it is also true that many such groups have failed to meet the needs of their members. In fact, autonomous action by small groups of people will not occur, or if it does occur will not succeed, unless certain conditions are present. These are:

1. that a number of people are dissatisfied with things as they are, and are agreed on something which they all feel as a specific want;

2. that they realize that this want is likely to remain unmet unless they do something about it themselves;

3. that they have, or have access to, sufficient resources to be able to achieve what they want to achieve. This implies that they have (or can get):

(*a*) enough knowledge to enable them to make a wise decision about what to do and how best to do it;

(*b*) enough resources of knowledge, skill, and equipment actually to do it; and

(*c*) a sufficiently strong incentive to keep them together while they carry the project through.

If the want is strong enough, and the other conditions are all present, then people will act without outside help. Unfortunately, more often than not they are not all present. This is why many potentially valuable need-meeting autonomous groups either do not form, or if they do form, quickly die: and this is why community workers, if they wish, can find ample scope for using the non-directive approach.

The worker's role in groups

This kind of work is now being called *community development*, and workers who undertake it are often called *community development workers*. Such workers specialize in using the non-directive approach in the work they do with autonomous groups. The essence of their work is to create sufficiently favourable conditions for successful group action without in any way infringing group autonomy either by making decisions for the group or by doing for its members anything that they could reasonably be expected to do, or learn to do, for themselves. This means in practice that the worker will:

1. *try to strengthen incentives for people to act—when these are weak —by stimulating them to discuss their needs in the hope that they will come to see them more specifically as wants.* (For example, a need which people might initially state only in such vague terms as, 'If only our children had somewhere to play', might in this way develop into a quite specific statement such as, 'We want, and intend somehow to get, a suitable play space for our children'. A restatement of their need in this positive form will greatly increase the chances that they will organize for some kind of group action.)

2. *help by providing information—if people need it—about how similar groups have organized for action;*

3. *help people systematically to think through and analyse the nature and causes of any problem they may encounter in the course of their project, and to explore the pros and cons of each and every suggestion for solving it; and*

4. *help by suggesting sources from which the group may be able to obtain any material help or technical advice in addition to what they can provide for themselves.*

The worker performs these functions partly by contributing any relevant factual information which the members lack, but appear to need, and partly by asking questions to draw their attention to relevant factors they would otherwise overlook. But he will not load his questions to suggest any specific answer, and he will not in any other way try to limit or direct their thinking by suggesting what he thinks they ought to do. In all he does, he concentrates on helping *them* to think.

The worker has one other important role in groups. This is to help resolve any inter-personal difficulties that may arise between the members. However strong the incentive that has brought them together may be, and even perhaps just because it is so strong, every member will be personally affected by the outcome—good or bad—of any decisions the group may take. Yet some of them may hold very different views about what these decisions should be. Such disagreements may easily lead to friction between the members, and unless they are resolved may even break up the group. Should such a disagreement happen, the worker is often in a much better position than anyone else to help resolve it. He is present in the group but he alone is not a member of it, and he does not commit himself to support anyone's viewpoint. On the contrary, by asking questions he tries to encourage the members of the group objectively to consider the pros and cons of *every* viewpoint in order that they should decide what best to do in the interest of them all.

The worker's role with individuals

What has been written above applies to non-directive work with a group, or with a committee representative of several groups. But a worker may also work with individuals in much the same way, for the underlying principle of enabling people to assume responsibility for implementing their own decisions for themselves is the same.

The potential advantages of the non-directive approach

Workers who use the non-directive approach do so because they believe that they can achieve their purposes better in this way. Its advantages, as they see them, are as follows:

1. *it enables them to accomplish more with their limited resources*

(No social or educational agency ever has enough material resources to do all the work it wants to do. By encouraging people to organize to meet more of their own needs for themselves, the non-directive approach enables an agency to spread its own limited resources more widely, since the agency provides less and the people more. There is also the additional advantage that people will generally look after what they provide for themselves more carefully than what an agency provides for them.)

2. *it helps to 'develop' people*

(Many agencies have as their primary aim the development of people in the sense that they want to help them, both individually and in groups, to develop the will and the competence to manage their own affairs. They value this, not only because it enables people to meet more of their own needs for themselves, but also because in the process of doing so they can increase their status and feeling of self-respect.)

3. *it helps the emergence of 'we-feeling'*

(People who work together in a group on a project they have all chosen in order to meet some need they all share tend to get to know and like and respect one another, and to think and talk of themselves more and more as 'we' rather than as 'I' and 'they'; and thus, if it was previously lacking, the germ of a feeling of caring for the welfare of other members is born which may later extend to people outside the group. It is this change of attitude towards others, which *may* result from a project, which constitutes the core of all true community development.)

4. *it provides many opportunities of educating and influencing people*
(Although a worker using a non-directive approach does not
try to lead or guide people to accept any preformed conclusion
of his own, he does hope to educate them, and also to influence
their attitudes and behaviour. He aims to educate them partly
by asking questions intended to help them to think more systematically and relevantly than they otherwise would, and partly
by providing any relevant information they need and would
otherwise lack. He can also hope to influence their attitudes and
behaviour indirectly, as we have just seen in (3) above through
what he contributes to the emergence of 'we-feeling'.)

Its limitations

Whether the worker actually reaps these potential advantages
of the non-directive approach or not will depend on the degree
of skill with which he uses it: but however great his skill may
be, he must always be ready to recognize that this approach has
limitations.

Thus it is implicit in the use of this approach that the worker
is never in control, and he has no guarantee whatsoever that,
as the result of the thinking he has helped people to do, they
will arrive at the conclusion he would prefer. All he can do is to
trust to his skill in the hope that with his (non-directive) help,
they will arrive at decisions which really are good for them. If
they fail in this, e.g. if they choose goals they lack the skill or
resources to achieve, they will lose confidence both in the
worker and themselves, and the worker's efforts will have resulted in harm rather than good. A very great deal, therefore,
depends upon his skill in helping them to think objectively and
systematically about where their own true interest lies.

Another limitation is that people may sometimes dislike and
reject the worker's non-directive approach because they do not
want the trouble and responsibility of thinking and deciding
for themselves. This may frequently happen when an agency
changes from the directive to the non-directive approach, for
one effect of the directive approach, as we have seen, is to make
people dependent, irresponsible, and unpractised in thinking

for themselves. Yet if the worker then tries to *impose* responsibility on them, however unwilling they may be, what then becomes of his 'non-directive' approach? This problem will be referred to again in the next chapter and in Chapter Seven.

CHAPTER THREE

Factors Affecting Choice

As we saw in the two previous chapters, a worker may either work *directively* by trying to get people to act on his conclusions about what is good for them, or *non-directively* by encouraging them to think out their own conclusions for themselves. The two approaches are therefore very different, but both are useful and neither is invariably 'better' than the other. Each has some advantages over the other and some disadvantages which the other avoids. Each is more suitable for some purposes than for others and for use in some situations than in others. On the whole, therefore, the worker who understands and values them both is more often likely to succeed than the worker who from force of habit or for any other reason restricts himself to using only one.

If both are useful, why then do so many workers use only one, and that in most cases, though not in all, the directive approach? There are many reasons for this which are quite unrelated to any normal criteria of efficiency. One is that the directive approach is the traditional approach to community work, and that like all established traditions it tends to perpetuate itself. Another is that the directive approach helps the worker to feel that he really is in control—however illusory in practice this feeling may sometimes turn out to be—and this is far more tolerable, even for people who are not authoritarian in outlook, than the feeling of strain and uncertainty that the worker so often has to endure when he is working non-directively. When working non-directively the worker can never feel entirely in control.

There are other reasons too. Even if a worker wants to adopt a non-directive approach he may not be free to do so. This is because many workers are not free agents. Their status in the community, or even with the agency which employs them, may depend on their ability to produce some quick and visible results which they cannot ensure, or ensure quickly enough, by working non-directively. Thus a youth leader, for instance, may feel that he has to work directively in order to satisfy his Management Committee or the parents of the young people that he is running 'a really worthwhile club'. Again, he is not really free to choose a non-directive approach unless he has acquired the skill he needs to use it. And he may have few opportunities of acquiring it for training of this kind is still, for most workers, hard to come by even if they want it.

But if a worker has skill in using both, how then does he decide which to use and when to use it? A great deal will depend on what he sees as the people's major needs and on what he thinks of the people who have these needs. If he thinks that they are either so ignorant and inexperienced or so young that they are unfit to decide for themselves where their own true interest lies; or so apathetic or irresponsible or lazy or dependent in attitude that they will not attempt to do anything to try to help themselves; or so hostile towards one another that they will refuse to work together; or so disorganized that they are incapable of working together: then he may well decide that the only way he can achieve anything is to decide, plan, and provide for them himself.

He will also be influenced by how he sees himself. Thus the more expert in diagnosing and meeting people's needs he feels himself to be, and the less he trusts the people he is working with to diagnose their own needs for themselves, the more likely he is to choose the directive approach. This is why so many health and agricultural extension workers tend to think for people rather than help them to think independently for themselves. By training and experience such extension workers may have become very expert within their own specialized field: and they feel, often quite rightly, that they know much better than the people what is good for them. The same is also true of many youth leaders who see their job mainly as one of leading and guiding young people who, because they are young and therefore immature, seem so much less well fitted to reach 'unguided' good decisions for themselves.

It is more than doubtful, however, whether even a skilled and experienced worker is always safe in deciding for people just how their needs can best be met, or even just what these needs may be. As a worker his standpoint and his purposes are necessarily somewhat different from theirs, and therefore just because he is a worker he can never hope to become completely 'one of them'. Thus when he makes a decision for them he can only do so in the light of *his* purposes and of the relevant factors which *he* sees. Since he is not and cannot be one of them, however, he may quite easily overlook some factors which are relevant for them: and in that case his decision will not be truly right for them. And the greater the difference between him and the people with whom he works—whether in age, education, training, or experience of living as they do—the harder it will be for him to see their needs as they see them, or to judge how acceptable to them his ways of meeting these needs will be. Many agency-sponsored and worker-sponsored projects in communities have failed for no other reason than this. A worker using the directive approach needs to be able to identify himself with his clients very fully if he is to avoid making decisions which may involve him in difficulties of this kind.

To the extent that a worker realizes that such difficulties are likely to occur and wants to avoid them, to that extent he may be inclined to favour the non-directive approach. This has the advantage that it does not involve him in making any specific decisions for people, for it is then his job to encourage them to make these decisions for themselves. If he does this, however, he incurs the disadvantage, inherent in the use of the non-directive approach, of never being sure that the people will choose what he would like them to choose or act in the way that he thinks best. Thus to avoid the one disadvantage he will have to accept another: and only he is really in a position to decide in the light of the circumstances facing him at the time which advantage, together with its accompanying disadvantage, he will choose.

If this were all he had to worry about it would be bad enough, but in fact he is likely to have to face yet another dilemma. On the one hand the surer he is that he knows what is right, and the surer he is in his own mind that the people are not to be trusted to decide, plan, organize, and act quickly and efficiently for themselves, the more inclined he will be to choose the directive approach. On the other hand, if he then decides, plans, and provides for people, how does this help to meet their basic underlying need of learning how to think, plan, and act responsibly and efficiently for themselves? In fact, it is likely to have just the opposite effect, for the more the worker decides, plans, and provides for people, the more dependent and irresponsible they are likely to become. Thus once again the worker has a difficult choice to make.

It would be presumptuous for anyone to say what a worker should do when he faces a problem of this kind. All that can certainly be said is that he should desirably recognize that the dilemma exists and needs to be resolved. This means that he must carefully assess his purposes for people in the light of both their present and their long-term needs. In crisis situations, e.g. when people are homeless or hungry or diseased, their material needs are dominant and they may be in no position to help themselves. In such situations, the case for the directive approach becomes overwhelmingly strong. When, however, the people's needs are chronic rather than acute, and their attitude so irresponsible that they show no real willingness to try to help themselves, then the directive approach seems far less applicable: and the case for stimulating people to think and act for themselves, and thereby develop themselves, i.e. the case for the non-directive approach, becomes correspondingly strong.

There is one final complication. Whichever approach a worker may decide on, he cannot use it to really good effect unless it proves acceptable to the people he is working with. Thus if people would rather decide things for themselves, they may resent a worker's attempt to decide for them, and withhold the co-operation he needs for success. Similarly, if a would-be non-directive worker seeks to impose on people the responsibility of deciding for themselves things they would rather have decided for them, then they too may feel resentful and refuse to co-operate. Somehow, whichever approach he chooses, the worker must make it acceptable to the people, and effective for his purposes with the people. For the worker the only sound criterion for assessing the value of either approach will be its effectiveness in helping him to achieve his purposes with people.

Hence although we believe very strongly in the value of the non-directive approach as a means of promoting development and growth in people, we also believe that workers should be careful to avoid imposing on dependent groups of young, or immature, or inexperienced people responsibilities for autonomous decision-making in excess of what they really are willing and able to bear. What the worker has to do with such people is to delineate initially only those areas of freedom and responsibility which he believes they will value and can learn to exercise with benefit and satisfaction to themselves. Then, as their confidence grows and as their competence increases, he will enlarge their area of freedom and responsibility accordingly.

Thus in some situations the worker may at one and the same time function directively in so far as he retains the power or intention to direct, lead, guide, persuade, or in any other way get people to conform to what he thinks they ought to do; and non-directively in so far as he defines and communicates to the people certain areas of freedom and responsibility within which he will leave them entirely free to act for themselves. Within these areas he will not express his own opinions and will not impose, or try to impose, any kind of veto, but concentrate solely on the non-directive functions of helping people to think, discuss, decide, plan, organize, and act responsibly and autonomously for themselves. And the more clearly he sees the development of people as his purpose, and the non-directive approach as the means of achieving it, the more he will want to use it with as many people and in as many situations as possible in relation to whatever wants and purposes they have or may develop.

There can be no question, therefore, of condemning one approach and supporting only the other. Neither can be judged good or bad except in terms of the worker's purpose, the relevance of this purpose to the needs and circumstances of the people, and the appropriateness of his choice of approach to the achievement of that purpose. However, when this has been said it may also be said that very many workers do habitually use the directive approach without ever seriously considering whether the non-directive approach might not sometimes, or often, help them to achieve their purposes better. Why this is so has been briefly explained earlier in this chapter, but the fact that it is so is unfortunate. One reason for writing this book is to explain both the uses and the disadvantages and limitations of the non-directive approach and thus provide some help to workers as to when to choose it; another, to explore what it implies in terms of role and function for workers who may then want to use it.

PART TWO

THE NON-DIRECTIVE
APPROACH

Introduction

WHAT we have said in the first part of this book about approaches to community work applies equally to work with individuals or to work with groups. In this second part we shall now examine in greater detail the scope for non-directive work with groups, and what this implies in terms of role and function for community agencies and their workers.

An agency may choose the non-directive approach for either or both of two reasons. Thus one reason may be that the agency diagnoses that the people have many more needs than it could possibly hope to meet out of its own unaided resources. It may then value the non-directive approach as a means of stimulating people to meet at least some of these needs for themselves. A second and even stronger reason may be that it feels the people's greatest need is to acquire more confidence and competence in thinking, deciding, and implementing their own decisions for themselves, and that a directive approach would tend to have just the opposite effect.

These two reasons for using the non-directive approach are both strong in those under-developed areas where the people's needs for local amenities are often very great; where neither the statutory nor voluntary agencies have anything like enough resources to be able to provide them; and where the people either cannot or will not help themselves until some form of outside stimulus or help is given. In such areas the non-directive approach has often been used in both rural communities and urban neighbourhoods with outstandingly good results. Thus in the villages the people have provided themselves with roads, or schools, or clean water supplies, or any of a host of other amenities according to what kind of need they have seen. Similarly, in towns people have cleared drains, cleaned or filled in wells, made playgrounds for their children, or constructed shelters under which they have met in order to learn to read and write. These are typical of the kind of material results achieved, but at the same time, so we are told, the people have changed in themselves by becoming more confident, self-reliant, and competent *as persons*.

In developed countries the scope for material projects of this kind is obviously more restricted: partly because most needs for the simpler material amenities are already provided for by the central or local governments, and partly because of the unavoidable but restrictive effects of government planning. Nevertheless, there is still much scope for agencies to encourage and help people to undertake self-directed group and community action. People in many villages still need village halls, playing fields, bus shelters, and similar amenities, and just because of planning restrictions they may need an experienced worker's help. Again, people newly resettled in a block of flats or on a new housing estate may badly want a play space for their toddlers, a playground for their school-age children, a room or hall where their young people, or their old people, or they themselves can meet. They may want to do something about providing these things but lack the knowledge or skill to provide them successfully for themselves. Here too they could do with an experienced non-directive worker's help.

But the play space, the playground, and the meeting-room or hall are no more than places where needs can be met. They do not meet the needs themselves. Whether needs are met or not depends on how the places are used. Does a nursery group develop? and a youth club? and a mothers' club? and a social group? and an old people's club? If so, how do they get started and how are they run? Do community workers run these groups for the people? But what if no community workers are interested or if the people want to start and run their clubs themselves? Is there not potentially as much scope in developed countries for community workers to encourage such self-help groups as there is in under-developed countries to encourage material projects? In fact, every club or group people might think of starting may be just as much a need-meeting project as the road, or school, or well in an under-developed country: and the people may be just as much in need of some outside stimulus or help either to get started or to keep going. Yet so far, in most developed countries, the scope for such non-directive work in helping self-help community groups to form has scarcely begun to be explored.

Community workers in developed countries, however, do feel that many adults and certainly most young people need help in acquiring more competence, and hence more confidence, in dealing with some of the many problems and frustrations that so often arise in the complex and rapidly changing situations in which they live. This has opened up two fields of non-directive work: the one, with individuals in some kind of special need—and much of the work now done with problem children, problem families, delinquents, alcoholics, and mental health patients is now seen to come within this field; and the other, with normal people who attend groups or classes in pursuit of their educational or social needs. Many agencies which sponsor groups or classes of this kind hope that the people who will join them will somehow more fully develop their potentialities as persons through the contacts they make with the worker and with each other. Youth Service agencies in particular have this aim in mind. They recognize that the young people with whom they work are still in the process of 'growing up into persons', and their prime object in all they do is to facilitate this growth or, to put it another way, to help them to mature.

In the chapters which follow we first define maturity and discuss how people do in fact mature. We then go on to consider what this implies for those agencies and workers who aim to assist adults or young people to mature. In doing so we particularly have in mind the problems that face youth workers: partly because the development of maturity in young people is their especial aim; and partly because the very degree of immaturity of some of the young people with whom they work makes this aim especially difficult for youth workers to achieve.

CHAPTER FOUR

Developing Maturity

BETTERMENT implies change, and most agencies aim to promote changes of two main kinds: changes for the better in the environment in which people live; and change for the better in the people themselves.

Changing people's environment for the better may mean anything from improving people's houses, or providing a playing field, a community centre, or a safe crossing-place on a busy road, to establishing a citizens' advice bureau, or a club for old people, or for young people, or for lonely people, or for physically handicapped people. Such changes are relatively easy to introduce. Agency workers know what to do, and when they have done it they see visible proof of what they have done.

Change for the better in people, however, is much more difficult to define and more difficult still to achieve. Just how can we precisely define 'better' for instance, when people are anyway already so different from us and from each other in so many different ways? Should the community worker define it in the sense that people who differ from him would be better if they became more like him by accepting his values, his standards of conduct and behaviour, and his ideas of what is and what is not 'worthwhile'? If so, this would suggest the use of the directive approach, but how can he be sure he is right in using it? This is a question that worries many community workers. If they answer it affirmatively they can hardly avoid implying that they are, or think themselves to be, in some way superior to and better than all those who differ from themselves, and this many of them are genuinely unwilling to imply. On the other hand, if they answer it negatively, what sure foundation are they left with on which to build their work?

Workers who adopt the non-directive approach find this

question much easier to answer. As we have seen, a worker working in this way does not try to guide or persuade people to accept his values or ideas, but concentrates on helping people to find their own values for themselves. He does this by helping them to learn to think more systematically and objectively about their purposes for themselves and for others. And, as we shall see, it is through just this process that people do, in fact, develop themselves by becoming more mature.

Maturity defined

But what is maturity? The Shorter Oxford English Dictionary defines it as a state of 'fullness or perfection of development or growth'. This does not help us very much, and perhaps we can get a better working idea of it by considering the nature of the changes in attitude and behaviour that this concept of human growth or development implies. Thus babies and very young children are by nature essentially immature, and hence their behaviour is also immature. If we study this (immature) type of behaviour, we notice that it differs from that of maturing or matured adults in certain important respects. Thus the behaviour of a baby is essentially self-centred and it is also greatly influenced by impulse and emotion. However, as he grows up so he will normally develop a more rational and socially responsible type of behaviour. He gradually becomes less dominated by impulse and emotion, and therefore takes more time to think before he acts. He also tends to become more objective in his thinking; more able to think further ahead; more able to deal with complicated activities; more willing to understand and take into consideration the viewpoints and interests of others; and more skilful in interacting with others in pursuit of his purposes. He thus becomes both more able to make realistic decisions about what best to do in any situation, and more skilful in putting such decisions into effect.

It is important to note, however, that all young people do not mature in this way as they grow older. In fact some, such as problem children and delinquents, may hardly mature at all; but apart from these and the problems they cause, many of our current political, economic, and social problems, one might think, would have been avoided, or would be solved more easily, if only more people were more mature.

It therefore seems relevant to inquire just what, if anything, community workers can effectively do to assist more people to attain a higher level of maturity, and especially what teachers and youth leaders can do to help the children and young people now in the schools and youth clubs to grow up into mature adults. Can young people, in fact, be given a better chance than their parents have had? and if so, just how can this be done? To the extent that we accept the development of maturity as a legitimate and desirable goal, as it certainly already is in the Youth Service, these are important questions that deserve clear and specific answers.

How people mature

Can we first consider how people do, in fact, progress from relatively immature to relatively more mature behaviour? Everyone starts by being immature, and maturity in the sense in which we have defined it is the product of a learning process which may, or may not, take place as a result of a person's attempts to achieve his purposes in interaction with others. In the case of very young children, most of such interaction will take place within the family, or in play groups, or in a nursery school. Then as children get older they interact with others in schools and in youth clubs; and then as adults at their places of work and as members of many kinds of formal and informal groups. Each of these situations is a potential learning situation.

In any situation and in relation to his interest or purpose at the time, a person will select the kind of behaviour which he thinks appropriate. If this brings a result which satisfies him, he will tend to behave in the same way in future similar situations. If, however, he finds the result of his behaviour unsatisfying, he will then either try to understand in what respect his own behaviour was at fault so that he can do better next time, or he will blame others for his failure, feel angry with them for frustrating him, and seek to pay them back in their own coin. If he does the former he is likely to learn from his experience and thus become more mature. If he does the latter, his reaction to his experience will have been a negative one, for he will have regressed into a more egocentric and emotionally dominated type of behaviour than before, and one that is likely to involve him in still more frustrating experiences in the future. Thus may begin a kind of chain regression which may end in one of two kinds of extreme immature behaviour: either, on the one hand, the openly aggressive behaviour of the criminal or delinquent; or, on the other, the progressive withdrawal from normal friendly social interaction which characterizes the social isolate. Both types of behaviour are equally symptomatic of a person's failure to mature. *So maturity = Community ?*

Thus whether a person successfully matures will depend partly on the kind of opportunities he has had of interaction with others; partly on how satisfied or frustrated he has been in each case with the result of the way he has chosen to behave; and partly on the way, positively or negatively, he has reacted to his frustrations and his failures.

What the community worker can do to help

Having got this clear, we can now consider what community workers can do in relation to their goal of helping people, according to their need, to develop a more mature type of behaviour. They can usefully aim to do two things: the one, to ensure that the people with whom they work have adequate opportunities of interacting with others in relation to purposes which are important, and therefore meaningful, to them; and the other, to provide whatever help they may need to enable them to react positively rather than negatively to difficulties and frustrations if and when they should occur.

Each and every person is, of course, continually interacting with others, but a good deal of this interaction is relatively insignificant as an aid to learning. For instance, a casual meeting between two strangers at a bus-stop is unlikely to produce a significant learning experience for either, since neither is likely to have a purpose he hopes to achieve with the other, and once having met and parted, they are unlikely to meet each other again. Interaction, however, becomes much more meaningful and significant when it is between two or more people who meet each other over a considerable period of time, and who need each other's help and co-operation in relation to purposes that really matter to them.

The case for encouraging autonomy in groups

This is why groups are of such potential importance. If a group really matters to its members, that is, if each member values it as a means of meeting some need or purpose of his own, and if the members are free to decide what they as a group will do, then there will be many occasions when they will need to interact significantly with one another, and from these many learning opportunities may result. Of course, significant interaction will also take place in many situations outside groups—in people's homes for instance, or at their place of work. Group situations, however, are usually much more easily accessible to the community worker than other situations and, in fact, most community workers do already do much of their work with youth clubs or in women's organizations, community associations, denominational groups, and groups of many other kinds.

Workers need to remember, however, that all groups are not organized in the same way. There are autonomous groups and dependent or sponsored groups, and the advantage we have claimed for autonomous groups is by no means as true of groups over which the worker exerts control, at any rate as far as all major issues are concerned. Such groups are really *proprietary* groups whose proprietor—whether statutory authority or voluntary agency—employs an agent such as a warden or a youth leader who, by taking all really important decisions for the members, deprives them of the learning opportunities they would have had had they needed to make such decisions themselves.

Proprietary, dependent, or sponsored groups, therefore, have much less potential for promoting maturity than autonomous groups in which members are entirely free to make their own decisions for themselves. Indeed, to the extent that members of proprietary groups are already immature, the overall effect of such groups may be to confirm them in their immature habits and inhibit further growth.

Unfortunately, all too few community workers realize this, and therefore all too few allow the groups with which they work much real autonomy. Thus even in the Youth Service, which specifically aims at helping young people to mature, most clubs are proprietary clubs which are owned by a statutory or voluntary agency, managed by an adult committee, and 'run' by a youth leader. Between them they customarily decide all major issues affecting the members and sometimes even, as a condition of membership, insist that all members shall participate in specified 'worthwhile' activities on certain nights of the week.

Most informal as well as formal adult education classes provided by Local Education Authorities are also of the proprietary kind, for it is the Evening Institute Principal acting as their agent who normally decides what classes there shall be, when and where they shall meet, and who shall be their instructor. We say 'normally', because an article published in *Adult Education* in January 1965[1] tells how the Local Education Authority in Oxfordshire handed over a major share of responsibility for the planning and provision of adult education in rural communities to the people themselves. The result, we are told, was that enrolments trebled, many new groups and societies formed and, surprising as it may seem, standards of work became higher than before. Such action, however, is still exceptional.

We are not arguing here that proprietary groups are bad, or that only autonomous groups are good. This is certainly not true. People's wants, purposes, and interests vary, and a person will only value his membership of any group, proprietary or autonomous, to the extent that he feels it helps to meet them.

[1] E. T. Dyke, 'Partnership in Oxfordshire', *Adult Education*, xxxvii, 5, Jan. 1965.

Many people, however, do want, and also need, more say in the affairs of the groups to which they belong, and incidentally therefore—though none of them would see it in this way— more opportunities of a kind that are likely to help them to mature. All we are saying here, therefore, is that wherever this want or need exists, the case for enabling more people to share in decision-making in groups is very strong; that for the community worker this implies encouraging autonomy in groups; and that the more he decides and plans for people instead of helping them to decide and implement their own decisions for themselves, the less likely he is to succeed in helping them to mature.

CHAPTER FIVE

Helping Autonomous Groups

In the previous chapter we suggested that how far a person matures depends partly on what kind of opportunities he has had of interacting significantly with other people, and partly on how positively or negatively he has reacted to his difficulties in trying to achieve his purposes with others. In this chapter we shall consider what community agencies can do to provide people with more opportunities of significantly interacting with each other in this way, and in the next chapter what they can do to help people learn from these experiences of interaction so that they do actually mature.

We have already noted that groups are important as centres of interaction, and that the interaction that occurs between the members of a group is usually much more significant in an autonomous group than in a dependent or sponsored group. Thus agencies which really want to help people to mature—and which value autonomous groups for that reason—will be interested both in enlarging the autonomy of any existing dependent groups and in helping and encouraging more autonomous groups to form. And in every case, in order to safeguard the autonomy of groups, the agencies will need to adopt a purely non-directive approach.

Attitudes towards helping groups to form

At present, very few community agencies see their task in this light. Most statutory and voluntary agencies limit the autonomy of the groups they sponsor and with which they work, and few are really interested in helping people to form autonomous groups to meet their own needs for themselves. Nor do they often seem very practically concerned about all the many people, including most of those whom community workers would judge as being in greatest need of learning to mature, who either do not belong to any group, or who do not stay long with the group they join.

Indeed, an agency may be so occupied with the groups it already has that it may even do nothing to meet the need for more groups of the same kind. For instance, we once visited a large rural community which had no women's groups, except devotional groups; and when we asked some of the women why they had not formed a women's group they said that they would have liked to form one, but that none of them had felt sure enough about how to proceed. Once we had asked the question, however, and they were given the information they had lacked, they acted on it and a flourishing women's group was quickly formed.

Another community had several women's groups, including one very large group which had had to restrict its membership to the maximum number its meeting-hall could take. This group had a waiting-list of forty, and the group's members were proud of the fact since it testified to the popularity of their group. Some of them, however, were worried about the women who could not join. Most of these were new arrivals and therefore especially in need of the companionship the group could offer. But neither the members of the group nor the women on the waiting-list were free to start an additional group, since their national organization had laid down that there could be only one such group in any one community. Not until this regulation had been altered, which was subsequently done, could a second flourishing group be formed.

Attitudes towards helping autonomous groups to form

While agencies can sometimes leave needs unmet, even for groups of their own kinds, the chances of people being helped to meet their needs for groups of other kinds are even worse. It is true that Community Associations and Councils of Social Service both do something in this field: but the wardens of community centres tend to concentrate more on organizing activities within their centres than on going out into the community to help people meet their needs on their own ground; while Councils of Social Service are still predominantly, though by no means exclusively, welfare organizations which think and plan and provide for people rather than helping them to think, plan, and provide more effectively for themselves.

Here again, relevant illustrations from two communities come to mind. Each of these communities has an old people's club, but the clubs are very different from each other. In one community the club was started by a small group of middle-class people as a welfare project *for* the old folk, and for years the old people themselves have never had anything to do with the running of the club. In the other community, when the need for an old people's club was seen, it was tackled as a community project. A committee was formed of representatives of every existing group to organize a community fête to raise funds, and the money raised was used to start a club. Soon after it was started, however, it was handed over to the old people, and since then they have run it as their own club for themselves. They are independent and enjoy being independent. They are proud of their club and proud of meeting their own needs for themselves.

But helping people to meet their own needs still seems to be the exception rather than the rule. What agency or association of agencies is there which is primarily interested in stimulating people to think about and define their own needs for themselves, including the needs which they could meet by forming a group of any kind? Indeed, what community worker is there, in any community, who is first and foremost interested in helping and encouraging people to meet their own needs as they see them?

These questions are not intended to imply criticism of the work that existing agencies are doing, but only to draw attention to work that is not being done, or not being done enough: and work, moreover, that has a particular importance for those agencies and their workers who aim to help people to mature. As it is, there are many people with needs and purposes that could be met by groups who do not join existing groups—

D

either because none of them really fits their need, or because
they are not congenial enough, or because they are too far
away. The only choice such people have is either to leave their
need unmet, or to establish a new group for themselves. But the
people most in need of such a group are often those who are
least able to start one, or to keep it going once they have started
it, without some help from people more experienced than themselves.

Promoting and servicing autonomous groups

How can this need be met, and met in such a way that it will
assist more people to mature? The primary need, surely, is for
workers skilled in working non-directively with people to
stimulate them to discuss and define their needs and form their
own groups to meet them. There are many such workers already
in the under-developed areas of the world, including the under-
developed areas of such developed countries as the United
States and Canada, but very few are yet working in the 'developed' parts of these countries or in other developed countries.
Some work of this kind, however, has been done by a few
voluntary agencies in Britain in recent years. One example, for
instance, is the work which has been done under the aegis of
the National Council of Social Service to start and service
autonomous clubs for women in new housing estates in industrial
areas. There is no prescribed constitution for these clubs and
their members are free to run their meetings how they like and
to choose any programme of activities they like. They therefore
attract women to whom the more highly structured meetings of
the National Union of Townswomen's Guilds and the National
Federation of Women's Institutes do not appeal, but who nevertheless value the help that the experienced but undemanding
worker can provide. In many of these clubs the members undertake voluntary work to help sick, elderly, or handicapped
people in addition to the programmes they provide themselves.

The small professional staff of the Community Development
Department of the London Council of Social Service has also
successfully worked non-directively with the autonomous

community groups which have been formed, often spontaneously, by the people resettled in London's new housing estates and blocks of council flats. These groups have now formed their own Association of London Housing Estates through which the member groups provide themselves with many services, including training. Yet another example is the recently started action-research project of the North Kensington Family Study which is stimulating and helping people in one of London's most depressed areas to organize themselves into small autonomous groups to meet some of the most pressing needs they feel.

Such workers, however, do much more than merely encourage people to form their own groups. They want to help them to achieve the purposes for which the people formed the groups. Therefore much of their work consists of helping the members of such groups to get whatever information or advice they may need in order to achieve their purposes for their groups; or with training in committee procedures, or in keeping accounts, or in any other skill the members of the group may need. In fact, such workers undertake for autonomous groups almost all the services that most voluntary agencies will normally provide for their affiliated groups, but without imposing conditions to which the groups are expected to conform.

This is well illustrated by what has often happened on new housing estates, and more especially in blocks of council flats. When a new block of flats is opened, the people who come to live in it usually become conscious of various social needs, and among them the need for something for their children and young people to do in the evening. But the established youth clubs are often too far away, and anyway both the residents and their young people prefer to have their own club for themselves. The residents may then form a committee, find adults willing to help, and start a club. They have the goodwill and they have the helpers, but they lack skill and experience. They need help, but where can they get it? Not from the established youth work agencies: they are already busy with their existing clubs, and anyway the people often do not want an agency to run their club for them. What they want is to run their own club for their own young people by themselves. They need help, and the help they need is with the problems they meet when trying to run a club. Any worker who gives this help works with adults, not with young people. Thus he does not work as a youth leader. His first job is to become known as a friendly undemanding person who in no way threatens the autonomy of the adults he works with, but who is a useful person to turn to when troubles threaten or problems arise. He has no specific programme except to help the adults sort out what to do in order to help their young people, and how they can best do it. One of his major functions, once he is really accepted, is to provide informal training courses of a practical kind in relation to what these adults need.[1]

Another function of such workers, or of the agencies to which they belong, is to represent the interests of autonomous groups with government administrators and planners at both national and local levels. We have mentioned earlier (p. 28) that the need for the detailed planning of land-use in developed countries unavoidably restricts people's freedom to undertake group or community projects which involve the use of land. Planning permission is always needed for such projects, and this may be difficult if not impossible to get. But planning can also greatly restrict, or even prevent, groups being formed at all if, when plans for rehousing people are drawn up, no provision is made for places where groups can meet; or if the provision made is of the wrong kind—a large hall, for example, when small rooms for separate groups are also needed—or in the wrong place, such as the centre of a town, if the main needs are in the out-lying residential areas.

Finally, there may also be a need for some agencies, both statutory and voluntary, to reconsider their existing approach to helping people to mature. Some of these agencies have been in existence for many years, and they may still be working

---

[1] This topic is more fully discussed in a short paper, 'Youth Organizations and the Changing Needs of Youth', written in 1960 and published in *Social Service Quarterly*, xxxvi, 1, in that year. Two years later two workers were attached to the Community Development Department of the London Council of Social Service to work in just this way.

directively when they would serve their purposes better by enlarging the autonomy of the groups with which they work. The only satisfactory criterion for choosing an approach is its potential effectiveness for the purpose for which it is used.

CHAPTER SIX

Working Non-Directively in Groups

FOR experiences in groups to help people to mature in the sense in which we defined maturity in Chapter Four, it is not enough that they should have the experiences: they also need to learn from them. To help them do this is one of the major functions, or rather *the* major function, of the non-directive community worker.

In autonomous groups the members themselves decide on their purposes for their group and on how they hope to achieve them. If the members are mature and experienced people, they will be able to decide realistically both what they want and how they can best achieve it. If they are less mature and less experienced, it will be harder for them to think realistically and they are therefore more likely to reach impracticable decisions, or decisions which may have some unforeseen adverse effect on the welfare of the group. The non-directive worker, however, if he is present at their meetings, can do a great deal to help. He will not tell the members of the group what he thinks they ought to do because this would deprive them of the opportunity of learning to think realistically for themselves: but he will try to structure, systematize, and enlarge the scope of their thinking, and in this way help them to reach a good decision for themselves. He will also hope that the thinking they do will help them further to develop their potentialities as persons.

But how can a non-directive worker structure, systematize, and enlarge the scope of people's thinking without reverting to a directive approach? It will help to clarify this if we consider how a group of people may move from feeling vaguely dissatisfied with things as they are to taking some action to change things in some way for the better.

Such an action results from a thinking process, and the dissatisfaction from which it begins may initially be very vague indeed. Once people begin to think about *why* they are feeling dissatisfied, however, they may become more specifically aware of certain needs, and these in turn may crystallize eventually as definite and specific wants. Only when they reach this stage may people begin seriously to consider taking some action to meet one or more of these wants themselves. If they do decide to act, they then have to decide on what action to take, how to organize themselves to take it, and when, where, and how to take it. Whether the people actually achieve a result satisfactory to themselves or not will depend partly on whether they have persisted through all the stages of this thinking and planning process, and then act as they have planned; and partly on whether at each of its stages they have thought effectively enough to reach really appropriate decisions.

Left to themselves without any external stimulus or help, many people, and more often than not those in greatest need, may never get beyond the initial stage of vague dissatisfaction. The non-directive worker, however, aims to supply both *stimulus*, in so far as it is needed, to get people thinking and to go on with their thinking until they reach some definite conclusions; and *structure* to ensure as far as possible that the conclusions people reach as a result of their thinking are practical and relevant to their need.

A non-directive worker can provide this stimulus and help in any of a wide variety of formal and informal situations. In a youth club, for instance, the 'worker' will be the youth leader or one of his helpers, and the 'group' either a formal group such as a members' committee, or an interest group, or an *ad hoc* informal group which consists of only a few members talking things over in the coffee bar. Similarly, in a church the 'worker' may be the vicar or one of his assistants, and the 'group' any of their parishioners they have discussions with in the course of their work. Whoever the worker may be and whatever the group, in so far as he aims to help them to do their own thinking for themselves, he will attempt to stimulate and structure the thinking process by asking questions. He will ask these questions initially to encourage people to think about their purposes for their group or club or church as the case may be, and assess to what extent they feel they are achieving them. If any dissatisfactions or criticisms are then expressed, he will ask further questions to test whether these are shared by the other members of the group.

In relation to any specific dissatisfaction, he may then promote further thinking by asking questions about its causes and about what changes the members think might help to put things right; then about what members think they could do to bring these changes about; and go on thus stimulating the thinking process with questions until the members have decided whether they will attempt to do anything themselves or not; and if they do decide to do something, what they will do and just what this implies in terms of who, and what, and with whom.

To take people right through to the end of this process, of course, may take a good deal of time, and it may continue intermittently through a whole series of meetings, informal or formal, with the same group or with several groups according to need and the way people's thinking develops.

The stages through which the members of a group may move from a passive state of feeling vaguely dissatisfied to some positive action designed to meet a specific want are summarized on p. 47, together with brief notes about what the non-directive worker does to move them on from any one stage to the next.

Stimulating people in this way, however, is only a part of the worker's job. He also needs to ensure as far as he can that the people think realistically enough at each stage to reach sound and practicable decisions. This is very necessary, for if through inexperience people are unaware of all the factors they may need to take into account, or if through immaturity they tend to disregard relevant but awkward facts, they may well decide to do something which is at best impracticable and at worst downright harmful to themselves.

STAGES IN THE THINKING PROCESS LEADING TO ACTION BY A GROUP

Members of the Group	The Worker (by asking questions)
Stage One Vaguely dissatisfied but passive	
↓	Stimulates people to think why they are dissatisfied and with what
Stage Two Now aware of certain needs	
↓	Stimulates people to think about what specific changes would result in these needs being met
Stage Three Now aware of wanting changes of some specific kinds	
↓	Stimulates people to consider what they might do to bring such changes about by taking action themselves
Stage Four Decide for, or against, trying to meet some want for themselves	
↓	If necessary, stimulates people to consider how best they can organize themselves to do what they now want to do
Stage Five Plan what to do and how they will do it	
↓	Stimulates people to consider and decide in detail just what to do, who will do it, and when and how they will do it
Stage Six Act according to their planning	
↓	Stimulates people to think through any unforeseen difficulties or problems they may encounter in the course of what they do. (He may again need to help them work through each of the preceding five stages in deciding how to tackle each problem)
Stage Seven Satisfied with the result of what they have achieved?	

If the worker thus needs not only to stimulate thinking but also to ensure sound thinking, what then can he do? Perhaps the best way to begin answering this question is to ask another, for if we ask ourselves what conditions in a group favour sound thinking, then to the extent that these conditions are not present in any group it becomes the worker's job to try to promote them. But what are these conditions? Perhaps we may agree that they can be listed as follows:

1. that the members have a very clearly defined and agreed purpose which they genuinely want to achieve together;

2. that they want to utilize to the full whatever knowledge and experience each and every member of the group may have which may in any way be relevant to the achievement of the purpose of the group;

3. that they have between them enough knowledge and experience, once it has been pooled and thoroughly considered, on which to reach sound decisions in relation to the purpose of the group; or, alternatively,

4. that they have enough knowledge and experience to know that they have not got enough, and therefore find ways of getting more by seeking it outside the group;

5. that they are sufficiently mature to subordinate their individual or factional interests to their common purpose for the group, and hence to put forward and consider every idea and suggestion objectively on its merits in relation to this common purpose, rather than each subjectively supporting his own idea because he made it;

6. that they are sufficiently skilled to think together, with or without a chairman, in a logical and orderly way in relation to their purpose.

To the extent that all or any of these basic conditions are lacking, so the members of any group will be hampered in their thinking and therefore also hampered in their purpose of reaching wise decisions for themselves. Thus if they fail to define their purpose clearly enough, or if some members do not whole-heartedly accept it, they will lack a clear enough focus for their thinking and are quite likely to find themselves arguing at cross-purposes. If they lack some of the facts they need to know, they are then likely to reach a decision which is faulty because they have ignored some of the facts. If they allow their individual or factional interests to predominate over their common group interest, any majority decision they reach—if indeed they are able to reach one at all—is likely to alienate the remaining members of the group. If they lack the skill to think and discuss in an orderly, logical, and therefore *structured* way, some of the points will be discussed too briefly; others, perhaps, will not be discussed at all; and none will be seen in proper relationship to the group's purpose as a whole.

Unlike the directive type of worker who tries to avoid these difficulties by 'guiding' the members of a group to the conclusions he thinks best for them, the non-directive worker concentrates on reducing their potentially bad effects by structuring, enlarging, and systematizing the thinking process of the group. He does this mainly by asking questions, but he avoids asking 'leading questions' which might restrict the thinking of the group. His sole purpose is to help and encourage the members of the group to structure their thinking more systematically and thoroughly for themselves.

The worker may decide to intervene with a question at any stage in a group's thinking according to the needs he sees, and only in relation to such needs. That is to say, he will not share in the members' discussion of what they should do or how they should do it: he will restrict himself solely to his function of facilitating effective group thinking and discussion.

The need for him to intervene will vary from group to group according to the maturity and experience of the members, but he may want to intervene for any of the following reasons:

1. *to make sure that the members of the group really are agreed about what they are aiming to discuss*

(Members of a group may sometimes agree on a common purpose only because it is stated so generally that each is able to interpret it according to his own idea of what it is intended to be. If these interpretations differ, the members may find themselves at cross-purposes in discussion and this may lead to confusion. If a worker thinks that such differences exist, he will try to bring them into the open by asking for some clarification of the purpose, or by stating it in more specific terms and asking if this is what the members mean. As they answer this question the members will incidentally define their purpose more specifically for themselves.)

2. *to ensure that they consider several possibilities instead of only one*

(By pushing his own idea a dominant member may inhibit other members from putting forward some different ideas of their own with the result that only the one idea is discussed. The worker may try to prevent this happening by asking, when one idea has been put forward, whether there are any others which might also be discussed. This creates an opportunity for the less pushful members to suggest alternative ideas so that every idea is noted. The merits and demerits of each idea can then be discussed in turn. The worker may ask his question not only at the beginning of a discussion but at any subsequent stage when there may be alternatives to consider.)

3. *to keep discussion focussed on one item at a time*

(Even when the members of a group have listed the possible alternatives, and are discussing one of them, they may stray from it without realizing that they have. The worker may then intervene to draw attention to the fact. He will not try to influence the members to return to their original point. They may decide to continue with one and abandon the other; or continue with one and return to the other later.)

4. *to ensure that the members of the group base their thinking on facts rather than on their assumptions about facts*

(Members of a group may discuss and decide an issue on the basis of their assumptions about facts rather than on the basis of facts they have tested for themselves. This is particularly likely to happen when the members of a group are planning a project intended to meet the needs of people other than themselves. They may then assume they know what people want without ever checking the truth of their assumption with the people they are planning for. Thus when members of a group make statements about what other people want, or are prepared to do, the worker may ask a question designed to encourage members to consider whether these are merely assumptions or whether they are based on ascertained facts: and if the former, how they can best ascertain the facts.)

5. *to ensure that the members of the group are aware of factors they need to take into account*

(If members of a group are either inexperienced or immature, it is very likely that they may fail to take some long-term considerations into account. For instance, they may plan to provide themselves or others with some amenity without really considering just how, when they have got it, they will use it and maintain it. The worker can be of great value to the members of a group if, by asking questions of the kind, 'Have you thought about how . . . ?' he draws their attention to points they need to discuss but would not have thought of themselves.)

6. *from time to time to help members assess what progress they have made and what still remains for them to do*

(Many non-directive workers work with small groups which have no chairman and which do not follow formal committee procedures. In such groups the members may sometimes ramble on in discussion without any clear idea of what progress they have so far made or of what still remains for them to do. When this happens, the worker can often help by asking if he is right in thinking that such and such points have now been cleared and such and such decisions taken, but that members are still not agreed on this point and that, and are these points they now need to discuss? Whether the members then agree with his summary or modify it, the worker will have succeeded in his purpose of helping to focus discussion more definitely on the areas of disagreement that remain.)

Apart from helping to structure and enlarge the scope of discussion in the ways outlined above, the worker can also help to improve communication and understanding between members in a more general way. Thus he can:

1. *help to clarify, when necessary, an unclear statement made by any member of the group*

(When people say something in a group, they do not always

manage to convey to the other members exactly what they mean. This can lead to the members talking at cross-purposes even about something on which they are really agreed. If the worker senses that this may happen, he can often help by restating more precisely the purport of what he thinks the member meant, and asking if this is what he meant to convey, e.g. 'I'm sorry, but I'm not quite sure I've got your point clear. Is it . . . ?' The member who made the contribution originally will then either agree that this is what he meant, or say again more clearly and specifically just what he had meant. Either way, the risk of misunderstanding will have been greatly reduced.)

2. *help to reduce unproductive argument between members*

(Members of a group may get so involved in arguing against each other—each for his own point of view—that they are liable to forget their overall purpose of reaching the best decision as a group. The worker can sometimes help them to realize this by suggesting that they may best serve their purpose for the group if they concentrate on listing and assessing the merits and demerits of *both* viewpoints instead of arguing for one viewpoint and against the other.)

Although it may appear at first sight that the worker's structuring and facilitating role is very similar to that of a chairman in a group, it is important to note that it differs in several important respects. Unlike a chairman, the worker is not a member of the group, exercises no authority over it, makes no decisions for it, and is not directly responsible for implementing any decisions the members of the group may make. Thus he is much less involved than a chairman in the actual content of a discussion, and correspondingly freer to concentrate as a neutral on his role of facilitating more thorough, systematic, and objective thinking and discussion by the members of the group. Even if they try to involve him further, as they may well do by asking him for his opinion when they differ among themselves, he will try to avoid giving it. Instead, he will return their question by restating for their further consideration all the points that have already been made for and against each of the alternatives they are considering, together with any further points which he thinks they might usefully consider. As far as he can he will also try to keep himself uninvolved by addressing any remarks he makes to the whole group rather than to a single member.

Because the non-directive worker neither has nor seeks *Nonsense.* power, he can only work in a way acceptable to the group. This is an additional reason, if one were needed, why he does not give his opinions, for by supporting one view he is likely to please some members of the group and alienate others, whereas he aims to work acceptably with them all. So he limits himself to asking questions which help people to think. Even these he has to choose and time with care, for if he intervenes too often this may also cause offence. In the end, therefore, much depends on his sensitivity to the atmosphere and feelings in the group, as well as on his skill in framing and asking questions in a wholly acceptable way.

CHAPTER SEVEN

Working Non-Directively with Young People

OUR theme in this book is that by helping people to think, decide, and act responsibly in relation to needs and purposes they define for themselves, the non-directive worker is helping them to mature: but as we saw in Chapter Two, however skilfully he works he can never be sure that they will always arrive at decisions which he thinks are really good for them. If, then, they arrive at a decision with which he disagrees, what can he do?

The short answer to this question is that this is a risk which he accepts, but which he minimizes by working in the way we described in the last chapter. After all, it is the group's decision not his, and if he has done this work properly the members of the group will have taken it with their eyes open. Also, at this stage, if the worker feels unhappy about it, he may feel he ought to say so, and say why, while accepting the right of the members of the group to decide for themselves. But even if he thus dissociates himself from the group's decision, he will not also dissociate himself from the members of the group as people. He will still want to help them. If he is right in thinking that they have made a bad decision, sooner or later events will prove him right. He can then do some of his most useful work by helping the members of the group review their decision in the light of these events, and thus help them to learn from their mistakes and mature in the process of doing so.

The dilemma of the youth worker

This is fair enough as far as work with most adults is concerned, but the situation is not quite so simple when the worker is working with young people. Just because young people are young, they are relatively more immature than adults, and it is the worker's main purpose to help them to mature. As we have seen, this involves the worker in providing them with opportunities of discussing and deciding among themselves things that really matter to them, and himself with corresponding opportunities of helping them to think. On the other hand, just because they are young, and therefore inexperienced and immature, they are more likely more often to reach 'bad' decisions in spite of all the worker can do: and just because they are young, the worker feels, and *is*, personally responsible for safeguarding their welfare to a much greater degree than if they were adult. Thus if he gives them freedom to decide for themselves and they use this freedom in a way that is harmful to themselves or to others, he is responsible. Yet if he denies them this freedom and decides and provides for them himself, he keeps them dependent, irresponsible, and immature: and what then becomes of his purpose of helping them to mature?

How can youth workers resolve this dilemma? Many have resolved it, not very satisfactorily from the point of view of helping young people to mature, by limiting the responsibilities of the members of their clubs to things that do not matter, or do not matter much: and one cannot but sympathize with them, for most of the adults in the neighbourhoods in which they work—and most of their Management Committees—expect the youth worker to conduct what they regard as a 'well-run' club, by which they usually mean a worker-directed club. And the worker who does not conform lays himself wide open to criticism should anything go wrong. In spite of this, however, many workers have experimented with varying degrees of self-government in clubs by delegating a good deal of responsibility for the management of affairs within the club to a committee elected by the club's members. Some of these committees have worked well, and some badly. Sometimes the members of such a committee have not really wanted the amount of work and responsibility involved; sometimes they have not been given enough help of the kind described in the last chapter; sometimes

E

they have taken decisions unrepresentative of the feelings of the rank-and-file members of their clubs.

Even if such a committee works well, however, its members are only a small minority of the members of the club. What about the others—the majority—who are not on the committee? For them the only difference may be that certain decisions affecting them are now taken by the committee instead of by the youth worker. How does this help *them* mature?

The plain answer to this question is that it does not. Indeed, the effect of establishing such a committee may be that the worker spends proportionately more of his time with the more mature and experienced of his members—those on the committee—and proportionately less with the less mature rank-and-file members who presumably most need opportunities of maturing. How can the youth worker, either directly or through his helpers, provide some non-directive stimulus to every member of the club?

Increasing autonomy of groups within the club

In fact, of course, the worker can only hope to promote his purpose with *all* the members by working non-directively in many situations within the club; and the Members' Committee is only one of these situations and not necessarily the most important one. There are normally many interest and social groups within a single club, as well as *ad hoc* project groups which may form from time to time: and it is by working non-directively with the members of these groups, and by giving them some real measure of responsibility for implementing their own decisions for themselves, that he can best provide himself with opportunities of helping them to mature.

In fact, such groups are ideal for the non-directive worker's purpose. Many clubs are large—so large in fact that no one member knows all the other members well. Most groups within a club, however, are relatively small. Their members habitually meet face to face. They have a common purpose which they wish to pursue, and often this purpose matters more to them than any purpose they have for the club as a whole. Usually, too, their numbers are small enough for every member to give his views, and if they should occasionally make a bad decision, its effects will usually be more limited, and therefore more tolerable, than if a bad decision were taken by a Members' Committee for the whole club. Moreover, as the generality of members get real experience of thinking, discussing, deciding, and implementing their own decisions for themselves in small groups and are helped to learn from whatever mistakes they make, so more of them will become more able to take on more responsibilities as members of club committees in the overall management of the club. The development of club autonomy should follow, not precede, the development of autonomy in groups within the club.

A group which is wholly autonomous in every respect has certain characteristics which are worth listing at this point. They are as follows:

1. its members are solely responsible for raising the funds they need to maintain themselves as a group;

2. they have absolute control in determining how these funds shall be spent;

3. they make and enforce their own rules for themselves (including rules controlling the admission and expulsion of members);

4. they decide on their own programme and how they will provide it;

5. if they need a helper or instructor, they recruit him, and dismiss him if they find him unsatisfactory;

6. they decide when a visitor (i.e. a non-member) shall be allowed to be present at any meeting of the group.

We do not know of any youth club or group within a youth club in which the members have all these rights and responsibilities, and we are not arguing that they should, although it is interesting to note that the members of gangs of young people, as distinct from members of clubs *for* young people, do.

As one considers each point on the list, one realizes how much most youth workers do in fact control the young people they work with; how little scope they give them for thinking, discussing, and deciding for themselves the things that really matter to them in their clubs; and how relatively little scope, therefore, they give themselves for helping young people to mature by working with them non-directively in the way we have described in the previous chapter.

Group autonomy limited only by established rules

Working non-directively with young people need not, however, imply giving them unrestricted licence to do whatever they might like to do without any regard to its effects on others. The youth worker does have, and should have, overall responsibility for ensuring that no one group of members, in deciding what it will do, is free to ignore the legitimate rights and interests of the other members of the club: and he or the club's Members' Committee, can and should make and enforce quite specific rules to this effect. Such rules—and the consequences of ignoring them—then become established facts which are known to all the members and which every group has to take into account when deciding what it wants to do; and should the need arise the youth worker will draw attention to them, *as established facts*, when he is working non-directively with a group. But within the limitations imposed by such established rules which, if a worker is anxious to enlarge autonomy, he will keep to a minimum, it is quite practicable for many groups to have much greater autonomy and hence many more opportunities of taking and implementing responsible decisions than they have at present.

Thus as far as finance is concerned, while it would be quite impracticable for the members of most youth clubs to raise and control the spending of the funds needed to maintain their clubs, they could often, perhaps, be given much more real responsibility for raising and spending money in their groups. Most would still be helped from club funds, but the extent of such help would be fixed in advance. The members would then know what funds they could rely on: and when they were planning what they wanted to do, and how much it would cost, they would have to plan realistically and responsibly in the light of the funds they had got, the cost of what they wanted to do and, if their funds were not enough, how by their own efforts they could raise more.

It is easy to realize that the non-directive youth worker, if he is present at discussions related to any item on the list, will have ample opportunities of exercising any skill he may have in helping young people to discuss and decide realistically in the light of all the relevant facts. The young people will feel really involved just because they know that whatever decisions they come to will have some direct effect, good or bad, upon themselves, *and that it will not be negatived by the youth worker, even if he personally disagrees with it,* provided it does not conflict with the standing rules of the club.

The worker not present as of right

One other point remains to be mentioned. The non-directive worker does not impose his presence on a group without being invited. (Nor does he bring visitors to the group without first asking the members of the group whether they are willing to receive them.) To be invited he has to establish himself as a person who is likely to be useful to the group and this means that the members of the group must know just what he can and cannot do to help them. To remain acceptable to the group, and hence to be invited to subsequent meetings or given 'the freedom of the group' without specific invitation, he has to behave in the group in a way acceptable to the group's members and to provide specific kinds of help that they value. This is the reverse of the kind of relationship that exists between worker and members in a dependent or proprietary group in which the worker is present as of right and the members by permission of the worker: and for the worker accustomed to working only with dependent groups, this very different relationship takes a lot of getting used to. But it is by establishing such a relationship and still being wanted that the non-directive worker get the clearest indication that he really is succeeding in his role.

To succeed, however, he will need considerable sensitivity and skill, and to the extent that he may feel that he has not got enough, training can help him develop them further. Just what kind of training, and just what this implies in terms of role and function for trainers engaged in this kind of training, is the subject of the third and fourth parts of this book.

APPENDIX TO CHAPTER SEVEN

WORKING NON-DIRECTIVELY WITH A CLUB MEMBERS' COMMITTEE

Soon after a club had started 'Beat Group Nights', the Club Leader began to receive complaints from people in the neighbourhood about excessive noise emanating from the club. Since he had recently attended a short course on working non-directively with groups, he decided to experiment with the non-directive approach by putting the complaints before his Members' Committee. He said nothing to indicate whether he thought the complaints justified or not. He merely asked the Committee to consider them and whether the existence of bad feeling in the neighbourhood which they indicated might create problems for the club.

The members of the Committee discussed the complaints and felt that they did indeed constitute a problem for the club. The Club Leader then suggested that they might like to discuss the problem: first, to establish just why it had occurred; and then in the light of this, what if anything they, as members of the Committee, could do to resolve it.

In the discussion which followed, he kept as close as he could to what he remembered of the role and function of the non-directive worker as described in Chapter Six—asking questions, clarifying viewpoints, and summarizing the course of discussion from time to time, but giving no opinions and making no suggestions himself. He records that the members of the Committee became intensely interested as they began to work systematically through the problem; that they refused to break off until they had finished although this meant that they stayed on far beyond the usual time for the ending of such meetings; and that by the end of the meeting they had listed and agreed on the following points:

A. *The Causes of the Problem*
1. *The Club Building* did not help because
   (*a*) of its situation (many people's homes were very close to it);

(b) its windows were not sound-proofed.
2. *The Club's Members* were inconsiderate. In particular
   (a) the Beat Group was very noisy;
   (b) members made a lot of noise starting up their motor-
      cycles at the end of the evening;
   (c) the Members' Committee had done nothing to reduce
      the noise.
3. *The Adults in the Neighbourhood*
   (a) did not like young people ('kids ain't wot they were');
   (b) were jealous of them (possibly);
   (c) did not understand or appreciate young people's
      activities;
   (d) the modern speed of living was too much for them.

B. *Implications for Committee Action*
  1. *Within the Club*—to reduce noise
    (a) fit extractor fans to keep the air fresh (the windows could
       then be kept closed);
    (b) fit a calibrated scale to the volume control of amplifiers
       and make sure that it is never set higher than a point
       which the Committee would fix;
    (c) as the club employs the Beat Group, the club must
       dictate the limits of the noise they make;
    (d) strengthen the club rules to control noise; insist that
       members with motor-cycles leave the club in small
       groups and keep the noise down; suspend persistent
       offenders from the club;
    (e) investigate ways of making members aware of the prob-
       lems of living in society with their neighbours, and so
       develop more understanding and consideration.
  2. *With Adults*, especially those living near the club
    (a) find ways of bringing adults and members together on
       an equal social footing, and so create more understand-
       ing and tolerance on both sides (open invitation?);
    (b) perhaps the 'old dears' who most constantly complain
       are lonely and are using the club as a target for their
       frustrations. Could something be done, perhaps in an
       indirect way, to help them, and thus help to improve
       relations between the club and them?

PART THREE

PROVIDING TRAINING

Introduction

IN the first part of this book we have suggested that every agency and every worker who aims at promoting betterment among the people with whom he works will use either a directive or a non-directive approach: *directive* if he tries to lead, guide, or persuade them to accept, or at least conform to, his own ideas of what is betterment for them; *non-directive* if he concentrates on stimulating people to think more systematically and realistically than they otherwise would about what they want for themselves, and about what they can do and how they can do it in order to achieve it.

We have also suggested that both approaches are useful, but that each has certain limitations that the other lacks, and that each is more appropriate for some purposes than for others and for use in some situations than in others. The worker therefore needs to be very clear about just what his purpose is in each of the situations in which he works, as well as about the limitations inherent in each of the two approaches, if he is to be able to choose the one that is more appropriate to his purpose: and, of course, to be really free to choose, he must be skilled in using both.

The idea of working non-directively, however, is still relatively new. Thus many workers, and more especially many voluntary workers, have never heard of it, or, if they have, either do not understand it or do not think they could achieve anything worthwhile by adopting it; and anyway lack the skill to work non-directively even if they wanted to.

For those who like ourselves believe that the non-directive approach, when properly understood and efficiently practised, is most effective at just those points at which the directive approach most often fails, this poses a major training problem. If what we believe is true then appropriate training needs to be provided, not only on professional courses of pre-service training for new workers but also for many of the paid and voluntary workers who are already in the field, and who have been conditioned by tradition and custom to use only the directive approach in the work they do with people. As we have seen, such people may mistrust the non-directive approach, and while they mistrust it they will not want to learn how to use it, or want to use it even when they have been taught how to. Thus before he attempts to train workers in the skill of working non-directively, the trainer may first have to try to get the members of his training group to rethink their existing ideas about working with people in the hope of inducing changes in their attitudes to people. But how can the trainer best promote such a rethinking? And how, if he succeeds, can he best develop among the members of his training group awareness of the role and functions the worker needs to assume when he chooses the non-directive approach? In answering these questions the trainer faces the same basic problem of choice—between a directive or non-directive approach—that faces every worker in every situation in which he works with people. It is these two questions and their implications for trainers that we consider in the remaining chapters of this book.

CHAPTER EIGHT

The Scope for
Non-Directive Training

EVERY community agency has purposes which it hopes to achieve with people, and when it provides training it does so because it hopes to make its workers more efficient in achieving them. The basic and, indeed, the sole criterion of success in training is that the workers work more effectively after the training than before it.

Most agencies adopt a directive approach to training in that they themselves decide quite specifically what content of knowledge, ideas, and skills their workers should learn: and most trainers see themselves primarily as instructors who transmit knowledge, ideas, and skills to the workers they train.

It is wholly natural that agencies should adopt this approach to the training of their paid workers, and not unreasonable, one might think, that they should apply it to the training of their voluntary workers also. After all, such voluntary workers will have elected to work for the agency of their choice, and may therefore be expected to subscribe to its purposes and to welcome any training designed to increase the effectiveness of the work they do.

All this may be true enough, but we are not here concerned so much with the reasonableness of using the directive approach as with its effectiveness in achieving the purpose of the training. This, we have seen, is presumably to increase the workers' efficiency, and this in turn makes it relevant to inquire whether it really is efficient for each and every training purpose.

Let it be said at once that a straight directive approach to training can be efficient for many training purposes, and more especially in preliminary or pre-service training, but only when certain conditions are met. The first of these conditions is that the ideas, information, and skills that the trainer aims to provide really are relevant to the jobs the workers are doing or will need to do. The second is that the workers realize this and therefore *want* the training the trainer aims to provide. And the third, that the training can be given by instructional methods.

What we have just said may seem to be no more than a statement of the obvious, as indeed it is, but it is still true that one or more of these prerequisites for effective training are often lacking on training courses of the directive type, and that agencies which rely too heavily on this approach to training are therefore often dissatisfied with the results they get.

To understand why, we must look a little more closely at just what each of these conditions implies.

1. *Ensuring that the information and skills provided really are relevant and adequate for the jobs the workers will have to do and for the situation in which they will have to do them*

When a trainer decides what ideas, knowledge, and skills his trainees need in order to do their jobs efficiently, he assumes that he knows better than they do what they need to learn. This will almost certainly be true in pre-service training, especially if the trainer has himself had a good deal of experience of doing the kind of job he is now training others to do: but it may be much less true in training provided for experienced workers by a trainer who has academic qualifications but no first-hand experience, or even no *recent* first-hand experience, of the kind of work they do. For him then to be sure that the content he decides on will adequately meet the needs of his trainees, he needs somehow to find out a great deal about the work his trainees do, the conditions in which they do it, and the kinds of difficulties they encounter while they do it.

One way, and we believe the best way, by which he can find this out is by adopting a non-directive approach to training on at least some in-service training courses. When he uses this approach, his purpose will be to get his trainees to define their major difficulties and problems—and hence their training needs—for themselves; and then help them analyse the nature of these problems and what

they can do in order to cope with them more successfully. This
means that the workers, not the trainer, decide what the content of the course will be, and in a real sense, while he is thus
non-directively helping them to train themselves, they will also
be providing him with many of the insights he needs in order to
decide, necessarily more directively, just what he needs to include on courses of preliminary or pre-service training.

2. *Ensuring that the trainees want the training the trainer aims to
provide because they realize that it is relevant to the jobs they have to do*

Even if the trainer knows, or thinks he knows, exactly what
training his trainees need, it does not necessarily follow that
they will always accept his training purposes as their own. In
fact, it can sometimes be very difficult for a trainer to get the
members of an in-service training group to accept and try out
some new idea they have not previously tried. On the whole,
the older and more experienced they are in doing their own
particular jobs, the harder this is likely to be, because they are
then more likely to resent someone else, i.e. the trainer, taking
it upon himself to decide what things they still need to learn in
order to do their jobs better. People who feel like this either will
not come for training if they are free to choose whether to attend
or not, or if they have to attend will come reluctantly and with
a prejudice against the purpose of the training.

If such a feeling exists, it can hinder a trainer's efforts to get
even a simple new idea accepted, but he will find it still more
difficult to get workers to change their existing attitudes, and
the ways they habitually work with people, for attitudes and
ways of working which he thinks are more appropriate and
efficient for the work they do: and he may encounter this difficulty in preliminary or pre-service training as well as on in-
service courses for experienced workers. This is because every
worker, including those undergoing preliminary training, will
already have had a good deal of experience of interacting with
other people as private individuals, if not as community
workers: and they will have already developed their own attitudes to others and their own ways of trying to influence others.
These attitudes and these ways of behaving towards other people may be

somewhat different from what the trainer thinks they ought to be, but the workers will not necessarily discard them just because the trainer thinks they should. They are only likely to do so when they have somehow first convinced themselves: and they are more likely to convince themselves if the trainer leaves them free to think for themselves by adopting a non-directive approach in this particular field of training.

3. *Ensuring that the training objectives are such that they can be achieved by instructional methods*

Provided the first two conditions are met, a great many training objectives can be achieved on directive courses of training and by purely instructional methods. Such methods are then entirely appropriate and efficient for the teaching of any technical skill in which there exists a close and predictable relationship between cause and effect. For instance, if the trainer wants to teach, and the trainees to learn, how to process photo-graphic film, the trainer's job is simple provided he knows how to do it himself. The rules to be followed are based on the known qualities of the film to be processed and of the chemicals to be used in processing it. For each kind of film, the compo-sition and strength of the solutions for processing it, the order in which they should be used, their temperature, and the length of time the film should be immersed in each is known, and must always be adhered to in order to get consistently good results. Thus all the trainer has to do is to explain and demon-strate exactly what has to be done, how it has to be done, and desirably why it has to be done that way. He can then get his trainees to process film themselves under his supervision until they are proficient. This is only one of hundreds of examples which could be given.

Unfortunately, the skill in working with people which is the primary skill of the community worker is not a skill of this kind. This is partly because the skill is so complex, and partly because every situation with which a worker may have to deal is in some way different from every other, so that no precise hard and fast rules can ever be said always to apply. Much, therefore, must always be left to the judgement of the man on the spot. What the trainer has to try to do is to develop in each of his trainees awareness of, and sensitivity to, as many as possible of the factors which may or may not be present in each of the situations in which he works; ability to make sound judgements about what to do in the light of whatever factors he realizes are present; and skill in putting these judgements into effect. *The trainer cannot teach these things by purely instructional methods. They are qualities and skills he has to try to help his trainees develop for themselves, and he can do this most effectively by using non-directive methods which stimulate them to think for themselves.* This is all the more necessary because, as we have seen in the previous section, his trainees may come for training with quite strongly held attitudes towards people, and ideas about how best to work with people, which they are not willing to discard merely because the trainer's ideas do not coincide with theirs.

Thus the non-directive approach to training provides an alternative to the directive approach at just those points at which the latter is least effective: and by using it in the training situations for which it is appropriate, the trainer incidentally helps the members of his training group to understand how they too can effectively use it in the work they do.

Trainers who use this approach recognize that they can operate most effectively by involving the members of their training groups in their own training of themselves. On in-service training courses they do this by first getting the participants to define their purposes as workers, then their difficulties in achieving these purposes, and thus their training needs for themselves. They then encourage them to pool their ideas and experience in order to understand the nature of these difficulties and what additional skills they need to solve them. All this involves discussion, which is time-consuming, but it is not time-wasting if it results in a training agenda with which the members of the training group all agree because it is *their* agenda based on conclusions they have reached for themselves, and not merely on conclusions that the trainer has reached on the basis of *his* thinking.

This indicates the key difference between the two approaches. The trainer works directively when he decides for his trainees

F

what values, attitudes, ideas, knowledge, and skills they ought to have, and just how he can best lead, guide, persuade, or instruct them to apply in their work the conclusions he has already reached for them. He works non-directively when his primary aim is to get them to think freely, yet systematically and objectively, about their purposes with people in the work they do and how they can do it better.

As we have seen, the trainer has far more scope for using the non-directive approach with experienced workers in in-service training than with raw recruits in preliminary or pre-service training: although even with inexperienced persons it can be used far more effectively than the directive approach when the trainer is dealing with values, purposes, and attitudes in community work and with the human-relations skills needed for it. The purpose of training is to increase efficiency. The trainer can try to promote this by telling the workers what their purposes, attitudes, and methods of working with people should be: but they will not give of their best in relation to their agency's purposes until they have first assessed these purposes, and their agency's methods of achieving them, and accepted them as their own. This is obviously true of voluntary workers, but equally though less obviously true of paid workers also. After all, there is usually a limit to the amount of work they can reasonably be expected to do, and when they give more than this they give it voluntarily. Realism in achieving the primary object of training, even with paid workers, suggests that much of it should be based on the non-directive approach.

One further point needs to be made. The essence of the non-directive approach in training, as in community work, is to stimulate people to think, discuss, and reach their own conclusions for themselves, since they are then much more likely to act on them themselves. However, this does not mean that the trainer will not provide them with relevant information to assist their thinking. Of course he will, but if he is working non-directively he will not in any way 'edit' this information in order to manipulate them into accepting his viewpoints as their own. Nor does it mean that he will neglect to instruct them in skills that can be taught. The difference is that, when he is working non-directively, he will not decide for them what skills they need to learn, but will teach them when, as a result of the thinking the members of his training group do, they realize the need for them.

CHAPTER NINE

The Nature of
Non-Directive Training

WE suggested in the previous chapter that although the directive approach is effective in teaching workers what they already want to know, it is much less effective as a way of teaching them what the trainer thinks they need when this is different from what the workers think they need: and least of all effective as a way of getting experienced workers to change some of their existing values, attitudes, ideas, habits, and ways of working with people for other values, attitudes, ideas, habits, and ways of working with people which the trainer—or the agency which employs him—thinks are better; or of training workers in human-relations skills.

We also suggested that the non-directive approach to training is most effective at just those points where the directive approach is least effective, and that promoting discussion plays a large part in it. The use of discussion methods, however, does not necessarily imply that the trainer is working non-directively, any more than the use of instructional methods implies that the trainer is working directively. Indeed, many directive-type trainers now use discussion methods as a less obvious means than lecturing of achieving their directive purpose: and every non-directive-type trainer will certainly need to use instructional methods whenever his trainees want them and are ready to profit from them. Thus no one approach should be identified with any one method. Any method may consistently be used with either, and the only criterion for choice of method, as of approach, is efficiency in relation to the training purpose.

This needs saying, for discussion methods are becoming increasingly fashionable, and some trainers now tend to regard such instructional methods as lectures, talks, and demonstrations as out of date. This is unfortunate as it leads to discussion methods being used for purposes for which they are inefficient and therefore unsuitable. *The key distinction is between the directive and non-directive approaches to training*—between the trainer who seeks to impose his judgements *by any method* on his training group, and the trainer who seeks, again by any method or combination of methods, to stimulate and help the members of his training group to embark on a self-directed process of training themselves.

When a trainer chooses to work non-directively, he has two basic ideas in mind, the one negative and the other positive. His negative idea is not in any way to try to direct, guide, or persuade the members of the training group towards accepting his own ideas, but to remain unbiassed and neutral throughout. His positive idea is to do whatever he can to promote systematic and realistic thinking and discussion among the members of the training group with a view to getting them

1. to clarify and define their purposes and appropriate roles and functions in the work they do;

2. to identify the major difficulties they encounter in achieving these purposes (with what kinds of people in what kinds of situation);

3. to investigate systematically the nature of these difficulties, how they have tried to deal with them, and why they are not satisfied with the results they have got; and

4. to pool their ideas and experience, and seek any relevant ideas and experience from others, as to how best these difficulties can in the future be more effectively overcome.

It is at this stage, when the members of a training group are aware of their need for knowledge or skills that they cannot adequately meet among themselves, that the trainer should operate in his instructional role. Nothing is more futile than for a trainer to persist in using discussion methods under such circumstances. When the members of a training group realize that they need some knowledge of skill they have not got, it is the trainer's job to help them get it.

It is still true, of course, that when the trainer is using the non-directive approach he will rely very heavily on his skill in promoting sustained and systematic discussion about the work the members of his group have to do and the difficulties they meet while doing it. In the course of the discussion he promotes, different members will contribute different viewpoints. By getting each of these viewpoints systematically considered and discussed, the trainer hopes to stimulate each member of the group to rethink his own assumptions, attitudes, and methods of work in the light of the ideas and experience of others. By remaining neutral to each and every opinion and by refraining from giving his own, the trainer is able to concentrate on his key function of promoting systematic and objective discussion without getting involved in argument and without attracting any emotional feeling against himself.

The theory is that such rethinking, to the extent that it takes place, will lead each individual member to modify, *as a result of his own thinking*, whatever of his purposes, attitudes, or ways of working with people he may now see to have been creating difficulties for him in achieving whatever it is that he really wants to achieve. Whether this will happen or not, however, will depend very much on how the trainer performs his functions. If he is unclear about what these are, or if he lacks skill in carrying them out, the discussion can easily become time-wasting; frustrating both to the trainer and to his training group; and even positively harmful if each of its members becomes emotionally involved in defending his own pre-fixed ideas.

What, then, are these functions? Basically there are only two: the one, to assist by providing *structure*; the other, to encourage *objectivity*. Just how the trainer can carry them out will be considered in detail in the chapters which follow.

CHAPTER TEN

Preparing the Ground

IT is difficult for administrators and trainers who have to organize and provide training to know all they really need to
know about the exact nature of their workers' training needs,
since they do not themselves do the jobs they train others to do.
Thus they need to find out, and one way of finding out is, as we
saw on pp. 68–9, by providing non-directive courses of in-service
training.

Discussion is an essential characteristic of non-directive
training, but it is time-consuming and needs to be conducted in
small groups. Since most courses of in-service training are
short, the non-directive trainer needs to prepare the ground
very carefully to ensure, as far as he can, that the training
time is used to good effect. First, he needs to define precisely
what purpose, i.e. just what training needs, he hopes the
course will meet; and then, in the light of that purpose, just
what kind(s) of workers he wants to attend, e.g. whether he
wants to restrict the course to one category of workers only, such
as paid field workers, or voluntary workers, or supervisors, or
administrators, or whether it would suit his purpose better if the
course were composed of several of these categories of workers
attending together. Thus if he wants to teach a skill, he will
want only those workers who need that particular skill, but if he
wants to improve relationships between different categories of
workers, he may want these different categories all represented
in the same training group.

Secondly, he may need to brief his prospective trainees as
adequately as possible about the purpose and nature of the
course before it starts. This is particularly important on short,
non-directive courses, for little effective training can take place
without the interest and full involvement of the trainees.

What the trainer can do in the way of preliminary briefing depends on many factors, and all we can do here is to give a few examples of how we have tried to meet this need in several quite different situations.

Example One: A two-day national conference

This was a national conference attended by some two hundred people, most of them committee members or secretaries, paid or unpaid, of local Community Associations. The chosen theme was, 'What job are the Community Associations doing?' This had been chosen in the hope of getting the people who came critically to examine the work of their Associations in the light of the purposes they aimed to serve, and what, if anything, they could do to help them achieve their purposes better.

Six months before the conference was to take place, a letter was sent to every Community Association outlining the purpose of the conference and enclosing a questionnaire. The questions were:

1. In what ways does your Association serve its neighbourhood as distinct from just its members?

2. Are you satisfied with what you have been able to do? If not, what kind of difficulties are you up against that prevent you from doing more?

3. In trying to serve your neighbourhood, have you ever tried to bring your point of view before your local government representatives and officials? If so, how did you set about it and with what result?

4. How have local party politics either helped or hindered the work of your Association in serving its neighbourhood?

5. Can you suggest one or more topics or problems related to the theme of this year's conference that you would like to have selected for discussion?

The purpose in sending out the letter and the questionnaire was partly to get the *Associations*, and not merely the representatives they would send, involved in preparing for the conference; and partly in order to obtain as much relevant information as possible from the Community Associations about the work they were doing. This information, which was collated in a briefing paper and circulated well in advance, indicated, *inter alia*, that more than half the Community Associations which replied felt that their work was hampered by the apathy of either their own members or of the general public. It gave as topics for discussion at the conference two questions which, from the replies received, seemed to be those the participants would most want to discuss. These questions, each with an appended note, were:

1. *How can a Community Association best stimulate and organize the energies of its members for service to the neighbourhood and for what kinds of service?*

(This question may also involve some consideration of community centres. To get and thereafter maintain a centre must absorb a great deal of the energy of the members and it may deflect their attention from the service of the neighbourhood to the service of the centre. Is this a real difficulty? If so, how is it best avoided?)

2. *Should a Community Association try to focus opinion on matters of public importance which are also the concern of the Local Authority and, if so, how?*

(This question raises the whole issue of relationships between Associations and Local Authorities, especially if an Association is supported with Local Authority funds and has the Local Authority officially represented on its Council. Does the Association thereby weaken its scope for free and independent action on matters of public importance?)

The briefing paper also stated that there would be twenty discussion groups, each of ten people, and the members would be allocated to groups according to the type of neighbourhood (e.g. new housing estate or established urban area) from which they came, and also according to which of the two questions they would prefer to discuss.

This was the preliminary briefing, but there were also two briefing sessions at the conference: one for the group discussion leaders[1] before the conference proper began, and the other at

---

[1] These were mainly Central Executive Committee members, most of whom had had no former experience of using non-directive discussion methods. They were

the first plenary session to make sure that everyone understood the preliminary briefing paper. The rest of the programme was only preplanned to the extent of deciding that the first plenary session would be followed by two discussion sessions in small groups, with a plenary session after each for a discussion of group reports by a panel of members elected for the occasion by their groups. The first of these plenary sessions was to be concerned with work on new housing estates; the second with the work in established areas.

Example Two: An area conference of a uniformed youth organization

The organization in question had known for some time that

---

given an oral briefing with opportunities of asking questions, and a mimeographed summary of the briefing talk for further study and reference. The text of the mimeograph was as follows:

Notes for Discussion Leaders

People meet in small discussion groups to exchange information and find out what other people think. They learn a good deal from one another and reach their own conclusions for themselves. No one can predict in advance what conclusions a group will reach, or whether it will reach any agreed conclusions at all. From some points of view this is a disadvantage. But there are also considerable advantages: everyone can take an active part and is helped to clear up his own ideas; and whatever conclusions are reached really do mean something.

The job of a discussion leader differs from that of a committee chairman. The chairman's job is to see that necessary decisions are taken, and he can wield a good deal of authority. The discussion leader's job is to help people to discuss. If he tries to force the pace he may easily sacrifice the real purpose and value of the discussion. All the same he has a job to do, for he can do a great deal to help the members of the discussion group explore their subject and reach conclusions about it. His main functions are:

   (i) to make sure that everyone understands exactly what the group is meeting to discuss;

   (ii) to remain completely impartial as between opposing points of view;

   (iii) to make sure that each viewpoint is understood, if necessary by restating it more clearly. (People often argue against each other interminably simply because they have never got the other person's viewpoint really clear.)

   (iv) to notify members when discussion wanders too far from the point. (The group may nevertheless want to follow up the new line and if they do the leader should not try to stop them. But he should make sure that they are aware of what they are doing.)

   (v) to provide opportunities for the less talkative members to speak if they want to. ('I see that X has been trying to get in for some time. Could we hear now what he has to say?')

   (vi) to provide a summary of the group's thinking from time to time and of any agreement reached. (This should normally be done several times during a session and, of course, at the end.)

it was no longer attracting and holding its members as well as in the past, and also that it was failing to hold enough of the young men who joined as junior leaders. It had therefore recruited a strong committee of knowledgeable and interested people from outside as well as inside the movement to find out why and suggest what should be done. When this committee's report was published, however, many of the movement's workers objected to most of the changes it proposed. They liked the old ways and said that many of the changes suggested would be impracticable anyway. It was therefore decided to hold a week-end conference to discuss and if possible reach agreement about what should be done. It was also decided to invite an outsider to conduct it as such a person would demonstrably have no axe of his own to grind.

Since many people felt deeply about some of the issues involved and the time available for discussion was very limited, the preparation of a suitable briefing paper was particularly important. The purpose of this paper was to focus the attention of the participants on the core of their problem in order to reduce argument about minor points on its periphery. Thus the briefing paper started with the acknowledged PURPOSE of the organization as stated in its official literature, and suggested that this was something which all participants would probably have in common. This was followed by a statement of NEED (to attract and keep more members and workers in order to achieve the purpose); a statement of PROBLEM (that fewer boys and junior leaders were in fact now being attracted and held); a statement of IMPLICATION (that numbers seemed likely to continue to decrease unless appropriate changes were made); and finally a QUESTION ('Have you not therefore to choose between accepting change or abandoning your purpose?').

This was followed by a statement of the major changes suggested in the report, and the participants were invited to discuss each of them in terms of the three questions listed below:

(a) Is the suggested change consistent with the PURPOSE?
(b) Is it practicable?
(c) If not, what practical alternative change can you suggest?

As in *Example One*, it was planned to begin the conference with a short plenary session to see whether the suggestions made in the briefing paper were acceptable to the participants. This was to be followed by two one-and-a-half hour sessions for discussion in small groups of some of the proposed changes: and these by a plenary session during which the groups would pool their findings and establish, as a conference, whatever agreements they had been able to reach on the proposals so far discussed. The same pattern was to be followed in discussion of the remaining proposals on the second day.

Example Three: A two-day meeting of the staff of a large, old-established youth club

For many years the workers at this club had worked directively with and for the club's members; and although there was a Members' Committee it was closely supervised. Every decision it took had to be approved by the Management Committee before it could be implemented. Even so, some of the workers felt that the Members' Committee was consulted too much about club affairs and given too much administrative responsibility. This led them to suggest at a staff meeting that the powers of the Members' Committee be reduced. The outcome was, however, the reverse of what they had intended, for although it was decided that the Committee should be enlarged by the addition of eight workers, all with full voting rights, it was also decided that the enlarged Committee should be given full powers over the running of the club; that the Management Committee be dissolved; that an Advisory Committee of workers be formed to take its place; and that the workers' functions in the club be limited to listening to what club members had to say, talking helpfully to them, and assisting (but not organizing and directing) them to do what they had decided to do.

These new arrangements produced unsatisfactory results. Many of the workers lost their old sense of purpose and complained that they now had nothing to do. The club committee members took their new responsibilities seriously, but were much less efficient than the workers had been. The club members were bewildered and unhappy. They weren't interested in 'democracy', and they wanted the workers to revert to running the club as before.

Conscious that they had a difficult problem to deal with, the workers decided to spend a week-end discussing it. They called in an outside 'trainer' to help them, both by preparing a preliminary briefing paper and by being present as a group worker at their discussions.

The briefing paper started with a concise factual account of the previous history of the problem. This was based on information supplied by the club. Then followed a statement to the effect that the workers appeared to be divided about their purpose for the club: some apparently wanting to develop the characters of (some) senior members by giving them responsibility for the management of the club; others feeling that their prime purpose should be to run the club efficiently for the sake of all the members, even at the cost of depriving such senior members of opportunities of exercising much responsibility for the management of club affairs.

The paper then asked, *'Does such a major division of purpose in fact exist? If so, is it clearcut, or does it reflect a reluctant choice between two purposes both of which are good but which appear to be incompatible with each other?'* If the latter is true, then the problem becomes one of *method*, not of principle, and what needs to be discussed is *how to get as many club members as possible involved in the responsible ordering of their own affairs with the minimum loss of efficiency in meeting other needs.*

Suggestions were then made as to why the club's previous decisions had had unsatisfactory results, and these were followed by suggestions for discussion topics at the meeting. These were:

1. Are we in fact agreed on our purpose(s) in the club? If so, do we include among them the development of maturity among club members through a process of meaningful decision-making and decision-implementing?

2. Do we consider that the club members, through their representatives, should have complete responsibility for managing

all the internal affairs of the club? Or should there be some 'reserved powers' kept by the adults? If so, what should these be?

3. Should the Members' Committee alone have delegated powers? E.g. are there any situations, other than meetings of this committee, in which groups of members might be involved in responsible decision-making and decision-implementing? If there are, what are they, and what scope do they provide?

4. How enjoyably and efficiently the members can learn to exercise responsibility will depend very greatly on how efficient the adults become in their 'helping' roles. Just how can adults help without taking charge? Just what is implied in terms of what they actually do?

5. The purpose of developing and educating young people by giving them responsibility is unlikely to succeed if responsibilities are imposed on them against their will, and with results that frustrate the average member who comes to the club to enjoy himself and/or pursue some specific interest or activity. What implications does this have for workers who want club members to learn how to think, decide, plan, and act for themselves?

Again, as in the previous two examples, it was planned to devote the first (plenary) session to a discussion of the briefing paper in order to test the acceptability of the suggested discussion topics; and, on this occasion in particular, to establish whether the workers would be able to agree on their overall purposes for the club. Until such an agreement was reached, it seemed unlikely that much real progress could be made in discussion on the other topics.

Example Four: A seminar for high-ranking government officials in an overseas country

This seminar was attended by all those heads of ministries of government departments whose co-operation would be needed to give their government's newly adopted community development policy—the details of which had still to be worked out—a really good chance of success. As in every other country in which community development has been introduced, it would have been unwise to have taken their co-operation for granted. After all, it is natural that long-established departments such as those concerned with agriculture, health, education, and local government should initially view with misgiving a new policy which would affect a number of departments; which was still not clearly defined; and which, they might think, would adversely affect the work they were already doing as well as causing them a good deal of extra work.

The seminar was to last for five days and was to be conducted by two neutral 'trainers' specially invited in from abroad. They decided not to attempt to produce a briefing paper for circulation in advance, but to do whatever briefing was necessary on the first day of the seminar itself. There were three reasons for this. The first was that the seminar was to last for five days. This meant that more time could reasonably be devoted to initial briefing at the beginning of the course than on the two-day meetings and conferences described in the previous examples. The second was that much of the background information on which to base a preliminary paper was not easily available to the trainers until they reached the country in which the seminar was to be held. And the third was that the trainers thought it would be easier to reach an agreed basis for the discussions in a face-to-face situation with the officers concerned.

The trainers started the briefing by referring to the government's directive to them and to the participants which stated the purpose the government hoped would be achieved. They then stated their purpose in the seminar, which was to get the participants to list the difficulties they anticipated they would have in implementing the new policy, discuss them, and decide how best they could overcome them. The trainers also defined their role as helping the participants in their discussions in any way they could, but as neutrals who would not, and indeed could not, put forward any opinions about what conclusions should be reached.

The briefing continued with an informal talk which outlined the directive and non-directive approaches described in Part One of this book, and identified community development with the latter. It indicated the advantages and disadvantages of each approach, and suggested that the efficiency of every ministry and department depended on being able to use both and knowing when to use either. It then described some of the problems that any use of the non-directive approach would probably entail. It dwelt particularly on the need for training, or retraining, workers at all levels if the non-directive (community development) approach were to be effectively used.

This talk and the discussion and elucidation of the various points that had been made took the whole of the first day. It was not until the second day, therefore, that the participants met to list the difficulties, including inter-ministerial and inter-departmental problems, they wished to work on during the rest of the seminar.

Certain common ideas underlie each of the briefings outlined in the four examples given. In each case the trainer's purpose was to stimulate and help the participants to think through their problems and reach their own conclusions realistically for themselves. For this, the first requirement was that they should agree on their purpose for the training group. Thus the first of the trainer's briefing tasks is to set down whatever information, and to ask whatever questions, seem most likely to help them to get this purpose defined. Only when the participants have done this will they be able to think fruitfully together, instead of at cross-purposes with one another. Such a clarification of purpose was particularly necessary in *Examples Three* and *Four*. Indeed, in *Example Three* the course was organized because the participants were already openly at cross-purposes with each other. In *Example Four* some of the participants only came on the course because they had to. Most of them initially had little faith in, and no enthusiasm for, their government's new community development policy: and they really only arrived at their own common purpose for the seminar when they faced up to the fact that they would have to live with the new policy, and decided to use the seminar time to see how they could make the best of it.

This indicates the trainer's second briefing task, which is to get the members of the training group realistically to face up to all the facts, however unwelcome some of these may be, that impose their own 'authority' on the kind of work they are able to do.[1] To get the participants to do this was a key function of the trainer in *Example Two*.

His third task, which follows logically from the second, is to get the participants to reach agreement about the kinds of difficulties and problems they will need to overcome in order to achieve whatever it is they want to achieve, and with due regard to the 'authority' of the situation(s) in which they have to work. These then become the training agenda for study and discussion by the group's members; and the outcome will be, the trainer hopes, that each member of the group, as a result of the work done by the group, will reach his own valid conclusions about whatever changes in organization, programme, training, or methods of work he may need to make in order to solve his problems and thereby achieve his purposes more efficiently.

[1] However great a person's decision-making power may be, his decisions will be ineffective unless he makes them with due regard to all the relevant facts of the situation within which he works. In this sense *the authority of the situation* is always greater than the authority of the person who can act effectively only within the limits it prescribes. People's attitudes and feelings are relevant facts in the situations in which the development worker works, and hence are part of the authority he has to accept when deciding how to work.

CHAPTER ELEVEN

Structuring Discussion

AT the end of Chapter Nine we stated that trainers using the non-directive approach have two basic functions when promoting discussion: the one, to provide structure; the other, to encourage objectivity.

That the trainer should understand and exercise his structuring function is extremely important. His use of structure is quite consistent with his non-directive approach because, in using it, he does not in any way try to lead or guide the group towards accepting any specific ideas or conclusions of his own. His sole purpose is to ensure as far as he can, and acceptably to the group's members, that they start by agreeing on what they want to discuss; that they all accept it as relevant to their training need; that they have defined it clearly enough to be able to exchange ideas and information about it usefully and to the point; and that, when discussing it, they discuss it thoroughly and systematically, and thus increase their chances of reaching conclusions acceptable to themselves.

If the trainer has prepared and circulated a preliminary briefing note before a conference or training course begins, he will already have begun to provide structure. But, as we saw in the examples given in the previous chapter, he will always need to find out whether everyone understands and accepts it when he meets the participants face to face at the beginning of the course. Its main value lies in stimulating the participants, before they come on the course, to think about their purpose for the course, and the means by which they can best achieve it. Thus, to the extent that it succeeds, it shortens the time that needs to be spent on preliminary discussions on the course itself. This can be very important on very short courses, e.g. on a week-end course, when some complex issue has to be discussed.

On longer courses for the general purpose of increasing the workers' sensitivity and skill in working with people, the trainer may prefer to delay all detailed briefing until he meets the participants face to face. In that case there will initially be no consensus in the training group about what the specific training agenda should be, and the trainer's first structuring job will be to get them to decide on one.

Our own approach in such situations is first to state the training purpose—which the participants will already have implicitly accepted by applying to come on the course—as one of increasing their skill in working with people; and then to say that presumably, like everyone else, they often succeed in achieving their purposes but also sometimes fail; and that it will make the training more valuable if they can identify the kinds of problems and difficulties they often encounter and feel least able to solve. Most of these problems are likely to arise from their inability to get all the help or co-operation they need from one or other of the following four categories of persons:

1. the people their organization aims to influence or educate;
2. their subordinates on whom they may have to rely to do the actual field work;
3. their colleagues either within or outside their organization over whom they have no power of control;
4. their superiors within the organization from whom they receive directives.

We suggest that they consider what kinds of problems they most commonly encounter with each of these categories of persons since these, once they have agreed on what they are, will indicate what their main training needs in human relations are, and thus provide a useful training agenda for the course. We also suggest at this point that since the purpose of the course is to increase skill, each problem should be stated as a need for skill by presenting it in the form of a question ('How to . . . ?').

When these points have been cleared, our next step in providing structure is to ask the members of the training group to divide into sub-groups, each of four or five members, to list their problems. At the same time we stress that their job in these groups is only to list the problems, *not* discuss them, and that there is no need for everyone to agree on every problem. Any and every problem that anyone feels strongly about should be listed.

CATEGORIES OF RELATIONSHIPS IN WHICH THE WORKER'S PROBLEMS ARISE

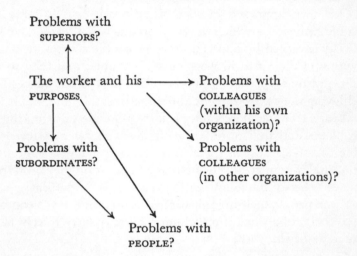

Problems with
SUPERIORS?

The worker and his ⟶ Problems with
PURPOSES   COLLEAGUES
(within his own
organization)?

Problems with   Problems with
SUBORDINATES?   COLLEAGUES
(in other organizations)?

Problems with
PEOPLE?

After a short time, usually fifteen or twenty minutes, the full group is reassembled to consider suggestions from the sub-groups. We find it best at this point to ask for one suggestion from any of the sub-groups, and then, when this has been stated, to ask the reporters of the other groups whether they also have the same or a very similar point, and if so will they please state it. When such points are stated, we try to get a form of words on the blackboard which satisfies everyone. We then ask for a second point—preferably from a different sub-group—and so on until all the points from all the sub-groups have been similarly recorded on the blackboard.

The members of the group are invited to edit this list by deleting from it items about which they are not all agreed, and to put the remaining items in order of priority. These items become the training agenda for the course. Any items representing training needs which can be met by providing information or teaching some technical skill will then be dealt with by straight instructional methods, leaving the main items on the list—the human relations problems—to be investigated in discussion.[1] The whole process of reaching an agreed agenda in this way normally takes from an hour to an hour and a half and in our experience it is time well spent.[2]

It is worth noting again at this point that although the process of reaching an agenda is highly structured by the trainer, everything he does is designed to promote free, independent, and systematic thinking by the participants themselves. He concentrates on this process and does not try to influence the *content* of the agenda himself.

1. DISCUSSING A PROBLEM

The trainer also structures discussion while each of the problems listed on the agenda is being discussed. Thus he aims to get the participants to discuss each problem in four distinct stages.

[1] See p. 93.
[2] For the reader who would like to have an example of an agenda developed in this way, here is the list of topics selected for study at a conference of some forty Youth Service trainers and administrators responsible for organizing and providing training.

1. How to overcome resistance to training
    (a) among the youth leaders who come for training?
    (b) among those who don't come?
    (c) among their superiors?
2. How to get leaders to question their attitudes and assumptions about the way to work with young people?
3. How to demonstrate to our trainees the relationship we hope they will adopt with their young people? If not by lectures, then what?
4. How to help youth leaders to acquire the know-how, and therefore the confidence, to allow more freedom to their young people?
5. How to ensure that the youth leaders agree with the purposes of the training we provide for them?
6. How to help the youth leader deal with the pressures from various quarters to which he will inevitably be subjected?

It is interesting to note that the first four items on this list also appeared on an agenda produced in the same way at a similar conference attended by a different group of Youth Service trainers and administrators six months later.

1. to establish agreement and common understanding about the scope and nature of the problem;

2. to diagnose just why it occurs;

3. in the light of this diagnosis to consider what they can most effectively do to overcome it; and

4. to draw out any general conclusions relating to the future conduct of their work.

Thus, for example, when the members of the Youth Service conference mentioned in note 2 on p. 91 were discussing the first of the problems on their agenda ('How to overcome resistance to training among youth leaders?'), the trainer first asked them to contribute some actual examples of such resistance and of the symptoms by which they recognized it. When these had been outlined and agreed to as typical—and the scope and nature of the problems had been thus defined—the trainer then asked the participants to consider just why they thought youth leaders did in fact often resist training in these ways. Then, when the reasons had been listed and agreed, he asked just what implications for changes these reasons might suggest for them as organizers and providers of training. That the trainer should have got them to consider these implications in terms of changes *they would need to make themselves* is extremely important. All too often when participants are facing a difficult problem they will tend to blame it on the apathy, prejudice, or ignorance of people other than themselves. This may well be true, but it is also entirely unrealistic as a solution to the problem. Training only really begins when the participants realize that they have to start with people as they are, and then try to see how they can work with them more successfully as they are.

These are the main stages in the structuring of problem discussions, but at each stage the trainer may also structure the discussion in other ways as and when the need arises. Thus:

1. *when a problem is being diagnosed, or its implications worked out, he may suggest that the participants should start by listing all the major points (causes or implications) they would like to discuss before starting on any one of them in depth;*

(This is often useful since it provides every member with an

STRUCTURING A NON-DIRECTIVE TRAINING COURSE

OUTLINE OF BASIC STEPS

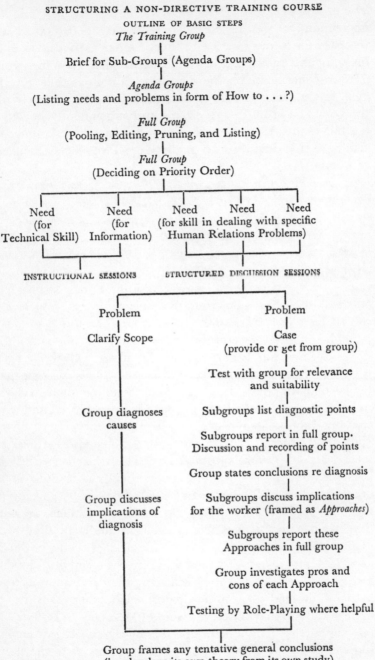

The Training Group

Brief for Sub-Groups (Agenda Groups)

Agenda Groups
(Listing needs and problems in form of How to . . . ?)

Full Group
(Pooling, Editing, Pruning, and Listing)

Full Group
(Deciding on Priority Order)

Need
(for
Technical Skill)

Need
(for
Information)

Need
(for skill in dealing with specific
Human Relations Problems)

INSTRUCTIONAL SESSIONS   STRUCTURED DISCUSSION SESSIONS

Problem   Problem

Clarify Scope   Case
                                     (provide or get from group)

                                     Test with group for relevance
                                     and suitability

Group diagnoses   Subgroups list diagnostic points
causes

                                     Subgroups report in full group.
                                     Discussion and recording of points

                                     Group states conclusions re diagnosis

Group discusses   Subgroups discuss implications
implications of   for the worker (framed as *Approaches*)
diagnosis

                                     Subgroups report these
                                     Approaches in full group

                                     Group investigates pros and
                                     cons of each Approach

                                     Testing by Role-Playing where helpful

Group frames any tentative general conclusions
(i.e. develops its own theory from its own study)

opportunity of getting his own particular point noted and recorded for future discussion. Once he has been able to make his point and knows that it will be discussed, he then feels much freer to concentrate on the discussion of points other than his own. If the group is a large one, the trainer may suggest that the points be listed in sub-groups and subsequently pooled in the full group. If so, he will then follow much the same procedure as that described on p. 98, Stage Two of the Discussion of a Case.)

2. *when discussion has strayed from the point, he may indicate what has happened while leaving it to the members of the group to decide whether to go back to the original point or continue with the new;*

3. *if the members of the group are discussing something they find they know too little about he may suggest how they can get the information they need;*

4. *he may summarize the course of discussion from time to time, tentatively suggesting what areas of agreement, if any, seem to have been established and what areas of disagreement seem still to remain.*

(This can be a very useful thing to do to bring life back into a discussion if it has begun to flag. Members will either agree with the trainer's summary or disagree with it at some particular point or points. In either case it helps members to clarify their ideas about just what they have so far achieved and what still remains for them to do.)

By thus structuring discussion, the trainer also furthers his second aim of promoting objectivity. This is partly because he is helping the group to work systematically according to an orderly and logical pattern, and partly because he encourages them to produce facts in support of their opinions. In both these ways he helps members to avoid misunderstandings that might lead to argument. When argument does occur, however, he will attempt to resolve it (and thus restore objectivity), by suggesting to members that they will serve their training purposes better if, instead of arguing against each other, they try to understand *why* they differ. He will be careful not to be tempted into supporting the views of one side or the other, but he will support every member's right to maintain his own viewpoint unless and until his study of the facts convinces him he ought to change it.

Discussion of problems on these non-directive lines can be very useful. 'Resistance to training' disappears. In fact, the participants are no longer conscious of 'being trained' because they are now actively engaged in training themselves. At the same time, the structure provided by the trainer helps them to avoid most of the difficulties and frustrations that commonly beset the members of discussion groups which are not being 'led'. Nearly always at the end of a session of this kind of non-directed but structured discussion, the participants feel that they have 'got somewhere', that they have reached some really worthwhile and practical conclusions, and that they have reached them for themselves.

Non-directed but structured discussion methods of this kind have been used with good effect in many situations both in 'developing' and 'developed' countries. Thus when these methods were used for the training of village development committees in northern Thailand (by a trainer who had studied them in London), the government department responsible for the training noted that 'the whole climate has changed completely like a miracle. . . . The responsiveness of the committee members to the new methods and the extent to which there has been a change of attitude are an outstanding achievement of the training.'[1] Many of the Youth Service trainers whom we have trained to work in this way in the United Kingdom report similar results.

Useful though this kind of general 'problem discussion' is, however, it has a limitation. It is ideal for stimulating people to purposeful action, or for getting them to review their assumptions, purposes, and methods in the work they do, and for arousing demand for some more specific training in human-relations skills. But it is much less satisfactory as a way of developing these skills. This is because such problem discussions

[1] Dr. Malai Huvanandhana and Mr. Sai Hutacharern, 'Mobilization of Village Resources through the Community Development Program in Thailand', a Paper presented by Thailand at the SEATO Community Development Seminar, 22 July 1965.

tend to be general and wide-ranging, while skill is best developed by studying something much more detailed, specific, and concrete. This is where discussion of cases becomes important.

2. DISCUSSING A CASE

When the members of a training group develop a training agenda by listing their problems in the way described on pp. 89–91, they indicate the kinds of difficulties which have prevented them from achieving their purposes, wholly or in part, in some of the situations in which they have worked. A 'case' is an actual example of a worker encountering a problem in the field. It describes the purpose of the worker, the situation with which he had to deal, the way he tried to deal with it, the result of what he did, and why he was dissatisfied with this result.

On in-service training courses lasting a week or more, it is entirely practical for the trainer to obtain cases illustrative of their problems from members of the training group. Such cases may sometimes be initially presented in spontaneous narrative by some of the group's members, but this is usually not a very satisfactory procedure. On the whole it is much better to ask the members to write their cases so that they can be pruned or expanded and otherwise edited, and then duplicated for distribution to all members of the training group. On very short in-service training courses there may not be time for this, and on preliminary or pre-service training courses the trainees will not have had the experience to provide cases for themselves. The trainer then has no choice, if he wishes to use cases, but to provide them himself from his store of cases contributed by members of former in-service training groups. Such cases, and more especially those which experience has shown to be very useful, may be further developed for presentation as tape-recordings or sound film-strips. These have the advantage of bringing a case to life more vividly.

It is much easier for the trainer to structure discussion of a case illustrative of a problem than a more general discussion of the kind of problem it presents. Indeed, the case itself is an important element in structure. Without in any way limiting the freedom of the participants to think out their own conclusions for themselves, it forces them to think realistically about what a worker like themselves actually did in a situation; about the result; and about just what he might alternatively have done to achieve a more satisfactory result. And the more they can identify themselves with the worker in the case—the more they accept that he and they have basically the same problem—the more relevant and effective for training purposes their discussion of the case is likely to be.

The trainer structures a case discussion in much the same way as he structures a problem discussion. Thus the main stages of the structure are basically the same as those already stated on pp. 91–92, but the structural pattern within each stage is now much more detailed. (This is clearly shown on p. 93.) These patterns must now be described. They are the outcome of much experiment and can produce consistently good results.

Stage One: Testing a case for relevance and acceptability

Even if a training group provides its own cases, no case should ever be proceeded with until it has been assessed by the members of the group to find out whether it really is truly relevant for them. It is essential that they should each be able to identify themselves to a considerable extent with the 'worker' in the case and with his problem. The trainer can help them decide whether they can do this or not by getting them to consider the following questions:

1. *Are we clear about the course of events?*

(i.e. what did the worker do, with what people, and with what results?)

2. *Was this result a failure, and if so, why?*

(This can be assessed by comparing the beginning and the end situations. It is very necessary to have this question discussed. Surprisingly often some members of the group will disagree over this. The resultant discussion is then very fruitful in revealing hitherto unsuspected attitudes and assumptions, and can be very educative both to members of the group and to the trainer.)

3. *Does the case illustrate the kind of problem we find difficult to deal with ourselves?*

(If this question is answered negatively, the case should not be proceeded with.)

Stage Two: Discussing the causes of the worker's failure

In the course of considering the above questions, the members of the group will incidentally be thoroughly briefing themselves in all the major facts of the case—the worker's purpose, the course of events, and the extent and nature of his failure. Thus by the time they have decided, if they do, that the case really is relevant for them, they will already be warmed up, as it were, for diagnosis.

The trainer then structures the pattern of discussion as follows:

1. He asks the members of the group to divide into sub-groups with four or five members in each, and in these sub-groups to list whatever ideas may occur to them which may serve to explain why the worker failed. These may take the form of comment on the nature of the difficulties the worker was up against but should also, and even mainly, state why what he did was inadequate to solve them. The trainer stresses that every suggestion that seems relevant to any of the members should be listed, even if other members query it; that the points should not be discussed or argued about at this stage; and that each sub-group should appoint a reporter.

2. The sub-groups are usually ready with their reports after about fifteen minutes. The trainer then re-forms the full group and takes points in turn from the sub-groups' reporters.[1] As each point is contributed he asks the reporters of the other sub-groups whether they think they have the same point, or nearly the same point. If they have, it will probably be worded rather

---

[1] It is important at this stage not to take every point from one sub-group before taking any points from the others. If this is done the last sub-group may be left with nothing to contribute, all its points already having being made by the others. This may sound unimportant, but it often gives rise to a quite unnecessary sense of frustration among the members of the sub-group last to report.

differently, and the trainer will then get the different versions considered with a view to getting a version which is acceptable to everyone. He will then put this on the black-board.

3. If some members disagree with a point because they think it invalid, when the trainer records it on the blackboard he adds a question mark. We have found this simple device quite invaluable for minimizing fruitless argument. For the time being the recording of the point on the board satisfies those who maintain it is valid; and the adding of a question mark those who disagree. Whether the point really is valid or not becomes clear later in the discussion.

4. When all the points from all the sub-groups have been listed in this way, the trainer then summarizes the salient points on which all the members seem to be agreed, noting particularly what they think the worker did wrong, either because of his *attitude* to the people with whom he was working, or through inadequate *skill*. He will also draw attention to any points (i.e. those with question marks against them) on which the members are not agreed, but neither then nor at any other time during the discussions will he press for agreement within the group. He will welcome agreement only when it is freely reached, for his main purpose is to stimulate every member to think for himself in the light of his own ideas and experience and the ideas and experience of others. If a member needs to change his ideas, he is more likely to do so if he feels completely free to think for himself than if he is preoccupied with defending his existing ideas against pressure and criticism from others.

Stage Three: Investigating implications

The trainer now asks the members of the training group to go back into their sub-groups to discuss, in the light of their diagnosis, how they might have succeeded better had they been in the worker's place. He asks them to think realistically and quite specifically about their *approach* in terms of the order of situations (where and with whom) in which they would try to achieve their overall purpose: and to state specifically what they would hope to achieve in each of these situations. He also says that if some members of a sub-group should favour one approach, and other members a different approach, they should not spend time in arguing the pros and cons of the two approaches, but get their points of difference clear and then record them both for discussion when the full group reassembles.

If each sub-group has recorded its approach or approaches on a large sheet of newsprint, when the full group reassembles these sheets can then be posted on the wall. Alternatively, if newsprint has not been used, the trainer will record each sub-group's approach on the board in turn, listing it in order of *situations*, and under each situation noting the *purpose* of the worker and how he hoped to achieve it. However, this alternative has the disadvantage that it can take up a good deal of time.

Once the different approaches—or variations of approach—have all been posted, or listed on the board, the trainer draws attention to the points of difference between them and notes them in order as problems of choice confronting the worker who has to deal with the problem in the case. He then suggests that the members should discuss the pros and cons of each of these choices in order, starting from the beginning of the case, and what each would demand in terms of *method*, i.e. just what the worker would need to do and just how he could most effectively do it in order to achieve his purpose. This gives rise to prolonged and very detailed discussion of quite specific points, some of which may get resolved fairly easily, but others, on which strong differences exist within the group, may prove intractable until they have been tested by role-playing.

3. ROLE-PLAYING

Role-playing is a technique which is often used in human-relations training. It usually involves the trainer getting two or more members of his training group to assume the roles of the persons involved in some hypothetical problem situation, and interacting with each other in relation to their feelings and purposes in that situation. Trainers use this technique in order to help their trainees to gain insights into how and why people tend to react to various forms of behaviour in the way they do.

It is a useful technique, but naturally much always depends on how far the role-players are able to identify themselves with the roles and purposes of the persons they are intended to represent, and to interact naturally and appropriately in accordance with such roles and purposes. This they are unlikely to do well unless they can first accept the role-playing situation as relevant for them, and feel wholly involved in wanting to solve the kind of problem it presents.

Problem situations which the members of the training group choose themselves for role-playing towards the end of their discussion of a case do not suffer from this disadvantage, for they are then used only at the end of a process during which the members will have

1. defined for themselves the kinds of problems they wish to investigate;

2. selected a case which they deem appropriate for the investigation of *one* such problem;

3. diagnosed why what the worker did in the case was inadequate to deal with the problem;

4. selected an approach or approaches which they think would increase the worker's chances of success;

5. defined each approach in terms of specific situations in which the worker will need to work; and

6. defined the worker's purpose in each of these situations. Any of these situations may be appropriate for role-playing, and each will have been defined by the members' own thinking about how to deal with the problem presented by the case. Their purpose for the role-playing is to test the validity of the conclusions they themselves have reached, and to develop the skill of working with people to put them into effect. The focus of interest in the role-playing is on just what the worker does to achieve his purpose, and with what effect. This effect is assessed from the reactions of the other role-players to the approach of the worker.

The effectiveness with which role-playing is used depends very much on how well the trainer performs his functions. These are as follows:

1. *Timing*. Since he is using role-playing as a technique to help members make progress with their investigation of a case, the timing of role-playing is important. The ideal time, as we have seen already, is when members are beginning to argue about the merits of two or more approaches to dealing with the problem it presents without much hope, *merely by discussion*, of resolving the differences that exist between them. The members of a group will then welcome role-playing as something entirely relevant to their purposes.

2. *Allocating roles*. The key role is that of the worker, and a natural choice for this role is any of the group's members who has just been arguing strongly in support of a particular approach, for role-playing gives him an opportunity of putting his idea to the test. The other roles will already have been fixed by the nature of the situation in which the 'worker' has chosen to work. The trainer asks members to volunteer for these and then arranges the role-playing situation in the middle of the room with the non-participating members grouped around as observers.

3. *Briefing the role-players*. The members of the group will already be aware of the general nature of the chosen situation since they will have defined it in their earlier discussion of the case. Therefore all the trainer now has to do is to ensure that each of the role-players is sufficiently briefed in his own particular role. He does this, not by telling each of them what his role should be, but by asking questions designed to help them brief themselves. Thus he will ask each of them to think himself into his role and say why he is present in the situation, what he hopes its outcome will be, how he feels towards the others who are in it with him, and how he regards the presence of the worker. In the process of answering these questions the role-players define their own roles for themselves and are then much more likely to play them naturally than if the trainer defines their roles for them.

The trainer completes the briefing by asking the role-players to clear their minds of any preconceptions about the worker they may already have formed during their discussion of the case, for the worker is now going to behave differently. They must start with their roles as they have just defined them for themselves and react to what he actually says and does in the role-playing, *not* according to how the persons whose roles they are playing reacted to the behaviour of the worker in the case.

4. *Getting results assessed.* The role-playing then starts, but the trainer will stop it as soon as he thinks that the worker has done enough to have had some effect, good or bad, on those he is working with. The trainer will then ask in order

(a) *the 'worker'* what he has been hoping to achieve and whether or not he feels that he has been succeeding; then

(b) *the other role-players* in turn what effect the 'worker' has so far had on them; and finally

(c) *the non-participants* for any additional observations they may wish to make.

If the replies to (b) above indicate that the 'worker' has so far succeeded, the trainer will ask why, and when this has been agreed role-playing will continue either at the next stage of the same situation or in a different situation. In either case another member of the group may take the worker's role. If, however, the 'worker' appears to have failed, again the trainer will ask why. If the reason appears to be lack of sufficient skill, he will suggest that the same situation be role-played again, with the same or a different member of the group acting as the worker. Thus the same situation may be played several times, each time a little better because of what has been learnt from earlier attempts, until a satisfactory approach has been achieved. On the other hand, if it appears that the failure was due to a wrong choice of situation, he will suggest role-playing a different situation taken from an alternative approach.

5. *Supporting the 'worker' who fails.* Anyone who fails in the worker's role inevitably reveals some lack of skill, and this is pinpointed by the other members of the group during their discussion of why he failed. Since it is usually the keenest and

H

often, too, the most skilful members of the groups who volunteer for the worker's role, they may find such criticism hard to take, especially when it is made by more cautious and less skilful members who are careful *not* to volunteer. The trainer can do a great deal to help by saying that it is much easier to sit back and criticize others than to do as well or better oneself; that those who volunteer learn much more than those who don't; and that each volunteer, after the first, starts with the great advantage of having learnt from any mistake his predecessor may have made.

Stage Four: Drawing tentative conclusions

A case illustrates a problem by describing one of the many situations in which it has occurred. The advantage of studying a problem in the context of a case is, as we have seen, that it promotes a much more realistic study of the problem than a general discussion would do. But in order to ensure that the members of a training group get the utmost value from such a study, the trainer will end by getting them to consider how what they have learnt can help them cope with similar situations better in the future. Any such conclusions may initially be very tentative, but it is important that they should be stated. The members can then test, develop, and refine them as they study more cases and get more experience in the field. Sound theory is based on a study of practice, and then developed and refined as the result of further experiment and practice. The study of cases on non-directive courses of training stimulates, helps, and trains workers to develop their own theory for themselves in the light of their own thinking about their own practice and experience.

APPENDIXES TO CHAPTER ELEVEN

APPENDIX 1: THE TRAINER'S (OR WORKER'S) ROLE IN DISCUSSION

He must remain *neutral* throughout. His job is to get the different viewpoints of members discussed in the group by the members and not himself to argue for or against any viewpoint. His job is primarily to facilitate systematic discussion *between* members. He does this by:

1. Not expressing his own opinions, or asking loaded questions ('Don't you think that . . . ?') or taking sides when members disagree.
2. Helping members to reach agreement on what to discuss and not assuming agreement without testing to ensure that it is genuine.
3. Helping members to keep to the point they have decided to discuss, e.g. when discussion wanders, to say so and ask whether members want to return to their original line or consciously choose the new one.
4. Creating an environment in which every member feels free to speak. (This involves finding acceptable ways of bringing in silent members when they appear to wish to speak.)
5. Clarifying what is being discussed by
   (*a*) ensuring that members are agreed about just what precisely they are discussing;
   (*b*) helping a member to clarify his contribution if for any reason it seems unclear;
   (*c*) indicating any major differences of viewpoint that exist within the group (as these become apparent) and encouraging members to investigate *why* they differ rather than argue against each other in favour of their respective viewpoints.
6. Summarizing briefly at appropriate times to indicate whatever progress has been made in discussion so far and what areas of disagreement still remain.
7. Providing relevant *information* (not opinion), if he has it, when the members lack all the relevant information they need.

APPENDIX 2: THE TRAINER'S STRUCTURING FUNCTIONS DURING DISCUSSION OF A CASE

1. *Testing the case for acceptability by asking*
   (*a*) what did the worker do and with what result? (Get the story clear.)
   (*b*) did he fail, and if so in what respect? (Compare initial and end situations.)
   (*c*) does the case present a problem of the kind we ourselves meet?

(d) could the worker have solved it if he had acted differently?

2. *Getting the case diagnosed by*

    (a) getting members in sub-groups to list points which may help to explain why the worker failed;

    (b) in the full group getting the sub-groups' points on the blackboard by

        i. taking one point from each sub-group in turn;

        ii. checking each point with the other sub-groups;

        iii. getting it acceptably stated on the board;

        iv. adding a question mark if it is not agreed by all;

    (c) getting members to sum up their diagnosis in terms of (i) the worker's attitude and/or (ii) lack of skill.

3. *Getting implications investigated in terms of* what *the worker should have done and* how *he should have done it by*

    (a) getting members in sub-groups to suggest a better *approach*, listing in order from the beginning of the case exactly what he should have done:

        in what *situation* (where and with whom);

        with what *purpose*; and

        by what *method;*

    (b) putting *one* approach on the board at a time. (One sub-group may have more than one approach. Several sub-groups may have the same approach.)

    (c) when all approaches have been listed, getting any basic differences and similarities between them noted;

    (d) getting each approach discussed in the light of the alternative suggestions;

    (e) testing by role-playing where this would be helpful.

4. *Getting conclusions stated by asking what, if any, are suggested by the group's study of the case.*

APPENDIX 3: AN OUTLINE SUMMARY OF POINTS DISCUSSED DURING A TWO-AND-A-HALF HOUR'S DISCUSSION OF A CASE BY A GROUP OF COMMUNITY DEVELOPMENT WORKERS IN AN OVERSEAS COUNTRY

(It was their first experience of case-study method.)

THE CASE

A newly formed village development committee invited a community development worker to its first business meeting. He was warmly greeted but he soon became very dissatisfied with the conduct of the meeting. Nearly every member of the committee seemed to have his own pet scheme: the store-keeper wanted a postal agency, the schoolmistress a playground for the children, and someone else a new lay-out for the village market. As the Chairman had no idea of how to control the meeting, nobody spoke to the Chair, several people argued different points at the same time, and no progress was made.

At last the worker felt he had to intervene. Luckily he was sitting next to the Chairman, so he pointed out what was happening and suggested that he (the Chairman) should call the members to order and ask them to address their remarks to him instead of arguing among themselves as most of them were doing.

Well, the Chairman then tried several times to call the members to order but without much effect. Meanwhile, time was getting on and the worker realized that he would soon have to be going. The best thing he could do under the circumstances, he thought, was to explain this to the Chairman, offer to come out again for the next meeting and show him how a meeting ought to be run. Accordingly, he made his apologies to the Chairman and put forward his suggestions as tactfully as he could. To his delight everyone seemed to think it a good idea and he came away feeling that there was now a real chance that things would go better next time.

However, a few days later he received a polite letter asking him not to come back until the members had had a few more meetings and got more experience, as they did not wish to waste too much of his time. This made him realize that they did not want him, but he still did not understand why. Could you have helped him?

NOTES OF POINTS CONTRIBUTED AND DISCUSSED

A. *Diagnosis* (Points recorded from sub-group reports.)

1. *The worker's attitude*

   (a) He was conceited although he didn't realize it.

   (b) He was too directive in his approach.

   (c) He expected too high a standard. (?)

2. *What he did wrong*

   (a) He did not plan the meeting in advance with the Chairman. (?)

   (b) When he intervened the first time, he criticized the Chairman and the members.

   (c) When he spoke the second time

      i. he implied that he had more important things to do elsewhere; and

     ii. again implied criticism of the Chairman and members.

Note. Although he appears to have assumed that he was skilled and they weren't, all he achieved was to get himself shut out.

B. *Implications* (From the blackboard summary of Approaches.)

Approach I	*Approach II*	*Approach III*
Before the meeting Brief Chairman in how to conduct it		
At the meeting Ask permission to speak	Ask permission to speak	Ask permission to speak

Summarize what
had been said so far
	Suggest a tea-break
	Use the tea-break to
	suggest to the Chair-
	man that ideas should
	be
	  i. listed
	 ii. discussed in turn
	iii. put in order of
	    priority
	    (Leave initiative
	    with him)
		Suggest that ideas
		should be
		  i. listed
		 ii. discussed in turn
		iii. put in order of
		    priority

*Isn't all this
Van Sireekun
rather manipulative
· clever*

C. *Notes of discussion of points from the approaches*

Approach I: Preliminary briefing of Chairman

This was quickly dismissed as impracticable because

      i. even if the worker arrived early, he could never be sure that he would have sufficient time with the Chairman on his own; and

     ii. it would be presumptuous of the worker to start advising the Chairman how to conduct the meeting when he had only just met him.

Members did, however, think that the worker should arrive early as it would give him a chance of getting to know the Chairman and at least some of the members before the meeting started.

Approach I: 'Summarize what had been said so far'

This was quickly dismissed as quite inadequate, even by the sub-group which had suggested it.

Approach II: 'The Tea-Break'

The pros and cons of this idea were discussed at some length because members liked the idea of the worker working through the Chairman and keeping in the background himself. They abandoned it in the end, however, because

i. they thought it would be presumptuous of the worker, who was the only stranger present, to suggest a tea-break; and
ii. anyway he could not be sure, during a tea-break, of getting enough time with the Chairman on his own.

Approach III

This left only Approach III. The trainer then suggested that this approach might be role-played to see just how the worker could have implemented it without arousing the resentment either of the Chairman or the members. The first two attempts failed by general consent, though each for a different reason. The third attempt was considered successful. In this attempt the 'worker', after getting the Chairman's permission to speak

i. started by complimenting the members of the committee on their keenness and public spirit as evidenced by the number of useful projects they were considering;
ii. continued by explaining just what he could do to help once they had decided what they were going to do;
iii. suggested that every idea should be listed in writing so as to ensure that none would be lost sight of;
iv. suggested that each should be separately discussed in order to ascertain just how much effort and sacrifice each would entail, and which would appeal to the largest number of their village people; and finally
v. suggested that with the help he hoped to be able to provide, they might, over a period, be able to complete not one but several projects.

D. *General conclusions the members reached at the end of their study of the case*

If one gives advice

1. to give it without referring to any shortcomings of the people to whom one gives it. Any suggestion of criticism should be

avoided. It is better to start by complimenting them on some
good point and link one's suggestion to that;

2. to frame it in such a way that the people will clearly see how
it can help them to do what *they* want to do. (e.g. the people
in this case did not want to be taught how to conduct a meeting: they wanted to choose a project and then get on with it.
Thus from their point of view the 'worker's' suggestions in
Approach III were much more helpful than those of the worker
in the original case. Incidentally, they were also likely to be
more effective in improving the conduct of the meeting.)

APPENDIX 4: NOTES ON SPECIFIC TECHNIQUES

(1) *Recording discussion points*

It is very important that the trainer should have enough blackboard or other suitable space for recording the points made in
sub-group or full-group discussions. Such recording provides every
member of the group with visual evidence of points already discussed
and agreed; of what is currently being discussed; and of what remains to be discussed. Thus it has an important influence in helping
to promote the development of structure.

It also helps in another way. People tend to be much more
meticulous in framing what they say when it is liable to be recorded
for all to see and comment on, and this helps to avoid misunderstandings creeping in later on.

One large blackboard rarely provides enough space. Even with
two, the trainer may still need to be economical in his use of space.

(2) *Sub-groups*

Small sub-groups are invaluable as a means of promoting a rapid
exchange and listing of ideas, and for actively involving more members more frequently in contributing to discussion. But members
should be discouraged from making their sub-groups centres of
prolonged discussion. This will keep members out of the full group
for too long and then it can hinder, rather than help, the progress of
the overall discussion.

PART FOUR

TRAINING TRAINERS

Introduction

In Part Three the need for training in the non-directive approach and the role and functions appropriate to the trainers who provide it were discussed. As yet, however, relatively few trainers work in this way, either because they do not appreciate its value, or because they are themselves untrained in how to train non-directively. Until this situation is remedied there is little chance of the non-directive approach becoming much more widely and effectively used.

How to get more trainers interested in this kind of training is therefore a major problem to those who believe that it can greatly increase the effectiveness of group and community workers. There are two parts to this problem: the first, and the harder, is how to get trainers who have always been accustomed to use a directive approach seriously to consider whether, perhaps, they ought not sometimes to work non-directively; and the second, how best to develop their skill in working non-directively if and when they come to value it.

The achievement of these aims is further complicated by the fact that most trainers are busy people who cannot easily take time off to attend a longish course even if they want to. This means that most trainers would be excluded by the time factor alone unless courses are kept short, and, in fact, the inside of a week is often the most one can realistically plan for. This difficulty, however, can be relatively easily overcome by breaking up what is in effect one longer course into several widely-spread short courses, all intended for the same people, and with each course taking their training one stage further. In the intervals between such courses the people who attend them have time to experiment and reflect, and in our experience such a linked series of short courses is often more effective than the same number of training days on one concentrated course.

The chapters which follow are based very largely on our

experience in training trainers both in the United Kingdom (mainly in the context of the Youth Service) and in some countries overseas. Some of these trainers have had high academic and professional qualifications, but others have become trainers mainly because they have had long experience of doing the kind of work they now train others to do. Some have been whole-time trainers; other have been administrators with part-time training responsibilities. All have had at least some responsibility for in-service training.

CHAPTER TWELVE

Arousing Interest

TRAINERS who have always used a directive approach are unlikely to modify their ideas merely because another trainer tells them that a non-directive approach is better. In fact, a great deal of harm has been done by people who uncritically accept the non-directive approach as a panacea for each and every problem with which a group or community worker may have to deal; who shut their eyes to its limitations; and who condemn as hidebound and out of date everyone who refuses to see eye to eye with them. People who do this are illogical as well as ineffective. They are ineffective because they grossly overstate their case. As we have already seen in Chapter Three, the directive approach is appropriate in at least some of the situations with which group and community workers may have to deal, and by denying this they arouse resentment, invite attack, and bring both themselves and the approach they advocate into disrepute. They are also illogical because by behaving as they do they are using a directive approach in order to 'sell' their ideas about working non-directively. There is a contradiction here between what they advocate and what they actually do.

For anyone who really believes in the value of the non-directive approach and therefore wants to get other people to realize this too, his best hope of influencing them is to attempt to do so non-directively. He is then behaving logically and consistently in accordance with his own belief and at the same time providing a live demonstration, as it were, of just what it means in practice. If the people with whom he uses it then find it acceptable and effective with them, this, more than anything else, will predispose them seriously to consider whether it might not also be of use to them in achieving their purposes in the situations in which they work.

Invitations to lecture to trainers or to 'direct' a conference or seminar or course for trainers have provided us with various opportunities of working in this way. Such invitations, however, in no sense imply that the people who will attend already value the non-directive approach. Indeed, the reverse is often true, for an invitation may mean no more than that a senior administrator feels that his trainers and workers are much too directive in the way they work, that this is adversely affecting the work they do, and that something needs to be done to put things right. Always we have found at least some people present who are strongly prejudiced against the non-directive approach, and all too often others who are equally strongly and uncritically prejudiced in favour of it.

What can be done in a situation of this kind? One possibility, in a lecture on the non-directive approach, is to start by stating that this is one of two basic approaches, and to define them as they have been defined in this book. One can then go on to say that each has some advantages and disadvantages that the other lacks, and that each is therefore more appropriate for some purposes than for others, and for use in some situations than in others. Each of these points can be illustrated with examples. Finally, one can suggest that it seems likely that most group and community workers, and their trainers, will be able to work more effectively if they are skilled in using both approaches rather than only one, since they will then be always in a position to use either according to their own assessment of need.

Such a lecture is itself an example of the non-directive approach. It does not state that one approach is always inherently better than the other. It stresses that both approaches are useful, but that they are different and sometimes complementary; that because they are different they face the worker with a problem of choice; that the choice he makes may greatly affect, for better or for worse, the result of the work he does; and that in order to make the right choice he needs to make it with due regard both to his purpose *and* to the facts of each situation in which he works.

In all this the lecturer accepts that each person is, and will remain, his own judge of what he really wants to do. The lecturer's purpose is to stimulate people to get *their* purposes clear, and become aware of all the many factors they need to consider when choosing their approach, as this may help them to become more efficient in achieving *their* purposes.

Since he does not query people's purposes but restricts himself solely to considerations of efficiency in achieving them, no one feels under attack. No one is told what conclusions he ought to come to; he is left to work these out for himself. All this kind of lecture does is to provide a logical, orderly, and factual structure which people can use to help them clarify their purposes and assess the effectiveness of the ways in which they try to achieve them.

We have found that this kind of lecture stimulates a thinking process which surprisingly often leads to people enlarging or modifying their ideas. Incidentally, it also often creates a demand for training in using the non-directive approach.

When we are invited to conduct a conference or course for trainers, we may start by giving much the same lecture, but basically the whole conference or course is used as a demonstration of non-directive training. This involves getting the trainers to clarify their overall training purposes; briefing them before they break up into agenda groups to define and list the major problems they encounter in trying to achieve these purposes;[1] getting them to pool, edit, and list these problems in order of priority when they reassemble into the full group; and then structuring their discussion of each of these problems in the manner already described in Chapter Eleven. By doing so, we both demonstrate the non-directive approach and put it on trial, for whether the trainers will become interested enough to want to use it themselves will entirely depend on how each privately assesses how useful the course has actually been to him. In our experience, most trainers who have been on such courses have found them useful, and it is this, more than anything else, that has attracted them to subsequent courses of skill-training.

[1] See note 2 on p. 91 for a list of trainers' problems produced in this way.

CHAPTER THIRTEEN

Teaching Skill

PROVIDED that all the trainers who attend a skill-training course already value the non-directive approach (see Chapter Twelve) and want to learn how to use it on the training they provide on their own courses, their trainer's job is then mainly to instruct them in method.

In many ways this is a much simpler task than coping with the problem of arousing interest discussed in the previous chapter, but it is complicated by the difficulty that many members of the training group may have in adjusting themselves to the requirements of an approach which is so radically different from the directive approach they have been accustomed to. The force of habit can be very strong: and in the practice sessions, however much they may want to concentrate on helping people to think, time and again they may find themselves defeating their purpose by stating their own opinions and getting themselves involved in argument. How best to help such members break this habit is a major problem, if not *the* major problem, on a skill-training course.

Such a course will usually consist of some lectures and demonstrations, followed by sessions of supervised skill-practice. We find that most trainers get hold of the basic ideas very quickly and that their main need is for supervised practice. Most of the training we provide consists of two linked short courses of a week each, both attended by the same people, and with the second course coming some months after the first.

1. LECTURING AND DEMONSTRATING

On such courses we keep lecturing to a minimum. Our most usual approach is to put the outline *Structuring a Non-Directive Training Course* (p. 93) on a blackboard, talk informally to that, and invite members of the group to ask questions at any point during the talk. We then distribute two papers reproduced in this book. One of these is *The Trainer's Role in Discussion* (p. 104) and the other *The Trainer's Structuring Functions during Discussion of a Case* (p. 105). These provide basic information about method, and the members of the course then have them available for constant reference during demonstrations, question sessions, and skill-practices.

We supplement this introductory talk with several demonstrations of method. The first of these is a demonstration of the method of obtaining an agenda of topics or problems for discussion. The members of the course need both discussion topics and cases for the skill-practice sessions, and this provides a natural opportunity for this demonstration. This consists of briefing the trainers for the agenda sub-groups in which they will list the problems they most want to discuss, and subsequently reconvening them as a full group to pool, prune, and edit the ideas they have listed in the sub-groups into an agreed list of problems for discussion in skill-practice sessions. This differs from the procedure they will themselves adopt in their own training groups only because *in this trainers' group*—the primary purpose of which is to learn method—they are invited to ask questions to elucidate points of method at any stage.

A little later on in the course, the method of structuring discussion of cases is also demonstrated through all its stages. Again, as in the first demonstration, the members of the training group are invited to intervene to elucidate any detail of method that may seem to them unclear, or the demonstrator may himself stop at any point to comment on what has been happening and on the functions he has been trying to perform.

I

2. BRIEFING OBSERVERS

There are many ways in which observers can be used in connection with group discussion. *On these skill-practice training courses for trainers we use observers for the specific purpose of helping the 'worker' in skill-practice sessions to become clearly aware of just what he has done, good or bad, during discussion in a group, and with what result.* Thus the observers are briefed to take no part in discussion, but to concentrate solely on noting and recording precisely what the worker does in order to (*a*) structure the course of discussion, and (*b*) cope with any difficulties that may be caused by the attitudes, relationships, and behaviour of any of the group's members.

To help them they are given a checklist (see p. 123) which they are invited to use as a basis on which to record their observations. This is gone through point by point during the briefing. The checklist is the one we currently use. It has been altered many times and no doubt will be altered again in the future. We say this, stressing that the checklist is intended merely as a guide, and that we expect that many members of the course will alter it to suit themselves as they gain experience in using it.

During the briefing we also suggest that they may find it helpful to record what happens during discussion in diagrammatic form. Two kinds of diagram are suggested; one to record progress with the content of the discussion and the other to record member participation in the discussion (see pp. 121, 122).

In the first of these diagrams, letters have been used to represent the order of individual contributions to discussion, although in practice it is preferable to use initials to help identify the actual members who speak. A vertical line indicates a contribution relevant to the preceding contribution; a horizontal line the introduction of a divergent point; and a diagonal line a reversion to the earlier point. Thus Diagram 1 (*a*) shows that both A and B contributed relevantly to the topic originally chosen for discussion; that C introduced a quite different (and irrelevant?) point which was followed by D; that E returned to the original point; that F continued with it; that G diverged to the point that C had brought in; that H reverted to the original point; and that the worker did not intervene at all.

DIAGRAM I: RECORDING THE DIRECTION OF A DISCUSSION

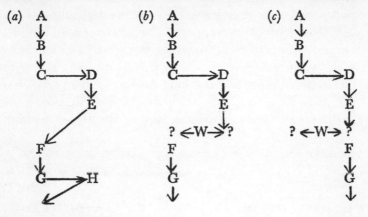

With the help of such a diagram the observer can indicate precisely what happened when the time comes for him to speak, and thus initiate a discussion about when, if at all, the worker should have intervened. Diagrams 1(b) and 1(c) indicate the course the discussion might have taken if the worker had intervened. In either case the worker's purpose would have been to draw attention to the divergence from the originally chosen topic and to ask the members of the group which line they would now prefer to take. Diagram 1(b) shows them reverting to their original line. Diagram 1(c) shows them continuing with the line first introduced by C. In either case the worker's intervention has achieved a positively good result.

Diagrams 2(a) and 2(b) record two different patterns of participation in discussion. Each diagram shows the position of each member of the group in relation to the other members, and the shape of a diagram of this kind will therefore usually show whether the members were sitting in a circle (as indicated above) or in an oblong or square as they would probably be if they were grouped around a table. In both diagrams the letter W indicates the worker and the other letters the members of the group, although here again in practice an observer would prefer to use the members' own initials in order to help him easily identify the actual members who spoke. When an observer is using a diagram of this kind he puts a stroke against a person's initial each time he speaks, and we also add a + to a stroke if the contribution happens to be a long one. In addition, if an argument develops between the worker and a member, or between two members, we indicate this by drawing a connecting line between them and marking the line with an arrowhead (as shown in Diagram 2(a)) each time a contribution by the one is directed to the other for as long as the argument lasts.

DIAGRAM 2: RECORDING ORAL PARTICIPATION IN DISCUSSION

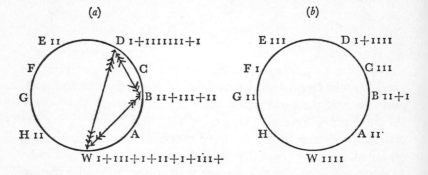

Thus Diagram 2(a) shows that the discussion it records was a very unbalanced one as far as member participation is concerned, since it was dominated by the worker and by members B and D. It records that out of a total of thirty contributions the worker made eleven, and that on six of these eleven occasions he spoke at considerable length; that B spoke seven times and D eight times, each speaking at length twice; that E and H spoke briefly twice; and that A, C, F, and G did not speak at all. It also shows that the worker twice got involved in specific arguments, once with B and once with D, and that B and D also argued with each other. Diagram 2(b), on the other hand, records a much more general pattern of discussion in which the

PROMOTING GROUP DISCUSSION: OBSERVER'S CHECKLIST

A. DISCUSSION IN GENERAL

   1. *Progress*   Much?   Little?   None?
   2. *Interest*   Much?   Little?   None?
              How general?   How well maintained?

B. CONTENT

Comment

Has the worker helped by

1. *remaining neutral*, e.g. by not giving opinions or taking sides?
2. *helping members to ascertain relevant facts*?
3. *supporting the right of minorities to disagree* and so discouraging superficial agreement?
4. *clarifying*
    (*a*) a member's contribution (if unclear)?
    (*b*) a difference of opinion between members when necessary?
5. *summarizing*?
6. *introducing structure*, e.g. by
    (*a*) getting the nature and scope of the problem adequately defined?
    (*b*) asking appropriate questions to ensure a logical order in discussion? (Why is it a problem? What can we do about it?)
    (*c*) ensuring that members are clear at all times about just what point is being discussed?
    (*d*) helping members to keep to the point *or* consciously to choose a new direction?
    (*e*) using sub-groups at appropriate times?

C. PARTICIPATION
Has the worker coped with
difficulties caused by members
1. dominating the discussion?
2. withdrawing from the discussion?
3. forming a splinter group?
4. arguing with each other?
5. all trying to talk at once?

worker made only four short interventions; in which everyone except H spoke at least once; and during which no argument occurred.

In presenting these diagrams during a briefing on observation techniques, we stress that there are many recording techniques; that those we have described are those we most commonly use; that members of the training group will find them useful to start with; but that as they get more experienced they may well develop alternative or additional techniques of their own.

We also stress that when members of the group are acting as observers they should restrict themselves to recording and subsequently presenting facts, and leave the worker and the members of the discussion group to discuss these facts and draw out for themselves their own conclusions about implications, in terms of what the worker did that he ought not to have done, or did not do that he ought to have done.[1]

3. PROVIDING SKILL-PRACTICE

Lectures, demonstrations of method, and the briefing of observers are essential preliminaries to the skill-practice sessions which form the main part of the course. These skill-practices

[1] In the skill-practice sessions during 'training of trainers' courses, observers concentrate on the worker and what he does to promote the progress of discussion in the group. While the observer may have noted that certain members of the group had tried to dominate the discussion, thus facing the worker with a problem, discussion of this observation will centre on what the worker did to deal with this problem, and whether what he did was right or whether he should have done something else, and if so just what, when, and how.

are of two kinds: conducting discussion of a *topic or problem*, and conducting discussion of a *case*.

DISCUSSING A TOPIC OR PROBLEM

During the demonstration of the method of obtaining an agreed agenda of topics and problems for discussion (p. 119), the trainers in the training group will already have listed those of their own training problems they would most like to discuss, and this list provides ample discussion material for the duration of the course.

We regard twelve as the optimum number of members of a practice group. The practice sessions usually last about an hour and a half. During this time three members of the group will each get a short practice in conducting discussion and at least another six will get practice in recording observations. At the end of each practice, i.e. three times during the session, the observers are invited to comment on the performance of the worker and these comments are then discussed by the members of the group. When all the points raised by the observers have been dealt with, another member of the group takes over the conduct of the topic or problem discussion at the point at which it had been stopped for the observers to come in, and the member who had conducted discussion during the previous practice becomes an observer.

It is during discussion of the comments made by the observers that most learning takes place. This is true of all the members of the group, not merely of the group member whose conduct of group discussion is under review. Every member of the group shares his interest in learning how the difficulties he has encountered can best be overcome.

With the help of their checklist and diagrams the observers can focus their comments on any such difficulties and on what, if anything, the worker did when he encountered them. Thus if the observers' direction-of-discussion diagrams show that members were frequently making 'off-the-beam' contributions, they will raise this for discussion in the group. The members of the group will then discuss it *as a worker's problem* in order to discover what implications it may have, not only for the worker who encountered it but also for themselves when they have the same kind of problem to deal with when conducting discussion in a group. First, they will seek to understand why the problem arose, and then how the worker could have avoided or solved it. Discussion may reveal, for instance, that the problem arose because from the very beginning some of the group's members had not been interested enough in the topic under discussion really to want to contribute relevantly to it; or because the scope of the topic had never been clearly enough defined; or because some members had been uninterested in any viewpoint other than their own, and therefore had not listened to what anyone else had had to say. However the members of the group may diagnose the cause of the problem, the focus of their interest while they are discussing it is always on what the worker could have done in order to avoid or solve it. It is in this way that they think out what they will do when as 'workers' they encounter similar problems themselves.

Similarly, if the observers' diagrams of participation show that a few members had intervened very frequently but most of the rest very seldom or not at all, or that two or more members had opted out of the discussion to carry on their own separate discussion for a time among themselves, the observers will comment accordingly. The members of the group will then discuss both why this happened and what the worker could have done to put things right. For instance, the splinter group may have formed for any of a number of reasons, each of which would have a different implication for the worker. Thus the reason may have been *either* that some members were uninterested in the topic under discussion and had therefore begun to talk about something else among themselves; *or* that they could not easily get in to make their contribution because they happened to be badly placed in the group; *or* that they lacked confidence to say what they wanted to say to the whole group; *or* because some other member always got in first; *or* simply because one member of the group had momentarily lost the thread of the discussion and had turned to his nearest neighbours for help.

Whatever the reason, once it has been established, everyone—
'worker', members of the practice group, and observers—considers together what the worker could have done either to prevent the splinter group forming or alternatively to bring its
members quickly back into full participation in the work of the
group.

What learning takes place during discussion of the observers'
comments depends, of course, partly on what problems the
worker encountered during the practice discussion and how he
dealt with them; partly on the skill of the observers in accur-
ately recording what actually occurred; partly on how acceptably they present their comments; and partly on how adequately
they are discussed.

Since many of the observers may have had no previous experience of observation, at first they are likely to miss some of
the relevant points from which the members of the group could
learn. We overcome this difficulty to some extent by dividing
the group into two sub-groups of six for the first practices, so
that while the members of one sub-group discuss the topic with
one of their members acting as the 'worker', all six members of the
other sub-group are observers. This has two advantages. Having
six observers often means that what one observer misses another
has noted: while the small size of the discussion sub-group eases
the job of the still unpractised 'workers' in coping with the
difficulties of operating in an unaccustomed role. There is also
always a staff member present as consultant-observer, and one
of his jobs is to come in after the trainee-observers have finished
their comments to comment on any major point they have
missed. Later in the course, when both 'workers' and observers
have developed more skill, the two sub-groups are then re-
united for practice in a single group with only two of their
members acting as observers at any one time.

The consultant-observer has other functions in addition to
that mentioned above. These are:

1. *to establish 'discussions of observations' as an essential part of
the course*

(It is very necessary to do this because the members of the

practice groups often get very interested in the subjects they have chosen for discussion. When this happens they are likely to resent having to stop at frequent intervals to discuss the comments of the observers unless the consultant-observer has initially explained the procedure he intends to follow, indicated the nature of the difficulty that may arise, and asked that members will accept that on this skill-training course *study of discussion method will take priority over interest in discussion content*, since the former is the more relevant to their purpose in attending the course.)

2. *to support the 'worker'*

(It is hard for anyone to accept without some feeling of resentment the very detailed analysis of his performance in conducting a group discussion that the 'practice worker' on this kind of course will often experience. However, the consultant-observer can do a great deal to make this tolerable, and even wanted, if he stresses beforehand that the job is a very difficult one, that mistakes are only to be expected, that everyone wants to learn, and that analysis of mistakes will help everyone to learn. He can also help by asking the observers to limit their comments, as far as possible, to statements of fact, and to avoid anything in the way of specific criticisms of the worker. They should not offer opinions about what the worker should have done, or should not have done, but should leave these to be worked out in general discussion by all members of the group. He stresses that although the observers are justified in making factual statements, no more weight should be attached to their opinions than to the opinions of all other members of the group.)

3. *to conduct discussion of the observations*

(This involves deciding when to interrupt discussion in the practice group; calling on each observer for comment; testing each comment for its acceptability with the worker and members of the practice group; and, by asking questions, helping the members of the group to diagnose the causes of any problems suggested by the comments and to discuss how, if at all, the worker might have coped with them more successfully.)

DISCUSSING A CASE

The practice discussions of cases are organized in much the same ways as the practice discussions of topics or problems. The members of the group take turns in conducting discussion. A staff member is present as consultant-observer and at appropriate times he intervenes with comments which are then discussed. Here again, as in the practice discussions of topics or problems, the comments are centred on the performance of the member who has conducted the discussion. Many quite detailed points get drawn to the attention of the group in this way: the need to economize in the use of blackboard space, for instance, when recording reports from sub-groups; the best way to record 'approaches' so that any significant differences between them become quickly apparent as shown in the sample blackboard summary on p. 108; and when to suggest role-playing during the discussion of a case. Discussions of comments made by the observers are always lively, and the contributions made by members of the group very much to the point, because each comment directs attention to some difficulty or problem that has just occurred in the group and to the performance of the 'worker' in his attempt to deal with it.

Most 'workers' find that the early stages of a case discussion are much easier to conduct than the more general discussion of a topic or problem because the former lends itself to a much more detailed application of structure. Once they have got the 'approaches' on the blackboard, however, they find the job of conducting the remaining stages (see pp. 100–4) very exacting but also, as they develop the necessary skill, very interesting and rewarding.

CHAPTER FOURTEEN

Obtaining, Selecting, and Editing Cases

TRAINERS who want to use cases need cases to use. In our experience the best providers of cases are the members of training groups. They can be stimulated to provide them if, when they have listed their problems according to the procedures outlined on pp. 89–91, the trainer asks each member of the group to write a brief descriptive account of what he did and with what result in some specific situation in which he encountered one of these problems and felt that he had not succeeded in coping satisfactorily with it. Each situation of this kind provides material for a case, and once the trainer has thus stimulated the members of the group to try to remember one or more of them, nearly everyone will usually be able to do so.

The trainer will then have a stock of potentially suitable cases for use with the group which produced them and he can continually add to his stock by following the same procedure with other groups whenever he can. In this way he can accumulate a wide variety of cases which he can, at need, use with training groups whose members cannot contribute their own cases for discussion, either because of shortage of time, or because they are inexperienced, or for any other reason.

Cases produced in this way, however, are only *potentially* suitable, even for the group which produced them, and most cases as originally contributed can be very much improved by careful editing before they are used. In fact, careful selection and editing of a case can greatly increase the chances that the members of a group will accept it when the trainer tests it with them for relevance and acceptability as described on pp. 97–8, and that they will be able to discuss it profitably if they do accept it.

Every case should satisfy certain basic requirements and cases which do not satisfy them should either be edited until they do, or if this should prove impossible, they should be scrapped. These requirements can be stated as follows:

1. *that it leaves no room for doubt about the identity of the person who encountered the problem*;

2. *that the problem it presents is one that quite commonly occurs and one that workers find it difficult to cope with*;

3. *that it states quite specifically what the worker did and with what result*; and

4. *that he might have succeeded if he had more skill.*

There are many other editing points too numerous to have specific mention here, although some of them are indicated by the editing of the three examples which follow. However, two points particularly deserve mention. The first is that even the slightest hint of criticism of the conduct of the worker in the case should be deleted. If it is left in the members of the training group will not want to accept the worker and his problem as typical of themselves and their problems, and this will defeat the purpose of the trainer in introducing the case.

The second point is that a trainer may edit a case differently according to the kind of training group he has specifically in mind. Thus the inclusion of detail about the kind of situation in which a particular problem occurs will strengthen the presentation of a case when it is used with members of a training group who all work in situations of a similar kind: but the same amount of detail will weaken a case—and should therefore be omitted—when the case is used with a training group composed of members most of whom do not work in situations of that specific kind. This point occurs in the editing of *Example Three* below.

The following case is in the form in which it was contributed for discussion by a member of the Youth Service.

Example One

The 'Commando Club' which has a strong tradition for outdoor activities arranged a week-end camp on their usual camping site. 'The Arabs', a mixed group from a different club, asked if they could share the camp with them. The 'Commandos' agreed and twelve members of the mixed group came to the camp accompanied by their leader.

On the Saturday evening the 'Commandos', their leader, and the leader of the mixed group went off for a hike, while the 'Arabs', the mixed group, preferred to stay in camp. When the hikers returned, they found the 'Arabs' lounging around the fire 'necking'. The leader of the 'Commandos' was annoyed and said so, whereupon the 'Arabs' became abusive. The 'Commandos' leader then said flatly that he would not have them in camp again and has since refused to accept another visit.

This is a poor case and if one assesses it to see how well it meets the requirements stated on the previous page it is easy to see why. There are two youth leaders and two groups of young people and the case is so presented that the reader is left to think out for himself whose problem is presented by the case and just what the problem is.

This could be remedied by editing, but even if this were done it is more than doubtful whether it could ever become a good case. One would expect most training groups of youth leaders to reject it, partly because most of them would feel that they might never get involved in a situation of that kind, and partly because the outcome or problem aspect of the case might seem to them too insignificant to worry about. This, therefore, is the kind of case to scrap.

Example Two

A Youth Centre has been established for several years *in its own premises* (1) with a good Management Committee and also a hardworking Members' Committee. When the Centre was established the canteen was staffed by a rota of lady helpers and this rota has worked satisfactorily for four years.

A full-time leader is appointed *and the two previous leaders are made assistants. This team works well in the club situation.* (2)

The leader suddenly decides that it should be the task of his senior girl members together with a few boys to staff the canteen. (3)

At a Management Committee he puts forward this proposal, pointing out that the running of a canteen is a responsible job and offers a training situation for his senior members.

The representative on the Management Committee of the lady helpers is upset at this idea, threatens to withdraw her services from the club and intimates that she will be able to persuade the other lady members to do likewise.

The Club Leader, however, has already committed his members to form a rota and this is due to start the following Monday.(4) He therefore tries to persuade the Management Committee that his idea is the right one, but their sympathies are with the lady helpers' representative whom they have known for four years and not with the leader who has recently been appointed.

The Chairman of the Management Committee sees this as a possible rift in the organization of the club and closes the discussion by saying that he will discuss the problem with the leader and the representative of the lady helpers after the formal business of the Management Committee has been concluded. (5)

This has the makings of a very good case. Today's trend in the Youth Service is all for getting young people to undertake more responsibilities for the day-to-day conduct of affairs within their clubs, and one of the major difficulties of a youth leader who tries to do this may be the reluctance of his adult helpers to hand over some of their responsibilities to young people. Thus very many youth leaders are likely to agree that this case illustrates a problem that is very relevant to themselves. The case is also a good one because it provides quite a clear picture of what the leader did and of the kind of difficulty he got into as a result of what he did.

This having been said, it is still true that the case can be considerably improved by editing. The points at which this might be done are indicated in the text of the case by italics and by the figures in parentheses. The first two points are very minor ones, for the italics merely indicate information which could be omitted as irrelevant to the problem contained in the case. Point (4) is more important, for the information provided by the words italicized refers to something the leader did at an earlier stage and would be more suitably provided at (3). It is, however, even more important that something should be done about the final paragraph, for it weakens the case from the point of view of leader-training by informing us that the Chairman of the Management Committee has taken over from the leader responsibility for dealing with the leader's problem. For use with youth leaders, therefore, the case would be much improved if the whole of the last paragraph were omitted.

If the case were edited in this way it would then read as follows:

A Youth Centre has been established for four years with a good Management Committee and also a hard-working Members' Committee. When the Centre was established the canteen was staffed by a rota of lady helpers, and this rota has worked satisfactorily for four years.

Then a new full-time leader is appointed who thinks that his senior girl members together with a few boys should staff the canteen. He discusses this with his Members' Committee and other club members who accept the idea and organize a rota which is due to start the following Monday.

He then seeks the approval of his Management Committee, explaining that the running of a canteen is a responsible job which provides a good training situation for his senior members.

The representative on the Management Committee of the lady helpers is upset at this idea. She threatens to withdraw her services from the club and intimates that she will be able to persuade the other lady helpers to do likewise.

Aware that he has already committed himself with his members, the leader does his best to persuade the Management Committee that his idea is the right one, but their sympathies are with the lady helper on the Management Committee whom they have known for four years, and not with the leader who has only recently been appointed. So the leader now has a difficult problem on his hands.

Could he have avoided it and still achieved his purpose, and if so, how?

Example Three

The leader of a church club of some thirty members, meeting once a week, decides after full consultation with the Management and Members' Committees and the church authorities to relax the rule of church membership and open the club to more people.

This move is resented by Richard, a member of long standing and a keen communicant, and by the technical group to which he belongs which is responsible for maintaining the club electrics (record player, etc.).

This group looks on newcomers with suspicion and Richard expresses his resentment (1) by avoiding the payment of subscriptions whenever possible. When the leader tackles him on this he becomes abusive, and the leader feels that he can take little definite action because the subscriptions are administered in a slack way, and there is no easy way to check up.

The problem reaches a critical point when the Members' Committee, of which the leader is chairman, (2) decides to tighten up the door procedure and raise the subs.

At the meeting, some of the committee who do not pay subs claim that they need not as they are in effect helpers. *The Chairman* (3) said that the responsibility as to whether they paid or not was theirs, but he advised that they should pay and put forward several reasons. After a full discussion they voted in favour of exempting themselves from subs. *Then the question of Richard was raised* (4) as he was not a committee member. The committee were strongly divided and recommended as a compromise that the leader should exercise his discretion in the matter.

Subsequently the leader tried to regularize the situation by asking Richard to pay up, but Richard was abusive. He left the club *and the church* (1) and took his technical group with him.

Could the leader have avoided this outcome?

This is also potentially a good case. It leaves one in no doubt about whose problem it presents, and the problem itself is one that any leader may encounter from time to time and have difficulty in dealing with. Once again, however, the case can be considerably improved by editing. Most of the detailed information (1) given at the beginning of the case should be omitted, since it helps to distract attention from the basic fact that the leader thought that Richard should pay and Richard, for reasons best known to himself, thought otherwise. Also, if the club is defined as a club of one particular kind—a small church club open on one night a week only—the case may appear less relevant than it really is to leaders, for example, of large open clubs which meet nearly every night of the week. This might influence them against accepting it in spite of the fact that the basic problem the case presents can face the leader in any kind of club.

K

The case can also be improved by editing it at points (2), (3), and (4) to bring out more clearly what the leader actually did. This can be done by rewriting the words underlined at (2) to make it clear that it was the leader who introduced into the Members' Committee the idea of tightening up the door procedure and raising the subs; by substituting 'leader' for 'chairman' at point (3); and by substituting 'Then the leader raised the question of Richard . . .' for 'Then the question of Richard was raised' at point (4). The purpose of all three emendations is to help focus the attention of the members of a training group more directly on how the leader tried to cope with his problem.

If the case is edited in this way it will then read as follows:

A club leader has noticed that Richard, a senior club member who leads the group which looks after the club's electrics (record-player, etc.), has got into the habit of avoiding paying his club subscription whenever possible. When the leader tackles him on this he becomes abusive, and the leader feels that he can take little definite action because he is aware that the subscriptions are not well administered and there is no easy way to check up.

The leader then decides to get the Members' Committee, of which he is the chairman, to tighten up the door procedure and raise the subs.

At the meeting of this committee some of the committee members who are also in arrears with subs claim that they need not pay as they are in effect club helpers. The leader replies that whether they should pay or not is for the committee to decide, but he suggests they ought to pay and puts forward several reasons. After a full discussion the members of the committee vote in favour of exempting themselves from subs. Then the leader raises the question of Richard who is not a committee member but who also helps in the club. The members of the committee are strongly divided and recommend as a compromise that the leader should exercise his own discretion in the matter.

Subsequently the leader tries to regularize the situation by asking Richard to pay up. But Richard becomes abusive and finally leaves the club taking the technical group with him.

Could the leader have avoided this outcome?

The impact of a case can sometimes be strengthened by editing it so that the person who encountered the problem tells his own story. If *Example Three* were rewritten in this way it might read as follows:

I am a bit worried about the way I handled a problem that I came up against in the club recently. I had noticed that one of my senior club members, a chap called Richard, had got into the habit of avoiding paying his club subscription whenever he could, and since the system for collecting subs had got a bit slack, he had been getting away with it for some time. Apart from that he was quite a useful club member for he and a few of his friends looked after the club electrics (record-player, etc.) and repaired them if they went wrong.

However, that was no reason why he should not pay his subs, but when I tackled him on the subject he became abusive, so I let the matter drop for the time being until I could feel I was on really strong ground.

I'm chairman of the Members' Committee in our club, and my next step was to get them to tighten up the door procedure so that no one would be able to get by without paying his subs. This wasn't at all popular with some of the committee members who also happened to be in arrears with their subs, and they took the line that as committee members they were really helpers and should not have to pay anything. I said that that was for the committee to decide, but that in my view everyone ought to pay and I told them why. The committee members discussed the pros and cons of this for a long time, but the upshot was that they decided to exempt themselves from paying subs.

I then raised the question of Richard who is not a committee member but who also does a lot to help the club. This led to still more discussion which ended with them telling me that I must do what I thought best.

I thought it over and decided that if I exempted Richard then a whole lot of other members would claim exemption too, so once again I asked Richard to pay up but he would have none of it. When I insisted, he left the club and his friends with him, and none of them has been back since.

Could you have handled this problem better?

A case can also sometimes be rewritten from the viewpoint of the person who, in the original case, was seen by the 'worker' as the cause of his problem. In *Example Two*, for instance, the youth leader's problem is with his Management Committee, and the case is suitable for use with a training group of youth leaders. But the final paragraph of the original case shows that the youth leader, through what he did, had also created a problem for the Chairman of the Management Committee. If the case were rewritten to present the problem as the Chairman saw it, it could then be used on a training course for chairmen and members of Management Committees. The training applications of many cases can be extended in this way.

But however carefully a trainer may edit a case, and however good a case may seem to him to be, he can never be sure that it really is good until he has tested and used it with a training group. This may reveal the need for further editing and it is only when this has been done and the amended case has satisfactorily passed the test of further use that the trainer can confidently add it to his permanent stock of 'good' cases.

There is one final point. Cases vary very greatly in respect of the difficulty of the problems they present and in respect of the level of skill, or lack of it, of the 'workers' who encounter them: and the training value of a case is greatly enhanced if the members of the training group are able to identify themselves with the way the 'worker' tries to achieve his purpose as well as with the problem presented in the case. The ideal case for any particular group is one which presents a 'worker' tackling a situation in much the same way as the members of the training group would normally have done themselves, and with much the same result. They then become thoroughly involved in the process of pooling their ideas and experience in order to understand just why the 'worker' failed and just how he (and by implication also themselves) could have done better.

Conclusion

IT has been our theme in this book that every 'worker' in every situation in which he works will necessarily use one or other of two approaches according to whether his intention is basically directive or non-directive; that each approach offers some advantages and incurs some disadvantages that the other lacks; and that in order to be consistently efficient in achieving his purposes the worker needs realistically to assess which of these approaches is the more appropriate one for him to use in each of the situations in which he works.

We have outlined the relevant factors of choice as we see them and have described the kinds of skill we think are needed to enable workers to use the non-directive approach to good effect. We have done this because we believe that many workers habitually use the directive approach in situations where the non-directive approach would suit their purposes better; and that many others who aim to work non-directively often defeat themselves: either because they sometimes try to do so when the situation is not right for it, or because in trying to be non-directive they adopt too passive a role. In fact, their role should be negative only in the sense that they refrain from giving their own opinions, since this would defeat their main object of getting people to think things out for themselves. In every other respect their role is a very active one. Getting people to think and decide realistically and constructively in the light of all the available facts about the things that matter to them demands real skill on the part of the worker. Only if he has this skill can he positively help them to arrive at really sound and valid conclusions that they will act on because they have reached them as a result of the thinking they have done themselves.

APPENDIX

A SELECTION OF YOUTH SERVICE CASES

Youth leaders, like many other group and community workers, have to be able to deal with a very wide range of human-relations problems. The cases which follow illustrate some of these problems and have all been successfully used on training courses designed to help youth leaders increase their human-relations skill. The cases vary in difficulty, some being more suitable for use with inexperienced leaders while others are hard enough to extend even a highly-trained and experienced leader.

Even a cursory reading of these cases, all of which are based on fact, highlights the need for some specific and practical form of human-relations training, which is why we have included them here. We also hope that any trainers in the Youth Service who may wish to experiment with the training methods we have described in this book may find them useful as an initial source of suitable training material. A wider selection of cases illustrative of problems encountered by group and community workers in developing countries has already been published in our earlier book, *The Human Factor in Community Work* (Oxford University Press, 1965).

I. PROBLEMS WITH MEMBERS

I. THE CLUB CANTEEN

A newly-formed small open youth club meets one evening a week in a hall used by other youth and adult groups every other night of the week. The leader is conscientious and well liked by the members. He organizes a wide variety of successful activities and has a roster of members of both sexes to serve for about an hour in the canteen and to clean up afterwards.

For some months the canteen runs smoothly until the caretaker complains that the kitchen was left in an unsatisfactory state after a club meeting.

The following week the leader approaches the two girls and one boy who had been responsible for the canteen at the last meeting of the club, and discovers that one of the girls had gone off with the boy, leaving the other girl to clear up on her own. The leader lectures the two culprits who answer back very rudely and then leave the club together never to return. This incident has a bad effect on the club. The leader loses the goodwill of many of the members; some activities no longer go on as well as before; and the leader is unable to find members willing to serve in the canteen and clean up afterwards. Could the canteen problem have been dealt with better in some other way?

2. THE BUILDING PROJECT

The leader of a large mixed youth club undertook a building project with his members. It was to last over a period of time and included building a workshop. To carry through the project on time it was necessary for the work to be undertaken at weekends.

The project was well within the capacity of the club members and it proceeded very satisfactorily, but because some of the work entailed skilled craftsmen, about 12 craftsmen-members became an exclusive group.

To retain the interest of the specialist group the leader permitted them certain privileges, but made it quite clear that they must not do anything that would cause offence to the community and give the club a bad name. The club members accepted his treatment of the skilled group and, indeed, were friendly with them, did the labouring chores for them, and kept them supplied with tea.

One Thursday morning the leader arrived at the club and found the roof of the front entrance decorated with a multitude of tools. A wheel-barrow was up the flag pole, thirty-foot ladders were dangling from the apex of the roof, adorned with picks and shovels. Unfortunately, not only was the club entrance fronting the high street, but also the Youth Employment Officer held court every Thursday morning and parents of club members and potential club members turned up to see him. The leader was unable to remove the offending articles physically by himself so he spent the day explaining away the escapade to members of the public.

That evening he held a meeting of the group, explaining the action he had taken and told them outright that they had not only let him down but also the club. He pointed out that there were limits to this kind of escapade, and that quite thoughtlessly they might have done irreparable damage within the community, on whom they generally relied for financing the project. One member of the group was most offensive to the leader, using foul language. The leader told him not to be insolent. The member then informed him what he could do with the building and said he had had enough and would not do any more work until the leader withdrew his remarks about being insolent. The leader said they could do without his help and that he was not indispensable. An hour later work came to a standstill. All the members of the group said they were going on strike until the leader withdrew his remarks about insolence.

The project came to an untimely halt. The club members generally were horrified by the behaviour of the specialist group, there was a lot of bad feeling within the club which became divided into various factions.

What went wrong?

3. THE MOBILE COFFEE BAR

The club is an open youth club which meets in a secondary modern school. Last year, the average attendance in the two evenings per week that the club is open was 150. During the summer recess the leader and his assistants constructed a large portable coffee-bar, attractively painted and really 'with it'.

Unfortunately the structure took about a quarter of an hour to erect and take down and naturally this had to be done each evening. Everything went well at first. The bar was very popular and the club strength increased.

The leader and his assistants erected and took down the structure each evening. After a while the leader started to ask for help in taking the structure down but was unsuccessful.

One night in desperation he announced that unless he got help in erecting and taking the structure down, he would not erect it again. No help was offered and so the lounge was left in the store. He repeatedly asked if anyone would help but always with the same result. In the end, the members got fed up with continually being asked to help, with the result that some of them began to come less often, and some even ceased to come at all.

What went wrong?

4. THE UNRULY MEMBERS

A group of 15/16-year-old boys arrived at the club premises and asked to become members. They were seen by the leader (who didn't really like the look of them) and warned that if they misbehaved they would be thrown out. He wanted more members, he said, but not troublesome ones. They filled in their application forms, and became probationary members.

Next club night, during the evening, the same boys began to

cause a disturbance, squirting water and causing the girls to scream. The leader went into the hall, physically restrained the boys, and lectured them on their behaviour in front of the other members. If they behaved like that again, he said, he would throw them out. Ten minutes later, the same thing happened. The leader immediately threw the boys out of the club amidst much resisting and swearing. The leader told them that they could not return until they learned to behave themselves.

The boys hung round outside the club, generally being a nuisance and trying to get back into the club. The leader remained firm.

The next week, the boys were again outside the club, and were again refused admission by the leader, in spite of their assertions that they would behave themselves. The boys continued to try to get in, and eventually broke a window. The leader promptly called the police but the boys had vanished by the time the police arrived.

The other club members resented the appearance of the police, and accused the leader of being unfair. Some members felt so strongly about this that they left the club.

Could the leader have handled this problem better?

II. PROBLEMS WITH MANAGEMENT COMMITTEES

5. YOU CAN'T PLEASE EVERYONE

A leader is running a large mixed club in good premises but with a shortage of adult helpers. His average nightly attendance is about 130. Nearly all his time is taken up with coping with administration problems and running social evenings for all who wish to come.

At a Management Committee meeting one member criticizes the club for its lack of 'worthwhile' activities. 'For all the good the club is doing,' he says, 'they might as well spend the evening in a local coffee bar or dance hall.' The leader is told by the committee to do something about this situation. He lets the members know that there has been a change of policy and that they will only be welcome if they are prepared to participate in one or more of the activities he has laid on.

The membership falls to an average nightly attendance of 40 who participate in a number of recreational and educational activities.

Corresponding with this fall in membership the leader receives complaints from local citizens that a lot of his ex-club members are lounging about the street corners, coffee bars, and dance halls and getting into trouble. It is evident that there is real concern about the situation.

Could he have avoided this?

6. THE JUMBLE SALE

A club leader wants to spend £35 on some new equipment for the club. He doesn't want to go to his Management Committee for sanction to spend this amount from club funds since he knows that the club is hard up, so he decides to organize a jumble sale as a special effort.

He explains his idea to his members who think it a good one and promise enthusiastic support, especially as he promises to buy the new equipment immediately after the sale.

Both the leader and the members work hard to make the jumble sale a success, but unfortunately it produces only £25. In view of the promise he has made to the members, the leader feels he must raise the other £10 quickly and decides to ask his Management Committee to make up the balance from club funds.

When he does so, the Treasurer objects. He argues that, as the club's name was used in publicizing the jumble sale, the proceeds should be paid into club funds and that it is for the committee to decide how they should be spent. He maintains that the leader has no right to organize money-raising events for special purposes unless he has got the committee's sanction first.

This leads to a long discussion, but in the end the committee decides by a majority vote that the money from the jumble sale must be paid into club funds, and that it should be used for payment of some of the outstanding accounts.

The club leader resents this decision which he thinks is very unfair. He is also very worried about having to explain to his members that they will have to do without the equipment he has promised them and about the effect this may have on attitudes and relationships within the club.

Could he have avoided this problem?

7. THE FACE LIFT

A full-time leader takes over a mixed youth club. A Members' Committee is in existence. He finds he is welcomed by all the members and that the Management Committee is friendly and seems to want to support him. The club, however, is split up into several cliques.

In order to integrate the members, the leader suggests at a

Members' Committee meeting that the club could do with a face lift. Perhaps they would like to consider this as a club project—all the members to lend a hand. The committee are most enthusiastic and he promises to put the project to the Management Committee.

At the next management meeting he explains his idea of integration, the method to achieve this, and the fact that he has the members' support if they, the Management Committee, agree. The Management Committee tell him to get out plans and estimates with the members and bring them back for the go-ahead next month.

Immense interest is shown by the members. Plans for a coffee bar and dance square are drawn up. Wallpapers, curtains, colour schemes, and new lights for the rest of the club are chosen and agreed by all the club members. A lot of talent comes to light. The total cost is small.

At the next Management Committee meeting the project is fully considered. The cost does not worry them at all, and they are all in agreement that if the project went through as suggested it would be wonderful. But member after member of the committee produces reasons as to why it would fail: 'We cannot have young people doing technical jobs', 'Monkeying about with electricity', 'What about the girls climbing ladders', 'What about insurance', 'The youngsters would not stick to it', 'The project would take too long', 'They would all get fed up before it was finished', 'Far too ambitious and big a project'! After long hours of argument with the leader the meeting threw out the project and suggested to the leader that he looked instead for a community project.

The leader reported the result of the meeting to the members, who were frustrated and angry. They accused the leader of misleading them and 'taking them for a ride'. He found himself very shortly rejected by the members.

What went wrong?

III. PROBLEMS WITH MEMBERS OF THE COMMUNITY

8. THE DRUG PEDDLER

A new purpose-built club had 350 members drawn from a good residential area in the town. One morning a C.I.D. officer called on the leader to tell him that a popular club member had been charged with passing 'purple hearts' at a near-by coffee bar. The leader suspended the member pending the magistrates' hearing. When the parents became aware of the situation a number of girls were for-bidden to attend the club. One parent, spokesman for several families, informed the leader that most of the girls might be allowed to return if the club members were officially informed that the lad had been excluded for all time. The leader would not agree to this and said that this was something that the Members' Committee would have to discuss if and when the lad was found guilty. The lad was eventually found guilty and fined. Under the guidance of the leader the Members' Committee considered the matter and decided to reinstate him at the end of the term which had three weeks still to run. With the temporary suspension this meant nearly a term's suspension in all. The leader then informed the spokesman of the parents that the lad had been punished by the law and by his club, and that he had promised the Members' Committee not to become involved in drugs in the future. He was then told that the parents would not accept this and that they would not permit their daughters to attend unless and until the lad was permanently excluded from the club. The leader explained the situation to his Management Com-mittee which approved of what he had done, but this did not bring back the many girls who were no longer allowed by their parents to attend the club.

Could the leader have prevented this from happening and still achieved his aim of helping the lad concerned?

9. THE DONATION

The leader of a self-supporting group (80 strong) of a uniformed organization received a donation of £100—the proceeds of Bingo sessions from the Community Association attached to a giant block of flats—in order to provide more camping equipment for the uniformed group, 50 per cent of the membership being boys from the flats. This donation the leader gratefully accepted. As a result of the acceptance of the £100 he and his group incurred the wrath of the parish church and local chapel congregations; and of the head-master of the large secondary school near by who happened to be a Borough Councillor and a bitter opponent of gambling. Though the donation enabled him to buy extra tentage, the lack of support and local resistance to all the subsequent money-raising efforts was so great that eventually the group, which had a small wooden head-quarters to maintain, was in grave financial difficulties, in spite of a growing membership and the goodwill of a number of interested parents.

What, if anything, could the leader have done?

10. THE NEAR NEIGHBOURS

A youth club was opened in the premises of an old primary school in a heavily residential area on a main road, with the playground adapted as a car and motor-cycle park.

The local residents were delighted to see the young people contained in a club with a proper programme.

A part-time paid leader, who was a local school-teacher, was appointed to run the club which was an immediate success.

After the club had been open for about three months the leader received serious complaints of noise from the retired residents living adjacent to the club; not only was the record player too loud, but noise from the car park of motor-cycles revving up was intolerable. The leader at once visited the complainants, heard the noise level, and promised to do all he could to reduce it—apologizing for the inconvenience. Action was taken, the windows were double-glazed, the record player controlled, and cars and motor-cycles forbidden to enter the old playground. This action considerably reduced the noise level outside the club. The residents continued to complain, threatened injunctions, and as a result relations between the residents and the club staff and members became very strained.

Could the leader have avoided this situation?

11. THE RESIDENTIAL NURSERY

A club which attached great importance to community service as one of its objects had sent a rota of members every weekend and in the evening to a local Residential Nursery for Children in Need of Care for some years.

Then a new matron was appointed who disliked using voluntary helpers, although she had to admit that they had their uses when staff shortages were acute. One weekend a visit of the Nursery Management Committee had been arranged, half of the staff were on the sick list with flu, and the two members on the rota failed to turn up without telling anyone.

The matron was furious, and wrote to the leader next day giving her opinion of the club and stating quite definitely that from now on the doors of the Nursery were closed to the members. The leader felt that the matron was ill-tempered and unreasonable and decided it was useless to ask her to relent. Knowing that the Chairman of the Nursery and the President of the club were great friends he asked the President to do something to help. The President therefore had a talk with the Chairman who agreed that the matron's attitude was unreasonable and that he would like her to accept the members back again. This she did and for the next three months the members were tolerated under sufferance, some of the nurses siding with the matron and some with the members. This situation, however, was thoroughly unsatisfactory all round and the members finally decided to give up the Nursery altogether, even though there were very few opportunities for other forms of service in the neighbourhood.

Did it all have to end that way?

IV. PROBLEMS WITH CLUB HELPERS

12. THE FOOTBALL TRAINER

A part-time youth leader has a club about 100 strong, the activities of which include football, netball, indoor games, drama, art, foreign travel, and weight-training. He was on good terms with his helpers. Then a demand arises for a *judo group* and the leader obtains the judo mats at a cost of £75, thus depleting his club funds.

The trainer/organizer of the very good *football group* then asks for £20 from club funds to buy new football jerseys and meet other expenses of his team (referees' fees, etc.). The club leader says that the club cannot spare so much money and suggests that the football team raise money by organizing a dance, and offers to help in every way he can.

The football trainer does not accept his suggestion. He says that the club leader is unfair to the football group and does not give them a fair share of the club's finances. The club leader replies that the football group had £60 from club funds the previous year and therefore should try to be self-supporting this year. He also accuses the football trainer of not caring for the club as a whole but only for the interests of his own section. Relations between the youth leader and the football leader become very strained and this soon has a bad effect generally on relationships within the club. Could the club leader have handled this problem better and, if so, how?

SET BY
BUTLER AND TANNER LTD. FROME
AND REPRINTED LITHOGRAPHICALLY BY
EBENEZER BAYLIS AND SON LIMITED
THE TRINITY PRESS, WORCESTER AND LONDON

3-72